UNCLAIMED VALOR

The History of the
One Hundred and Thirtieth Regiment
Pennsylvania Volunteer Infantry

TERRENCE W. BELTZ

Mechanicsburg, PA USA

Published by Sunbury Press, Inc.
Mechanicsburg, Pennsylvania

www.sunburypress.com

Copyright © 2025 by Terrence W. Beltz.
Cover Copyright © 2025 by Sunbury Press, Inc.

Sunbury Press supports copyright. Copyright fuels creativity, encourages diverse voices, promotes free speech, and creates a vibrant culture. Thank you for buying an authorized edition of this book and for complying with copyright laws by not reproducing, scanning, or distributing any part of it in any form without permission. You are supporting writers and allowing Sunbury Press to continue to publish books for every reader. For information contact Sunbury Press, Inc., Subsidiary Rights Dept., PO Box 548, Boiling Springs, PA 17007 USA or legal@sunburypress.com.

For information about special discounts for bulk purchases, please contact Sunbury Press Orders Dept. at (855) 338-8359 or orders@sunburypress.com.

To request one of our authors for speaking engagements or book signings, please contact Sunbury Press Publicity Dept. at publicity@sunburypress.com.

FIRST SUNBURY PRESS EDITION: May 2025

Set in Adobe Garamond | Interior design by Crystal Devine | Cover by Lawrence Knorr | Edited by Debra Reynolds.

Publisher's Cataloging-in-Publication Data
Names: Beltz, Terrence W., author.
Title: Unclaimed valor : the history of the One Hundred and Thirtieth Regiment Pennsylvania Volunteer Infantry / Terrence W. Beltz.
Description: First hardcover edition. | Mechanicsburg, PA : Sunbury Press, 2025.
Summary: With no military experience and little training, they faced hardened Confederates at Bloody Lane the stonewall at Mayre's Height and would hold the line stopping the Confederate Stonewall Jackson's advancing troops at the Battle of Chancellorsville. Through their diaries, letters, memoirs and personal accounts, these men tell their heroic story.
Identifiers: ISBN 979-8-88819-294-8 (hardcover) | ISBN 979-8-88819-410-2 (paperback).
Subjects: HISTORY / United States / Civil War Period (1850–1877) | HISTORY / Military / General | HISTORY / United States / 20th Century .

Designed in the USA
0 1 1 2 3 5 8 13 21 34 55

For the Love of Books!

This book is dedicated to the memory of
HENRY I. ZINN

COLONEL HENRY I. ZINN, COMMANDER,
130TH REGIMENT PENNSYLVANIA VOLUNTEER
INFANTRY
(Library of Congress)

CONTENTS

Acknowledgments		vii
Preface		ix
Introduction: A Sense of Duty		4

CHAPTERS

1	Deeds, Not Words	7
2	Guarding the Capitol	29
3	Seeing the Elephant: The Antietam Campaign	41
4	A Respite at Harper's Ferry	81
5	Death Comes to a Commander: The Fredericksburg Campaign	101
6	A Camp Near Falmouth	126
7	Holding the Line: The Chancellorsville Campaign	140
8	Home Again	156
Conclusion: "Manhood Shall Be the Test of Citizenship"		158
Afterword		166

APPENDICES

A	Additional Photographs	190
B	Commanders and Staff, August 1862	202
C	Special Order #122	207
D	Regimental Strength and Casualty Statistics	209
E	Regimental Roster	210

Bibliography	267
Index	272
About the Author	276

ACKNOWLEDGMENTS

A WORTHWHILE project of this scope requires the ongoing support and assistance of a host of professors, historians, friends and family to whom I am eternally grateful. I would first like to thank my wife, Patricia for her encouragement, proofing, keen transcription assistance and moral support. Without her support, I could not have attained this accomplishment.

The kind assistance provided by the following organizations and institutions was invaluable: Antietam National Battlefield Park; Fredericksburg & Spotsylvania National Park; Chancellorsville Battlefield Park; U.S. Army Military History Institute; National Archives and Records Administration, National Archives at College Park (Photographic Department); Pennsylvania State Archives; Pennsylvania Capitol Preservation Committee; State Library of Pennsylvania; Cumberland County Historical Society; Newville Historical Society and the Shippensburg Historical Society. Additionally, my gratitude to Dr. Robert C. Kenzer, History Professor, the University of Richmond, Richmond, Virginia, who was my academic advisor and thesis director.

I am indebted to both Ms. Dorothy Bonafield and Mrs. Susan M. Boardman, descendants of men of the 130th Pennsylvania, for sharing copies of their ancestors' diary and photograph.

Lastly and most importantly, I wish to thank my late mother, Darl L. Beltz, née Thomas, for her love and encouragement. It was her endless work as our family genealogist who gave me this door to open.

During a trip to York, Pennsylvania, when I first began this endeavor, I felt it necessary to visit the grave of my paternal great-grandfather, William H. Seifert, who served in Company C of the regiment. Not finding a visible marker knowing that I was in the correct cemetery location, I was able to uncover the fallen sunken stone hidden under three to four inches of overgrown sod, out of sight for countless years, revealing the inscription "Gone, but not forgotten." As I was later able to raise his marker from obscurity, my hope is that my work will also uncover the forgotten deeds and sacrifices of those brave men of the 130th Regiment Pennsylvania Infantry.

PREFACE

By July 1862, faced with a succession of mounting battlefield losses and expiring enlistments, President Abraham Lincoln's administration needed volunteers to fill a critical gap in the war effort. By then, the once patriotic fervor in the North had significantly declined, and countless returning veterans refused to support the cause and did not re-enlist; while potential recruits who had learned of the realities of war avoided recruiting offices. The supply of men was dwindling and organizing regiments became difficult. In June 1862, although contemplating a military draft, Congress gave the President authority to raise an additional 300,000 troops through imposed enlistment quotas to be filled by each state. Concerned with a low turnout, the term of enlistment was set at nine months.

On Independence Day, July 4, 1862, the governor of Pennsylvania, Andrew G. Curtin, swiftly appealed for new recruits.

THE GOVERNOR'S PROCLAMATION
An Appeal to the Patriotism of the People

PENNSYLVANIA, SS
In the name, and by the authority of the Commonwealth of Pennsylvania, Andrew G. Curtin, Governor of said Commonwealth

A PROCLAMATION

More men are required for the suppression of the Rebellion. Our regiments in the field are to be recruited to their original strength, and in addition new regiments are to be formed.

Pennsylvania has hitherto done her duty to the country. Her freemen are again called on to volunteer in her defense that the blood of her sons who have already fallen, may not have been shed in vain, and that we may hand down to our posterity the blessings of Union and civil and political liberty, which we derived from our fathers.

The number of men now required, and the regulations for the enlistment, will be made known forthwith in General Orders. Meanwhile the men of Pennsylvania will hold themselves in readiness for prompt compliance with the necessary demand upon the gallant and patriotic spirit.

Our noble Commonwealth has never yet faltered, and must stand firm now when her honor and everything that is dear to her are at stake.

Given under my hand and the great seal of the State, at Harrisburg, this fourth day of July, in the year of our Lord one thousand eight hundred and six two, and of the Commonwealth the eighty seventh.

A. G. CURTIN

By the Governor,
    Eli Slifer.
        Secretary of the Commonwealth[1]

---

1. *The York Gazette*, July 8, 1862, "The Governor's Proclamation."

THE FOCUS OF this study concerns itself with the vital role that the men of the 130th Pennsylvania performed during its nine-month term of enlistment. One of eighteen nine-month regiments recruited during the month of August 1862, this regiment served with silent distinction on the killing fields of Antietam, Fredericksburg, and Chancellorsville. Many of these nine-month regiments have often been ignored, overshadowed by the more notable and sensationalized three-year regiments. These regiments often played critical roles during significant engagements yet received little recognition. For instance, both the 130th and 132nd Pennsylvania Volunteers were, in part, responsible for the Army of the Potomac's success at "Bloody Lane" in the Battle of Antietam. Yet, little is known or written of their deeds on that infamous day in America's history. Although hundreds of Civil War regimental histories have been written, many of the nine-month unit histories are nonexistent, including the 130th Pennsylvania.

This regiment was selected as it typifies common Pennsylvanians torn between duty to their county and devotion to their families. This study is not intended to re-write the history of significant eastern theater Civil War battles, but to provide a historical perspective into the critical role the soldiers of the 130th Pennsylvania played in them. To accomplish this study and accurately portray the realities of war that the men faced on a daily basis, I have drawn heavily upon primary source materials such as soldiers' diaries, letters, memoirs, newspapers, official regimental records, and federal records. In building an organizational framework in sequencing military events, I have relied upon Francis A. Walker's *History of the Second Army Corps*.[2]

---

2. Francis A. Walker, *History of the Second Army Corps*, (New York: Charles Scribner's Sons, 1887; reprint Gaithersburg, Maryland: Old Soldier Books, Inc., 1997.) Page citations are to the reprint edition.

INTRODUCTION

A Sense of Duty

By July of 1862, faced with a succession of mounting battlefield losses and expiring enlistments, President Abraham Lincoln's administration needed volunteers to fill a critical gap in the war effort. By then, the once patriotic fervor in the North had significantly declined and countless returning veterans refused to support the cause by not re-enlisting, while potential recruits who had learned of the realities of war avoided recruiting offices. The supply of men was dwindling and organizing regiments became difficult. In June 1862, although contemplating a military draft, Congress gave the President authority to raise an additional 300,000 troops through imposed enlistment quotas to be filled by each state. Concerned with a low turnout, the term of enlistment was set at nine months.[1]

The individual motivations prompting enlistment in the Union Army in the summer of 1862 are debatable. For instance, Mark A. Snell hints that an impending draft triggered volunteerism in York, Pennsylvania, particularly with members of companies B, C, I, and K of the 130th Regiment Pennsylvania Volunteer Infantry.[2] Yet, after reading the letters, diaries, and memoirs of many of these men, I found no single reference to a soldier volunteering out of fear of being forced to serve via military draft. Instead, there are many references to "a spirit of loyalty" and a "sense of duty" prompting their enlistment. Perhaps they enlisted with the sentiment that their services were now necessary, to once and for all put an end to the rebellion. Oftentimes, however, soldiers were reluctant

---

1. Mark A. Snell, *Union Soldiers and the Northern Home Front*, (New York: Fordham University Press, 2002), 82–84.
2. Snell, 84–85.

to express their genuine thoughts to pen and paper, particularly with issues concerning their manhood. I found no instance when a soldier openly stated in a diary entry, letter, or memoir that he had enlisted merely to avoid the draft.

Other notable Civil War historians addressing the motivations of Union enlistees have reached similar conclusions. My work points to evidence similar to that offered by James M. McPherson's *For Cause & Comrades* supporting the concept that "duty and honor" were strong motivating factors in an era dominated by the traditional values of Victorian mores.[3] McPherson dwells deeper, borrowing a concept from John A. Lynn, maintaining that there are three categories of motivations: "initial motivation," "sustaining motivation," and "combat motivation" that relate to why a soldier would enlist, why he would stay in the army, and what prompted him to face the danger of battle.[4] Although a soldier may have been motivated to enlist in response to an impending draft, during his service, his motivation could change over time, despite being sick of war. A soldier would not let down his comrades. With few exceptions, most soldiers felt that it was better to die in combat rather than being cast as coward if he ran.

McPherson also contends that "community pressure" prompted enlisting.[5] Based upon my research, I fully concur, particularly where in smaller towns everybody knew everybody. I would argue that community pressure equally influenced an individual's sustaining and combat motivations. Quite often, small town newspapers would provide detailed personal accounts of its "citizens in blue." To be disgraced by desertion, dereliction of duty, or similar intolerable acts would haunt the returning citizen-soldier for life and negatively reflect upon his family.

Neither McPherson, nor Gerald F. Linderman in *Embattled Courage*, mention "family" as being a motivating factor to serve. Throughout my research I continuously found brothers, fathers and sons, and cousins serving often in the same company or regiment. On numerous occasions, the enlistment of an older brother would soon be followed by his younger sibling. In many of the letters home by members of the 130th

---

3. James M. McPherson, *For Cause and Comrades*, (New York: Oxford University Press, 1997), 4–5.
4. McPherson, 12.
5. McPherson, 13.

Pennsylvania, the soldiers would inquire about the well-being of their brothers and cousins serving in other units. On occasion, they would chastise those who had not yet enlisted, and poke fun at those who were later drafted, claiming "it was about time!"

In concert with McPherson, Linderman also cites manliness, duty, and honor as significant factors prompting enlistment.[6] He also introduces another factor—that of religion.[7] Linderman discusses the correlation between courage and godliness. If a soldier believed in God, putting himself in God's care would provide him the courage to endure the test of combat and even death. Often a soldier with no prior religious conviction would find God, while others would become more religious. Religion played a significant role in the 130th Pennsylvania. Initially, the regiment lacked a chaplain, which was a continual concern for the regimental commander and was the topic of many of the soldiers' letters. Until the regiment's chaplain arrived, some of the more religiously-versed officers filled in for him. In some of the soldiers' letters, the reference to God was revealed. In a September 21, 1862 letter to his wife, the regiment's Quartermaster Officer, John R. Turner, wrote:

> As I write the wind blows strong some appearance of rain I now stop and lay me down to sleep and pray the Lord my soul to take and also to protect you all at home as you lay upon your beds at home no doubt you think of me often and as soon as you go to bed no doubt I am remembered by you and the children in your prayers.[8]

This regiment typifies common Pennsylvanians torn between duty to their county and devotion to their families. This study is not intended to re-write the history of significant eastern theater Civil War battles, but to provide a historical perspective into the critical role the soldiers of the 130th Pennsylvania played in them. To accomplish this study and accurately portray the realities of war that the men faced on a daily basis, I have drawn heavily upon primary source materials such as soldiers'

---

6. Gerald E. Linderman, *Embattled Courage*, (New York: The Free Press, 1987), 13.
7. Linderman, 8–14.
8. John R. Turner to his wife, September 21, 1862, Cumberland County Historical Society, Carlisle, Pennsylvania. Hereinafter cited as Turner Letters.

diaries, letters, memoirs, newspaper, official regimental records, and federal records. In building an organizational framework in sequencing military events, I have relied upon Francis A. Walker's *History of the Second Army Corps.*[9]

---

9. Francis A. Walker, *History of the Second Army Corps*, (New York: Charles Scribner's Sons, 1887; reprint Gaithersburg, Maryland: Old Soldier Books, Inc., 1997.) Page citations are to the reprint edition.

CHAPTER 1

Deeds, Not Words

FROM THE ARMY OF THE POTOMAC
Seven Days Hard Fighting

The Army correspondent of the Associated Press, who claims to have arrived at Fortress Monroe direct from General McClellan's headquarters, reports that after seven days hard fighting McClellan, pressed by superior numbers, was forced to retreat to a point on the James river near Turkey Island, where what remains of his army is under cover of the gunboats, and where we are told, it is now being reinforced. The battles, it is said, have been "the most destructive of human life that the world has ever seen . . ."

—*The Hanover Spectator*
Friday Morning, July 11, 1862[1]

TO THE CITIZENS of Hanover, Pennsylvania, it became obvious that the war was not to be short-lived, as they had originally anticipated. President Abraham Lincoln was becoming concerned. What the Union had suffered in military defeats in the Peninsula Campaign, its soldiers had suffered in declining morale. Major General George S. McClellan continued his appeals for additional men to fill the ranks of his depleted Army of the Potomac. With the glamour and excitement of war replaced with the cruel and inhumane realities, scores of the tried veterans had

---

1. *The Hanover Spectator*, July 11, 1862, "Seven Days Hard Fighting."

PENNSYLVANIA GOVERNOR
ANDREW CURTIN
(Pennsylvania State Archives)

had enough and would not re-enlist when their original term of enlistment would soon expire. In mid-1862, young men were not rushing to the recruiting offices as seen in 1861. With the monthly pay of $13.00, it was difficult enough for a soldier to support himself and his family and experience the misery, depravations, and the possibility of death.[2]

On June 6, 1862, the Lincoln administration responded to this dilemma by issuing General Order No. 60 that restored the volunteer recruiting service.[3] The federal government quickly requested 150,000 volunteers, which would increase the figure to 300,000 by Special Order No. 94 on August 9, 1862.[4] In effect, General Order No. 94 "Regulations for the Enrollment and Draft of 300,000 Militia," mandated that if the states could not raise their assigned quota by August 15, 1862, a

---

2. U.S. War Department, Revised United States Army Regulations of 1861 (Washington: Government Printing Office, 1863), 362. Hereinafter cited as Revised Regulations for the United States Army, 1863.

3. The Civil War CD-ROM: The War of the Rebellion: A Compilation of the Official Records of the Union and Confederate Armies, (Carmel: Guild Press of Indiana, Inc., 1996), 109. Hereinafter cited as OR.

4. OR, Series III, Vol II, General Order #99.

special militia draft "of all able-body citizens between the ages of eighteen and forty-five" would fill the deficiency for the particular state. The Commonwealth of Pennsylvania was required to provide eighteen new regiments.[5] Congress gave the President the authority to set the length of service not to exceed nine months.[6]

August 15 arrived with Pennsylvania not meeting its quota and thereby putting the wheels in motion for a special militia draft. Governor Andrew G. Curtin called for an accounting of all eligible men in Pennsylvania. Due to early enrollment difficulties, the draft was delayed until September 15, with a subsequent postponement resulting from Confederate General Robert E. Lee's invasion of the North requiring 50,000 emergency volunteers to defend the state's borders. The state's draft lottery eventually took place, but not until October 16, 1862.[7]

The Shippensburg News reported the postponement of the draft on August 23, 1862, citing that it was postponed until the 4th of September "for the purpose of allowing further opportunity for enlistment . . . and each county, borough and township will be credited with the number of men already furnished, so that the weight of the draft will fall equally heavy upon all sections of the country."[8]

Although not questioning Governor Curtin's actions, the article cited that a draft could cause some townships and boroughs within York County to be treated unequally, since "Some localities had already been almost drained of their able-bodied men by volunteer enlistment, whilst others have not sent a corporal's guard to the Army."[9] This nine-month alternative was contrary to the government's intention to obtain recruits to serve a three-year term. To the volunteer, however, it was perceived as being more honorable than being forced to serve under the draft, and it was only for nine months.

The impending draft prompted communities to take action. By obtaining sufficient volunteers, they would receive enough enlistment credits to remove the requirement for the draft in their districts.[10] The

---

5. William J. Miller, *The Training of an Army: Camp Curtin and the North's Civil War*, (Shippensburg, PA: White Mane Publishing Company, Inc., 1990), 101.
 6. Snell, 83.
 7. Snell, 84.
 8. *The Shippensburg News*, August 23, 1862, "The Draft Postponed."
 9. Ibid.
 10. Snell, 84.

City of York was no exception. *The York Gazette* reported a war meeting held on July 23:

> WAR MEETING IN YORK LARGE AND ENTHUSIATIC GATHERING OF PEOPLE
>
> Washington Hall was crowded to the utmost capacity on Wednesday evening last, in response to a call of many citizens, "to take into consideration the condition of the county in relation to the war, and devise means for encouraging enlistments of volunteers."[11]

A president, vice president, and two secretaries were appointed with a committee of ten men being selected to draft resolutions expressive of the meeting that was unanimously adopted. In part, the York war meeting resolved that:

> Whereas, The President of the United States has made a requisition upon the loyal people of the Union for an additional number of volunteers, to aid in suppressing the unholy rebellion, now existing in our land; and whereas, the Governor of Pennsylvania has fixed the quota to be supplied by York County, at three companies of volunteers, and urged the loyal citizens throughout our borders to take active measures for the encouraging of volunteering, and whereas, York County should not be behind any sister counties, in the patriotic work of sustaining the government in this hour of peril, therefore, Resolved, That we pledge our warmest efforts in furnishing the number of men required, and as many more as possible.[12]

These efforts included a $15,000 fund appropriated from the county coffers to pay bounties "of not less than fifty dollars" for each volunteer who enlisted under this current quota. The borough of Hanover paid each recruit an added $25 bounty giving each recruit a total bounty of $75.[13]

---

11. *The York Gazette*, July 29, 1862, "The President's Call for Troops in 1862."
12. Ibid.
13. Snell, 83.

York County quickly raised its quota, as The York Gazette reported on August 15, 1862: "The quota of three companies assigned to York had been more than filled." The paper further proclaimed that:

> Such a response speaks well for the patriotism and loyalty of our people. We have, excepting in the last quota, sent the greater part of one regiment into the field, and we would pledge ourselves, if allowed the privilege of volunteering, to raise another regiment. The people of York will not allow any other County to go before them in their efforts to carry on the war to a successful issue.[14]

On July 29, 1862, Cumberland County appropriated $20,000 "from the county funds to be obtained by a loan, if necessary a sum not exceeding twenty-thousand dollars to be appropriated at the rate of $50 per man, to every soldier who shall join companies to be raised in Cumberland County..." At the same time, Cumberland County passed a resolution "to pay the families of those who are now in the service of their county and are now sick, wounded or prisoners, and whose families are in a destitute condition, a sum sufficient to the support of said families."[15]

Bounties were offered at both the national and local levels in an effort to provide relief to the soldiers' wives and families. Federal legislation had been passed on May 11, 1861, that allowed counties, cities, and towns to appropriate funds for their relief by levying taxes or issuing bonds. First enlistment volunteers of the 130th Pennsylvania Regiment were entitled to receive a $100 National Bounty that would be paid at the time of their discharge, or to their legal representative if the volunteer was killed or died in service. For first re-enlisted volunteers they would receive $2 in addition to his formal pay, and $1 for every subsequent enlistment.[16] In an effort to fill the vacancies created in existing regiments, the Federal government amended the National Bounty provision by eliminating the bounty and advance pay for anyone volunteering for any new regiments after August 15, 1862.[17]

---

14. *The York Gazette*, August 15, 1862, "York County's Quota."
15. *The Carlisle Herald*, August 1, 1862, "War Meeting—$20,000 Appropriated."
16. *The Carlisle Herald*, September 20, 1861, "Bounties, Soldiers' Pay, Etc."
17. *The York Gazette*, August 19, 1862, "General Order of the Secretary of War Relative to Volunteers and Bounty."

Assuredly, the motivations to enlist were as varied as the volunteers. Many merely sought adventure, the allure of the romance of war that they had so wrongly perceived. Others signed on merely to receive the bounties. Despite their individual motivation, the majority of volunteers found in the recruiting lines were there with the sentiments of "right" and "duty." Patriotism, yes, but even more, it was a symbol of honor and manhood. The spirit to serve one's country in the great cause was the impetus for most to take their solemn oath of allegiance "to protect and defend against all enemies, foreign or domestic."

John D. Hemminger, who was recruited in Newville, reported that in response to the President's call, recruiting offices in Carlisle, Mechanicsburg, Newville, and Shippensburg met their quotas in a few days.[18] In

PRIVATE JOHN D. HEMMINGER, CO. E.
(U.S. Army Military History Institute)

---

18. John D. Hemminger Diary, Michael Winery Collection, (United States Army Military History Institute, hereinafter cited as USAMHI, Carlisle Barracks, Pennsylvania), 1. Hereinafter cited as Hemminger Diary.

Deeds, Not Words 13

the opening remarks in his diary, Hemminger recounted not yet meeting the age requirement of eighteen:

> Prompted by a spirit of loyalty I offered my humble service to help suppress the rebellion but was refected [*sic*] on account of not having attained the age of eighteen years. In the description, my age was put down as 18 years although I was lacking more than six months of the required years for enlistment. I was born on Saturday February 22, 1845.[19]

Sixteen-year-old Edward W. Spangler of York County noted how he volunteered with his mother's permission:

> On August 4, 1862, President Lincoln called for 300,000 volunteers to serve for nine months. In consequence, another war meeting was held by the citizens of York, for the purpose of taking measures to fill the county's quota—four companies which were quickly recruited. In the fall of 1861, I was rejected on account of my youth and small stature as a drummer boy in the 87th Regiment Pennsylvania Volunteers then forming on the York Commons—eight Companies from York County and two from Adams. About August 5, 1862 having obtained my mother's written consent, tearfully given, to my enlistment in the army, in company with brother Frank, two years my senior, we resigned our store clerkships. I was then a little over sixteen years of age and weighed ninety-two pounds.[20]

Edward Spangler would not be the youngest member of the unit. John C. Brown of Newville "ended" the war at the age of sixteen after enlisting as a private in Company E, 130th Pennsylvania Regiment at the age of thirteen.[21]

Within days after his 1859 graduation at Dickinson College in Carlisle, Pennsylvania, John Hays wrote to his college friend, Frank S. Findlay in Arlington, Virginia:

---

19. Hemminger Diary, 1.
20. Edward W. Spangler, *My Little War Experience*, (York: York Daily Publishing Company, 1904), 16.
21. *Star and Enterprise*, Newville, Pennsylvania, July 10, 1913. Although a John C. Brown is not included in Company E's official roster published in Samuel P. Bates' *History of Pennsylvania Volunteers, 1861-5*, recruits would sometimes use aliases in cases of those underage.

RECRUITING POSTER, YORK COUNTY
(Library of Congress)

Though the dividing lines between North and South and East and West may separate us and though our minds become imbued with the principles of that section of country in which our lot may be cast and our feelings as much imbittered as those of the hottest in the strife yet when the watchword 'concordia' shall be heard loud and clear above the din and noise of the contestants all bitter feelings, all differences in opinion, and all that may tend to separate us will be forgotten and our hands joined in the old-time grip of brotherly love.[22]

Soon after graduating, Hays joined into a law practice in Carlisle only to answer his call to duty in August 1862. He would in time be promoted to Major, becoming the 130th Pennsylvania Regiment's Adjutant, and would suffer the remainder of his life from wounds received at Chancellorsville.

In a September 1862 letter to his wife, Mary, Captain Henry I. Zinn expressed his feelings about serving, that were not unlike those who

---

22. Raphael S. Hays II, *John Hays*, (Carlisle, Cumberland County Historical Society, Carlisle, Pennsylvania, 2000), 12.

PRIVATE EDWARD W. SPANGLER, CO. K.
(*My Little War Experience*, Edward Spangler)

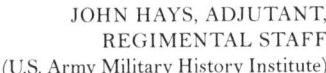

JOHN HAYS, ADJUTANT, REGIMENTAL STAFF
(U.S. Army Military History Institute)

served under him: "I do not feel so much like soldiering as formerly, but a sense of duty, and the hope that things will soon get better, prevent me from being despondent . . . so I make the best of my situation and take things as they come."[23]

Mechanicsburg native John B. Landis perhaps most accurately expressed the mindset of those new Pennsylvania recruits who decided to join the cause by rushing off to save the Union:

> On Saturday morning August the 9th, 1862 I joined a delegation of young men who had volunteered to enter the army of the Union. The whole country had been shaken to its foundation by the first year's experience of the war; and no young man who had any patriotism in his heart felt that he was doing his duty unless he shouldered a musket in defense of his country . . . The lump that rose in my throat as they gave me a tearful yet cheering farewell came near choking me. I scarcely dared to give a look back, for in that one moment of farewell came visions of battle, wounds, prison and death itself. But as quickly as it came it dissolved in the fire of patriotism as with song and cheer we sped down the hill toward town.[24]

An August 1862 article published in the Shippensburg News summed up not only the attitudes of the newspaper, but of every reader:

> Everyday that the present terrible war proceeds we receive fresh illustrations of the touching and beautiful self-sacrifice of the loyal people. Deeds not words, are generally the eloquent teachers of this, one of the paramount duties and instincts of the hour . . .[25]

---

23. Henry I. Zinn to his wife, August 13, 1862. As cited in Pennsylvania Antietam Battlefield Commission, *One Hundred and Thirtieth Regiment Pennsylvania Volunteer Infantry: Ceremonies and Addresses at Dedication of the Monument at Bloody Lane, Antietam Battlefield*, September 1904 (n.p., 1904), 54. Although all of the cited letters of Henry I. Zinn were to his wife Mary, some were addressed, "Dearest Mary," while others were addressed, "Dearest Wife."

24. John B. Landis Memoirs, (Antietam National Park Service, Department of the Interior, Sharpsburg, Maryland), (n.p.), 3. Hereinafter cited as Landis Memoirs, Special Collections, Antietam National Park service, Department of the Interior, Sharpsburg, Maryland.

25. *The Shippensburg News*, August 23, 1862.

Deeds, Not Words 17

CORPORAL JOHN D. LANDIS, CO. F,
(Cumberland County Historical Society, Carlisle, Pennsylvania)

This new flood of Pennsylvania volunteers inundated Harrisburg during the first two weeks of August 1862 to begin their journey that would forever change their lives. Harrisburg had been selected as the site where the state would organize and train its men. In addition to serving as the Commonwealth's capital city, Harrisburg provided rapid transportation for both men and materials as four railroads converged into the city as well as the recently opened Pennsylvania Canal.[26] The initial site selected to serve as the point of rendezvous and limited training (and often with none) was the 80-square-acre Dauphin County Agricultural Fairgrounds that was located one mile north of the state capital building. Originally named Camp of Rendezvous, and later renamed Camp Curtin in honor of Pennsylvania's governor, the facility would become the largest camp in the North, serving over 300,000 men from Pennsylvania, Ohio, Wisconsin, New York, and New Jersey.[27] The sudden August 1862 influx of new volunteers necessitated a second camp, located one and a half miles east

---

26. Miller, 5.
27. Miller, 237.

of the city, dubbed Camp Cameron in honor of the Secretary of War. This camp was immediately followed by a third camp located in fields north of Camp Curtin where the new 130th Pennsylvania Regiment would be organized. The new camp was named Camp Simmons, in honor of a Harrisburg soldier recently killed in the Peninsula Campaign. During that time, Camp Curtin was often referred to as the "Old Camp."[28]

The new recruits came from all stations in life, arriving individually or in organized companies. Most often, the localities organized their own companies of volunteers or provided their already-established local militia. William Laughlin and Joshua Sharpe, who had been given authorization by the governor to raise a company for nine months service, organized the future Company E of the 130th Pennsylvania Volunteers in Newville in July 1862.[29] A group of volunteers, called "The Shippensburg Guards," arrived at Harrisburg in similar fashion to become Company D.

They came by train, wagon, boat, or on foot. They were the teachers, farmers, tailors, carpenters, clerks, blacksmiths, and common laborers who formed together in August 1862. Many of those who arrived between August 10 and 15 were brought together into ten companies and designated the 130th Regiment Pennsylvania Volunteer Infantry. Companies A, G, D, F and E, were recruited from Cumberland County; Companies B, I, and K from York; Company C from York and Montgomery; and Company H from the counties of Cumberland, Dauphin, and Chester.[30]

Upon arriving at Camp Simmons the men, organized into volunteer companies, were assigned to new regiments, and were quickly issued brooms, rakes, tin cups, forks, and knives. The men of the 130th were not unlike most other inexperienced recruits, relying on their own initiative to keep warm that first night. Corporal John Landis recounted his unforgettable experience on August 9:

> Evening came on, we were not yet organized and had not tents. I remember with what care a comrade and myself selected a board

---

28. Miller, 107.
29. Unknown author, "Captain William Laughlin," 130th Pennsylvania Regiment Folder, Newville Historical Society, Newville, Pennsylvania, n.d.
30. Samuel P. Bates, *History of the Pennsylvania Volunteers, Volume II*, (Harrisburg: B. Singerly, State Publisher, 1870. Reprint, Wilmington, NC: Broadfoot Publishing Company, 1994), 203.

CAPTAIN WILLIAM LAUGHLIN, CO. E   CAPTAIN JOSHUA SHARPE, CO. E
(Newville Historical Society)   (Newville Historical Society)

pile for a bed, putting up a board for a roof to protect us from the night dews.[31]

Soon after the men arrived, they had to overcome their first obstacle of being examined by a surgeon who would attest that they were indeed fit for service. "Despite each examining officer's passing an examination by the surgeon general and a board of officers, many became less than thorough as the war progressed." Miller noted the examining doctor's questionable standards: "Often a quick look in a man's eye and mouth and a hearty thump or two on his chest was sufficient to determine a man's fitness for military service."[32]

John D. Hemminger vividly recounted his first medical experience at Harrisburg:

---
31. Landis Memoirs, 3.
32. Miller, 60.

> We were ordered to appear before a band of examining surgeons one at a time being admitted . . . divested of every particle of clothing the examination was conducted very much like a dealer wont to before purchasing a horse. And concluded with a description of the subject by age, weight, height, complexion, color of hair and eyes.[33]

When Edward Spangler's turn came to be inspected, the examiner commented, "Young man, you are only five foot two—two inches too short." Spangler remembered that he immediately stood on his toes and declared, "Try it again." The examiner winked, replied, "That's all right."[34]

In his words, future Corporal Landis of Company F recalled the scene in an even more descriptive manner:

> We marched to a house near the river bank to await examination. Here I had time to study the crowd about me, as I was lying in the shade of a locust tree, I saw the squads go in and out, to and from examination . . . Finally my own time came, I was nearly twenty-one years old, slight, only five feet seven inches tall, and poor in physical appearance. I passed with a blow to the collar bone and scarcely a look.[35]

Beginning that Saturday evening through August 15, typically by company, the men of the 130th were officially "mustered into the military service of the United States for a period of nine months unless sooner discharged by a termination of the war."[36] "The oath taken was to support the Constitution and defend the flag and country against all foes," Hemminger noted.[37]

August 1862 was colder and rainier than normal, continuously exposing men, used to the comforts of home, to the exposure of these unusual conditions affecting the general health in camp. The combination of a severe change in a diet of questionable quality, coupled with substandard

---

33. Hemminger Diary, 1.
34. Spangler, 18.
35. Landis Memoirs, 3.
36. Spangler, 18.
37. Hemminger Diary, 2.

and often unsanitary living conditions, resulted in higher-than-normal cases of dysentery and diarrhea followed by typhoid, assorted fevers and respiratory illnesses.[38]

On Sunday, August 10, the volunteers received their tents, which they pitched in the southeastern portion of Camp Simmons. Their day was busy in preparing their camp and receiving visitors coming to see their loved-ones perhaps for their last time. The mustering in continued through Monday with some new recruits, including Private Samuel Brehm of Company E, standing guard for the first time. Private Brehm documented his viewpoint of being a soldier thus far: "Think sogering [*sic*] tolerable good business—rather wild."[39]

Tuesday morning was a beautiful morning with indications of a warm breeze. Both the morning and afternoon were uneventful. On Tuesday evening there was a dress parade for the men of Companies A and F with the ladies of Harrisburg presenting them "colors." Afterwards, Corporal Landis recorded the event:

> One brave fellow over six feet tall, with light hair and high cheek bones, by the name of Crist, went so far as to go into town and buy a great butcher knife, which he stuck under his belt, as he went around the Camp bellowing to be let loose on the Rebels. But the poor boy hadn't smelled powder yet, and his big knife was afterward put to the peaceful uses of dividing the salt pork for his comrades in the cook's tent, under his hands, instead of being used upon our erring brothers on the other side.[40]

An infantry regiment in the Civil War contained ten companies lettered A through K omitting J. The letter J was unused since it was easily confused with the letter K in hand written orders and reports. A colonel commanded a regiment with additional staff officers of a lieutenant-colonel, a major, an adjutant and quartermaster officer, both with the rank of lieutenant, a surgeon, and an assistant surgeon. Additionally authorized were the positions of regimental sergeant major, a

---

38. Miller, 61.
39. Samuel H. Brehm Diary, August 11, 1862, Newville Historical Society, Newville, Pennsylvania. Hereinafter cited as Brehm Diary with corresponding date.
40. Landis Memoirs, 4.

regimental quartermaster sergeant, a regimental commissary sergeant, a hospital steward, two principal musicians, and twenty-four musicians for a band. A captain commanded each company, which was divided into two platoons, with one platoon commanded by a first lieutenant and the other by a second lieutenant. Each platoon was divided into two squads, each supervised by a sergeant. A company was additionally authorized one first sergeant, four sergeants, eight corporals, two musicians, one wagoner, and from sixty-four to eighty-two privates.[41]

The sudden departure from the toils and responsibilities of everyday life caught many soldiers with a sincere concern for their families' welfare. How was a family to survive without its breadwinner? Who would take care of them in the soldier's absence? Twenty-seven-year-old schoolteacher Captain Zinn, of Company F, from Churchland, Cumberland County, wrote to his wife on August 13, 1862, from Camp Simmons, expressing these concerns. Little did he know that within four days of his first letter home that his responsibility would multiply tenfold from being the captain of a company in charge of one hundred men, to becoming the commander of the regiment with the overwhelming responsibility of about 1,000 men.

> Dearest Wife: . . . orders have been received to prepare four regiments immediately, and as my company is one of those to go, I cannot get off. I have no idea at all where we will be sent. It leaves me in a predicament, as I have not yet made any provision for you nor myself. My uniform and other things I need are still at home. If I can possibly get off, I shall go home soon in order to arrange my affairs. You will have to exercise your business tact and try to collect certain outstanding accounts due me. Above all, take good care of yourself and the children, and take things calmly. I shall write you soon again and if I find I cannot get home I shall then give you directions how to send me things. Until then believe me.[42]

---

41. *Revised Regulations for the United States Army*, 1863, 505.
42. Henry I. Zinn to his wife, August 13, 1862.

Thursday August 14 brought with it the election of company officers, a common practice both North and South. The members of each company would elect their captain. The elected captain, in turn, would appoint the company's noncommissioned officers. The command position for the 130th Pennsylvania Regiment came not from political influence, wealth, background, or military experience, but from the drillmaster at Camp Curtin. In a letter sent to Governor Curtin on September 2, 1862, requesting that commissions be issued, Captain Henry I. Zinn remarked, "I was selected by Capt. Tarbutton to take command of the Regiment and have had command up to the present time."[43] Tarbutton, a middle-aged Harrisburg resident, was given the rank of captain at the outbreak of the war and initially assigned to Camp Curtin.[44] He was tasked to teach the officers and non-commissioned officers how to march, and the basics of squad and company drill, so they could then teach their men.[45] Captain William Tarbutton served concurrently as drillmaster and post adjutant, and later as the nine-month units arrived, he was the Vice Commander, commanding Camp Simmons, the satellite of the Old Camp (Camp Curtin).[46] It can be assumed that he selected the men he believed could best perform the duties of the regimental commander from the officers within the newly-formed regiment, based upon his first-hand observations and military experience. This temporary selection was contingent upon Governor Curtin's confirmation.

Two subsequent documented requests were made in attempts to become the 130th's Regimental Commander. On July 28, 1862, an application was filed with Pennsylvania's Adjutant General A. L. Russell by A. G. Barney who requested command of one of the newly-formed volunteer regiments. On August 27, 1862, Barney followed up his application with a personal letter to Governor Curtin, requesting that he be considered to take command of the 130th considering his previous regimental command experience.[47]

---

43. Captain Henry I. Zinn to Governor Curtin, September 2, 1862, 130th Pennsylvania Regimental Records. RG-19, Box 81, Pennsylvania State Archives, Harrisburg, Pennsylvania.
44. Bates, 207.
45. Miller, 72.
46. Miller, 107.
47. A. G. Barney to Governor Curtin, August 27, 1862, 130th Pennsylvania Regimental Records, Pennsylvania State Archives.

BRIGADIER GENERAL WILLIAM H. FRENCH,
COMMANDER, 3RD DIVISION, SECOND CORPS
(National Archives and Records Administration,
Brady Collection, College Park)

Brigadier General William H. French, commander of the 3rd Division, Second Corps, to which the 130th would soon be assigned, recommended a second nominee. Brigadier General French's September 9, 1862 letter to Lieutenant Colonel J. H. Taylor, Chief of Staff of the Second Corps, cited that the 130th Pennsylvania had reported without any field officers. He requested that Lieutenant J. H. Wilson (United States Army Topographical Engineers) be "assigned to the regiment as acting colonel and that the governor of Pennsylvania be asked to confirm the appointment." Further, General French went on, "A very few days only under its present organization or rather the want of it will demoralize nine hundred fine men. The captain commanding [Captain Henry I. Zinn] reported to me that his men were beyond his control and acquiring habits of thieving, straggling and marauding."[48] General French's request was subsequently

---

48. Brigadier General French to Colonel J. H. Taylor, September 9, 1862, 130th Pennsylvania Regimental Records.

Deeds, Not Words

endorsed by the Second Corps Commander, General E. V. Sumner, who added, "I would respectfully urge the appointment."[49] On September 20, 1862, Lieutenant J. H. Wilson petitioned Governor Curtin for the position in a letter citing that "if granted that I can make the 130th Regiment a credit to Pennsylvania and extremely useful in the Great Cause."[50]

The actual commissions issued by the Commonwealth of Pennsylvania would arrive much later.[51] The mustering-in process continued through Sunday August 17, for those who had not yet taken the oath

MAJOR GENERAL EDWIN V. SUMNER,
COMMANDER, SECOND CORPS
(National Archives and Records Administration,
Brady Collection, College Park)

---

49. Ibid.
50. Jas. H. Wilson to Governor Curtin, September 20, 1862, 130th Pennsylvania Regimental Records. Three days prior to Lieutenant Wilson writing his letter to Governor Curtin, an internal election of the regiment's field and staff officers occurred.
51. Hays, 16.

of allegiance.[52] For others in the regiment, the day was uneventful with some members returning to their homes for their last "good-byes."

During the next two days, the men were issued their uniforms, equipment, and new 1861 model Springfield rifles.[53] Company E's Private John Hemminger carefully recounted that they received:

> Then was issued to each member of our company an outfit of clothing consisting of 1 pair of pantaloons, a dress frock coat, 1 pair of shoes, a cap. 2 shirts, 2 pair of drawers and 2 pair of socks. In addition we each received a wool blanket, Knapsack, Haversack. and canteen. For the above outfit we were charged the sum of $30.00 to be accounted for at the expiration of the term of service as against the allowance each one was entitled to receive.[54]

With this issue each company had received its required clothing and equipment, with the exception of a rubber blanket and a shoulder strap for the cartridge box.[55]

Corporal John Landis of Company F recalled the procedure of issuing uniforms in a somewhat more humorous manner:

> We now began to look more like soldiers, although many of us took on quite ludicrous appearances. One man's clothing was too large and another's too small. A big cap on a small head or a little cap on a big head, gave an odd look to many a one. But after exchanges were made, most of us looked presentable. But getting on our accoutrements and learning how to roll up an overcoat and blanket were the next problems.[56]

Company G's Private John S. Weiser was able to find a free moment on August 16 to write home to his parents telling them of his first experiences of military life:

---

52. Ibid.
53. Hemminger Diary, August 17, 1862.
54. Hemminger Diary August 16, 1862.
55. Hemminger Diary August 17, 1862.
56. Landis Memoirs, 4.

We get plenty to eat such as Government peas and good Beef and splendid shoulder with coffee for supper and Breakfast and Bean and Rice [soup] with Potato for dinner, I fare very well all the time as I am on the right side of the Cooks[.] [W]e have two cooks that cook for the whole Company[.] [W]e were formed into a Regiment the beginning of the week but it was broken up and we are in another new, but don't know what one it is yet[.] [W]e are under marching orders and can't tell how soon we will leave as there are two Regiments leaving every day.[57]

Camp Curtin served as both a camp of rendezvous and instruction. On a typical day the nearby fields were alive with commands being shouted teaching squad, company, and battalion movements necessary to both save lives and be successful on the battlefields yet to come. Regiments received training that could prove the difference between life and death to the soldier and success or failure to the unit. The 130th would be forced, at least temporarily, to forgo this opportunity. On Monday morning, August 18, the 986 men of the newly-formed 130th Pennsylvania Volunteer Regiment were given three days rations and ordered to pack up and be ready to leave Camp Simmons.[58] Their time had so quickly arrived.

According to Private Hemminger, the morning of August 18 was "bright and clear and by 9 o'clock in the morning with organization of the regiment complete." The men of the new 130th Pennsylvania marched out of camp headed towards Harrisburg.[59] They marched up Market Street to the Susquehanna River and crossed over the large wood "Camel back" bridge to Bridgeport where train transports were awaiting them. Private Hemminger continued in his diary: "In marching over the old bridge the regular step of nearly one thousand men carried the structure to oscillate so much that for a few moments great alarm was felt for fear that the thing might collapse."[60]

The Northern Central Railroad cars at Bridgeport came in a wide assortment. Company E was crowded in open boxcars with sides about eighteen

---

57. John S. Weiser to his parents, August 16, 1862, Civil War Miscellaneous Collection, U.S. Army Military History Institute (USAMHI), Carlisle Barracks
58. John R. Turner to his daughter, Kittie, September 28, 1862.
59. Hemminger Diary, August 18, 1862.
60. Ibid.

inches high with planks laid over for seats. At 12:00 P.M. the train reached the city of York, giving many York soldiers the opportunity for one last good-bye from their loved ones.[61] At 3:00 P.M., the regiment arrived at the Calvert Street Station in Baltimore, disembarked, and marched up Calvert Street past Monument Square to the Camden Station of the Baltimore and Ohio Railroad. The regiment was taken to the rooms of the Union Relief Committee at the Camden Station and given a good supper.[62]

Corporal Landis of Company F described his first journey in blue:

> This began to seem a little like soldiering; loaded down with blanket, haversack, canteen, tin-cup, musket, &c. and moving out . . . with our engine headed southward, we began to feel that we were indeed to take up an army life. I remember with what interest we watched the state line between Pennsylvania and Maryland, and how when we crossed it the boys cheered loud and long, for they were entering the enemy's country.[63]

Arriving in the streets of Baltimore, Corporal Landis began to realize that the patriotic sentiment he shared with his comrades was viewed differently in neighboring Maryland: "The streets of Baltimore were very quiet as we marched through. How different from Harrisburg . . . how quiet. Only dark side glances were cast upon us. Window blinds were drawn, or opened sufficiently to reveal the scowling glances cast upon us from behind them."[64]

Shortly before 10:00 P.M., the 130th reboarded the train, continuing their tiresome journey to Washington. En route, Private Hemminger became stricken with severe stomach cramps. The regiment, finally arriving in Washington around 12:00 P.M., was quartered for the night at the Soldiers' Retreat, a spacious wooden structure, at the railroad depot and later provided supper by the Soldiers' Relief. Private Hemminger was taken to a room at the Soldiers' Retreat and examined by a physician who found his "suffering greatly alleviated but in an exhausted condition."[65]

---

61. The Shippensburg News, August 23, 1862.
62. Ibid.
63. Landis Memoirs, 4–5.
64. Ibid.
65. Landis Memoirs, 4–5; Hemminger Diary August 18–19, 1862; Merkel Landis, Esq., "History of the 130th Regiment Penn Volunteer Infantry," *The Evening Sentinel*, December 28, 1929, 3; Brehm Diary, August 18, 1862.

CHAPTER 2

Guarding the Capitol

At daybreak, August 11, the regiment awoke to its first view of the nation's capital. Private Spangler recounted, "We had never before seen an edifice so large, majestic, and imposing in appearance. Its present lofty dome, with its tiers of columns . . . its summit surmounted by the colossal statue of liberty, was then erected only a score of feet above the adjacent wings, with a huge crane projecting from the opening."[1] After breakfast at the Soldiers' Relief, the regiment formed "with colors flying and moved under a hot sun up Pennsylvania Avenue, unpaved and full of ruts."[2] While on their march down the avenue the "Hallelujah Chorus" was started by some of the men and quickly joined by the whole regiment and "it became a volume of sound that made the windows rattle and stirred the hearts of Union men in the Capitol City."[3] The regiment crossed the Long Bridge that spanned the Potomac River into Virginia and proceeded to Camp Wells, a distance of three or four miles.[4] This was the regiment's first experience of marching with the added burden of a knapsack. Private Lewis Masonheimer of Company A described it as, "A very ugly article for a soldier."[5] Attesting to what he thought a long march, Private Samuel H. Brehm of Company E commented, "Walked the whole distance and was rather fatigued."[6] The regiment arrived at their destination, Camp Wells, which was part of a thirty-seven-mile ring of twenty-three fortifications

---

1. Spangler, 19.
2. Lewis Masonheimer Diary, August 18, 1862, in possession of Dorothy Bonafield Snyder; Spangler 19.
3. *The Shippensburg News*, August 23, 1862.
4. Spangler, 19.
5. Masonheimer Diary, August 19, 1862.
6. Brehm Diary, August 19, 1862.

LONG BRIDGE, WASHINGTON
(National Archives and Records Administration, Brady Collection, College Park)

built to protect the Capitol, which was situated across the Potomac River in Virginia, two miles in the rear and southwest of Arlington Heights on the farm of General Robert E. Lee."[7] The men settled into their new camp, put up their tents, and prepared themselves for their first night on Virginia soil. Private Hemminger, still feeling quit ill and unable to march with the regiment, was sent by Captain Joshua W. Sharp by ambulance to the Trinity Church Hospital in Washington for further treatment.[8]

August 20 was uneventful for most in the 130th. Many lay in camp resting from the long trip from Harrisburg. Others, including Private Brehm, were detailed with a twenty-four-hour guard duty.[9] This day gave Colonel Zinn his first opportunity to write home to his wife since leaving Harrisburg: "I have never been so busy in my life as now. It may sound very nice to be the commander of a regiment, but I have come to the conclusion that a colonel earns all he gets . . . I am very much interrupted by persons coming in so that I can hardly write a dozen lines without two dozen interruptions . . ." His letter further complained that "No permanent appointments have yet been made for the regiment;

---

7. *The Shippensburg News*, August 23, 1862; Landis Diary, 5.
8. Hemminger Diary, August 19, 1862.
9. Brehm Diary, August 20, 1862.

therefore things do not go off very smoothly."[10] Given the command and staff responsibilities, Colonel Zinn and his staff lacked the proper authority of their positions, which could jeopardize their effectiveness.[11] He further described the living conditions as "a little rough, but that is owing to a want of proper management . . . the location is very good but the water is somewhat scarce."[12]

Others within the regiment also had time to write short letters home describing their wartime experiences thus far. Private John S. Weiser of Company G wrote to his parents describing the surroundings as being somewhat desolate and his living conditions rather limited:

> We . . . arrived here yesterday evening all very well this camp is seven miles from Washington City it is the most desolate country I have ever seen . . . I just came from a brook two miles from camp where I was washing two Shirts and a pair of drawers the first I washed since I have been in the Service last evening after we pitched our tents, our bunk went out and brought in a lot of tomatoes and we cooked them for supper this morning we had onions for breakfast When I say bunk I mean the men that stay in the tent that I do there are fourteen of us in the tent.[13]

Captain William Laughlin, who commanded Company E, thought well of his first days at camp, writing to his nephews on August 20, 1861: "Boys we are on the sacred soil of Virginia encamped in a blackberry field and all well and comfortable . . . with good water and plenty of it."[14]

The quality of the men of the 130th Regiment thus far was held in high regard. Colonel Zinn claimed that the regiment was composed of "fine material, and most of the officers are gentlemen."[15] Captain Laughlin held a similar opinion: "We have a very pleasant Regt there has not been a fight or a drunk man that I know of since we have been in camp."[16]

---

10. Henry I. Zinn to his wife, August 20, 1862.
11. Although Henry Zinn was appointed the regiment's commander, the rank of a colonel, he continued to use his rank of captain until October 1, 1862, when the formal officer commissions would arrive from the Pennsylvania Governor's Office.
12. Henry I. Zinn to his wife, August 20, 1862.
13. John S. Weiser to his parents, August 20, 1862.
14. William Laughlin to his nephews, August 20, 1862, Newville Historical Society.
15. Henry I. Zinn to his wife, August 20, 1862.
16. William Laughlin to his nephews, August 20, 1862.

The 130th Regiment celebrated two events the next day, Thursday, August 21, with the first regimental drill and the birthday of Company F's Corporal John Landis. Corporal Landis wrote on his birthday: "This day Aug. 21 was my birthday, and my twenty-first anniversary, too. So from that day forward I felt a little more a man."[17]

For the next several days, the regiment's routine consisted of both company and regimental drill, along with picket duty and swimming the "rapid current of the falls of the Potomac."[18] Cooking was at company level with appointed cooks who provided a "monotonous supply of bean-soup" cooked in large iron kettles "often burnt in the cooking, for our noonday meal."[19]

Meanwhile that day, Private Hemminger, still in a Washington hospital, received a visit by his friend, Private Simon M. Whistler, also from Company E. With permission from a hospital surgeon, he and Private Whistler visited the Capitol and other places of interest only to return to the hospital to witness the cruelty of war. A number of wounded had just arrived, including an Irishman who had both of his arms amputated near the shoulder. Amazingly, the Irishman marched back and forth through the ward singing songs and telling funny jokes and observed that he could not understand why the rebs would take both his arms and leave his head.[20]

Company K was detailed to protect the famous Virginia Mansion "Arlington" owned by Confederate General Robert E. Lee.[21] Private Spangler described the mansion:

> "A stately brick structure with slave quarters and stables . . . with a picturesque view of the Capitol City. The old portraits of the Custis and Lee families were still hanging over the parlor walls. The interior architecture . . . was a perfect reproduction of an aristocratic Virginia interior of a century ago. All about the place had the aspect of antiquity and former wealth"[22]

---

17. Landis Diary, 5.
18. Spangler, 21.
19. Ibid.
20. Hemminger Diary, August 22, 1862.
21. Spangler, 20.
22. Ibid.

U.S. CAPITOL, UNFINISHED
(National Archives and Records Administration, Brady Collection, College Park)

It was rumored that Company K was to be detached permanently to provide guard duty at the Arlington mansion for their entire term of service. The rumor was quickly quelled after a week's service when the company was ordered to march about six miles up to the Potomac River to the regiment's new encampment at Fort Marcy near the Chain Bridge.[23]

After several attempts, on August 23, Private Hemminger was able to convince the surgeon, Dr. Davis, to discharge him. Under protest, the doctor relented and issued the discharge and pass, although he claimed that Private Hemminger was "unfit for duty" and that he should remain for a week or two longer.[24] Private Hemminger immediately set out to

---

23. Ibid.
24. Hemminger Diary, August 23, 1862.

ARLINGTON HOUSE, 1864 (Library of Congress)

locate his regiment that was somewhere across the Potomac River in Virginia. He went on to add, "Further on I was taken on by one of Uncle Sam's forage wagon going in the direction of Arlington. With permission of the driver I mounted the seat by his side . . . arriving at the Regiment's camp at 5 o'clock P.M. almost tired out, but glad to be again with the boys."[25]

Private Brehm observed that Sunday August 24, was a less demanding day, with a 9:00 A.M. inspection followed in the afternoon with a "short discourse in Camp by a member of the Reg. The theme, sin. Its origins, character, effects. Very suitably applied to the profanity in Camp." A dress parade concluded the duty day that evening.[26]

After only four days of drilling, the regiment was temporarily separated. "Three companies of this regiment have been sent to man forts in the neighborhood. Captain Porter's company [A], and Company F, have been ordered to Fort Albany, while the other companies have been sent to Fort Craig," Colonel Henry I. Zinn informed his wife.[27] This assignment was short-lived as Private Masonheimer recorded in his diary

---

25. Ibid.
26. Brehm Diary, August 24, 1862.
27. Henry I. Zinn to Mary, August 24, 1862.

August 25: "Marched to Fort Albany one mile from Long Bridge and back to camp at night."[28]

There was a strong indication that the regiment would soon be moving. On August 24, fifteen teams were sent to move the regiment; however, no official orders had been received authorizing the move. The teams were sent a few hundred yards to move the nearby 125th Pennsylvania Infantry Regiment.[29] Company E had been sent three miles to Manassas Gap for their first experience at picket duty and would return at 4:00 A.M. on August 26 to see their fellow soldiers having breakfast and being instructed to pack up and be ready to march with no time or opportunity for sleep.[30] Since the teams arrived late on August 26, the regiment would begin its seven-mile trek to their new camp at Fort Marcy.[31] Ft. Marcy was located on a ridge near the Leesburg Pike, about one mile from the Chain Bridge on the Virginia side of the Potomac River.[32]

Colonel Zinn was beginning to understand military service when to his wife he wrote, "There is no probability of our remaining long in any position." Further, Colonel Zinn remarked, "The Regiment is to be drilled as heavy artillery."[33] He had somehow received tentative advanced notice of the intentions of the War Department. This garrison-type duty would require the regiment to man the heavy artillery on Washington's outer defenses. While this duty would have come as positive news to their families, it would not be to most of the men in the 130th who were ready to get into the fight. Fortunately, or not, the regiment was destined to fulfill its obligation to the nation as it had begun, as an infantry regiment.

Not long after settling into camp, Private Hemminger was among those detailed for camp guard and was given the countersign of "Baltimore" by the officer of the day in order to identify friend or foe. The officer further instructed the guards "not to allow any person to approach or cross the given line that could not give the countersign."[34] As a testament to the greenness of the men, later in the day an unidentified guard heard

---

28. Masonheimer Diary, August 25, 1862.
29. Henry I. Zinn to Mary, August 24, 1862.
30. Hemminger Diary, August 25–26, 1862.
31. Masonheimer Diary, August 27, 1862.
32. Hemminger Diary, August 27, 1862.
33. Henry I. Zinn to Mary, August 24, 1862.
34. Hemminger Diary, August 27, 1862.

approaching footsteps and quickly shouted to the approaching stranger: "Halt who comes there." The reply came back promptly: "A Friend." The unidentified guard then replied: "approach friend within three paces of guard and say Baltimore or I'll shoot."[35]

Later that day the reality of war unveiled itself to the men of the 130th when they heard heavy cannonading for the first time coming from the distant direction of Manassas.[36] Excitement stirred the air as rumors spread throughout the camp that a large number of Rebels were nearby and could soon be expected. Private Brehm's concerns of enemy action increased as he wrote, "Reports still worse in the afternoon. In the evening, the regiment is drawn up on the pike [Leesburg Turnpike] and undergo a drill on firing. Receive orders to be ready at a moment's warning."[37]

As many had expected, at 2:00 A.M. the next morning, August 29, the regiment was awakened and ordered out to repel the possibility of invading Rebels on the heels of Union Major General John Pope's Army in the area of Manassas. Corporal Landis wrote in his diary how "by a roundabout route [the regiment] took a position near the banks of the Potomac, among the tall wet grass and weeds, where we remained until daylight, when with nothing but our arms we marched to Fort Ethan Allen."[38] Not long after arriving at Fort Ethan Allen, the regiment back-tracked and bivouacked on the hill between Fort Marcy and Fort Ethan Allen.[39] Later that afternoon the regiment witnessed General George B. McClellan's Army of the Potomac passing up the Potomac.[40] Private Brehm recorded this significant evening in his diary: "This night our bed is the soils of the 'Old Dominion' and the firmament our pavilion. The stars seem to stand over us as sentinels to guard us from all besetting danger."[41]

Just as the evening of August 29 had ended, the next morning began with heavy cannonading heard all day, reaching its crescendo at 3:00 P.M.[42] This meant to the men of the regiment that Major General Pope and his

---

35. Ibid.
36. Brehm Diary, August 27, 1862.
37. Brehm Diary, August 28, 1862.
38. Landis Memoirs, 5.
39. Brehm Diary, August 29, 1862.
40. Landis Memoirs, 5.
41. Brehm, Diary, August 29, 1862.
42. Landis Memoirs, 5.

Army of Virginia were being forced from their position and any hope of Union victory seemed doubtful. Private Hemminger heard the sounds of heavy cannons from the direction in Centreville: "The tide of battle was against us . . . Our forces were repulsed in yesterday's engagement, and are falling back to this place."[43] The battle would remain distant to the men of the 130th, who would not encounter the rumored approaching throng of the Confederates that day. On August 30 the regiment was ordered back to its former position at Fort Marcy, with the men striking their tents on familiar ground.[44]

Sunday morning, the last day of August, brought with it rain that lasted the entire day, along with a stream of escaped slaves, dubbed "contrabands," heading into Washington seeking refuge. Private Masonheimer recorded that "Every contraband a different story. Numbers of families flitting down the road towards Washington."[45] That morning, the absence of cannonading was noticed by the men of Company E as they were receiving their scripture lesson, the 10th Chapter of Matthew, by Lieutenant Joshua W. Sharpe, who was filling in for the yet to be assigned regimental chaplain.[46] Later in the afternoon, the firing began coming from the same direction as the day before. Rumors were spreading throughout the camp like wildfire about the fighting taking place only a few miles west of the regiment's camp.[47] Private Masonheimer recalled that "Many reports concerning yesterday's fighting afloat but nothing definite as yet."[48]

With only picket duty to perform, most of the men had the day to themselves. Company F's Corporal Landis and one of his comrades took the opportunity to venture outside the regiment's campsite to investigate a nearby cabin to learn a little about the Southern culture:

> "With one of my comrades, I went to a cabin where we found a jolly old colored Auntie, with whom we soon contracted for a hoe-cake . . . The real slave, old Chloe, was not at all afraid of

---

43. Hemminger Diary, August 29, 1862.
44. Brehm Diary, August 30, 1862.
45. Masonheimer Diary, August 31, 1862.
46. Brehm Diary, August 31, 1862.
47. The fighting taking place near Centreville, Virginia, would become known as the Battle of Second Bull Run.
48. Masonheimer Diary, August 31, 1862.

Yankees. I became interested in her, and tried to get some idea of her life and childhood. I found her, however, to be one of those happy, contended old "mammys", whose thoughts did not seem to run above the satisfaction of her physical wants for the day. True, no doubt she was to her master, who was in the service in the Southern Army, but the great question, which racked the country, in her happy ignorance she was never destined to see. So, whether she fed "yank" or "reb", she was alike contented."[49]

The day also brought news that a Washington newspaper had reported how the 130th had been engaged in battle and were badly cut up. In his August 31, 1862 letter to his wife Meg, Captain Laughlin, commander of Company E, wrote from Fort Marcy: " I heard of an account of a battle being published in one of the Washington papers in which it states the 130th Regt Penna were engaged and badly cut up for fear that some of you might see it in some of the papers and believe it, I thought I had better write and let you know not a word of truth in the statement. . . ."[50] False reports like these lessened the confidence in the reporting of many of the well-respected newspapers of the day. About the same time, the men had heard a report that Confederate Lieutenant General Thomas J. Jackson and his staff had been captured, along with a good portion of his army.[51] Confusion and rumors were daily ingredients in this camp not unlike any camp in any war. As their time in the army progressed, undoubtedly, the men of 130th learned to question the reliability of what they heard in camp and read each day in the newspapers.

On August 31, the regiment received news that it, along with the 127th Pennsylvania Infantry Regiment, had been assigned to the Reserve Corps of the Potomac.[52] The assignment would be a short-lived one, lasting only a week. The regiment's fate was soon to be decided due to a turn of events unfolding only twenty miles west of them near the small Virginia town of Manassas.

The next day brought not only the first day of September, but also news that their Union Army had been defeated at the battle of Second

---
49. Landis Memoirs, 6.
50. William Laughlin to Mag, August 31, 1861.
51. Henry I. Zinn to his wife, August 31, 1862.
52. *The Shippensburg News*, August 30, 1862.

Bull Run. Corporal John Landis witnessed the solemn return of Pope's defeated soldiers:

> The road [Leesburg Pike] was full of retreating soldiers and we first became aware of the defeat and disaster of Second Bull Run. The straggling towards Washington continued the next day, Wednesday [September 3, 1862], some of the soldiers having had nothing to eat for two days. We ourselves were on half rations. Infantry, Cavalry and Artillery were moving for Harper's Ferry we were informed, and Alexandria.[53]

Company E's commander, Captain William Laughlin, wrote in a letter that "You ought to see the returning soldiers they are the hardest looking set of men you ever did see but at the same time they are determined to put down this rebellion."[54]

Confidence in the Union campaign was being questioned by both the troops and their officers after seeing first-hand their defeated comrades passing by and retreating to the safety of Washington. Colonel Zinn shared his personal sentiment to his wife Mary: "My opinion of the war is that we are worse off now than a year ago, and that the rebellion is not much near put down than then . . . The old army is about played out, and the salvation of the country depends on the new levies.[55]

During the next two days, the men practiced company and regimental drill, performed picket duty, and listened to rumors of a possible Rebel confrontation. Private Hemminger noted on September 2 that they still had a lot to learn about soldiering, "This morning the company was taken out for drill. We practically know nothing about the Manuel [sic] of Arms and less about executing movements."[56]

Rumors spread through the camp late that evening that the Rebels were approaching Washington. In response, the regiment was ordered to form along the Leesburg Pike and nervously anticipated a confrontation that never came. After a full day of work on September 4, the regiment was ordered back to Fort Marcy, still anxious to know the whereabouts of

---

53. Landis Memoirs, 6.
54. William Laughlin to Mag, August 31, 1862.
55. Henry I. Zinn to Mary, September 5, 1862.
56. Hemminger Diary, September 2, 1862.

the Confederate forces.[57] With little time to rest, Companies E and I were ordered out on picket duty for the next two days. "We marched out the Leesburg turnpike road to a place called Pleasant Hall and stationed along an old abandoned road. Darkness had set in before arriving at this place. We captured two Rebel prisoners and an old horse, Our only food on this outing was green corn," recounted Company E's Private Hemminger.[58]

That same day, a steady stream of about 25,000 troops marched past the regiment's camp at Fort Marcy. Major General Franz Sigel passed by the regiment and was given three cheers. Later on that evening of September 3, the regiment was honored with both Major General McClellan and Major General Fitz-John Porter who visited the regiment and had supper with Colonel Zinn.[59]

As large bodies of Union troops began encamping near Washington on the Upper Potomac on September 4 and 5, anxiety increased in camp according to Private Hemminger, since the men did not know "the whereabouts of the confederate forces and their intentions of their Commander."[60] "I was greatly struck with the beautiful sight of numerous camp fires on the hills round about on the night of Friday," recalled Corporal Landis.[61] The influx of Federals concentrated around the outer defenses of the Capitol was an indication that something was being planned and the 130th would soon be a part. On Saturday, September 6, the order was given to cook two days rations, but with no orders to move, the regiment remained in place until the following day.[62]

The Federal movement into Maryland began on September 6.[63] Private Hemminger was impressed with the "Large bodies of the Army are march[ing] down the pike and crossing into Maryland over the Chain Bridge. Indicating that Gen Lee is about to cross the Potomac. If not already invading Maryland."[64] The men of the 130th Regiment were soon to join the march into Maryland not knowing either their destination or destiny.

---

57. Hemminger Diary, September 4, 1862.
58. Hemminger Diary, September 2–3, 1862.
59. Masonheimer Diary, September 3, 1862.
60. Hemminger Diary, September 4, 1862.
61. Landis Memoirs, 6.
62. Ibid.
63. Hemminger Diary, September 6, 1862.
64. Hemminger Diary, September 6, 1862.

CHAPTER 3

Seeing the Elephant: The Antietam Campaign

WHEN THE ORDER to move out finally came early on Sunday afternoon, September 7, 1862, the regiment numbered 930 enlisted men and officers who were prepared for their first march with the Army of the Potomac.[1] Private Hemminger recorded his experience that morning:

> We each received a cartridge box strap for over the shoulder, also a [poncho] used in time of rain. Today we also received brass letters and numbers to fasten on the front of our caps designating the company and Regiment we are members. Painters were busy stenciling the company and Regiment on our knapsacks.[2]

Anticipating a long march, the men were instructed only to pack their knapsacks with things that they needed on the march. As his comrades, Private Hemminger was then ordered to leave his knapsack behind that contained "a change of clothing a new rubber coat. Stamps and stationary."[3] The men were equipped only with their gun, rations, blanket, and the clothing they were wearing.[4] At 2:00 P.M., orders were finally received directing the regiment to be ready to march within an hour.[5]

At exactly 3:00 P.M., the regiment left the safety of Fort Marcy and began its march. The regiment joined in with Brigadier General William

---

1. John R. Turner to his daughter, Kittie, September 28, 1862.
2. Hemminger Diary, September 7, 1862.
3. Ibid.
4. Brehm Diary, September 7, 1862.
5. Hemminger Diary, September 7, 1862.

BRIGADIER GENERAL WILLIAM H. FRENCH
(U.S. Army Military History Institute)

H. French's Third Division, which was assigned to Major General Edwin V. Sumner who commanded the Second Corps.[6]

Traveling down the Leesburg turnpike to the Chain Bridge, the regiment crossed over the Potomac River where Private Hemminger caught a quick and unimpressive glimpse of Major General Franz Sigel who commanded the First Corps returning from the loss at Second Bull Run: "His hair reaching his shoulder straps is not becoming to the active Soldier life."[7] Once across the bridge the regiment moved northward up the north bank of the Potomac River for several miles, finally reaching the intercepting turnpike that led to Frederick, Maryland.[8] Private Spangler vividly recalled, "It was our first day's march with the army. The heat was sultry and oppressive, and after we had gone but a short distance on the turnpike, all superfluous clothing was doffed."[9] The regiment's grueling eighteen-mile march passed through the Maryland town of Tennallytown, continuing

---

6. Masonheimer Diary, September 7, 1862.
7. Masonheimer Diary, September 7, 1862.
8. Hemminger Diary, September 7, 1862.
9. Spangler, 21.

late into Sunday evening. The men marched by the light of the bright moonlight arriving about 10:00 P.M. The "very tired and fatigued" unit bivouacked at the Montgomery County fairgrounds near Rockville.[10]

Once the regiment left Fort Marcy, the practice of company cooking was abandoned and each soldier was left to prepare his own meals. Cooking utensils consisted of a quart tin cup and a small tin pan. The cup was used to boil coffee, and to soak hardtack in water, which was then fried in a pan with pickled pork—an unpretentious meal but eaten with gusto after a hard day's march.[11]

Monday, September 8, came early with the regiment rising at dawn. As most men were getting themselves ready for what the day would hold, Private Hemminger's young curiosity overcame him:

> Just beyond the grounds I saw a church edifice and people entering therein. My curiosity led me that way. [F]or I never [b]efore had seen worshipers assemble at sun rise. Upon inquiry I learned they were of the Catholic faith, and were meeting for the morning mass. I entered and remained for a short time. a silent spectator to a Service conducted in a tongue I could not understand.[12]

He finally made his way back to his comrades in time to resume their march at 10:00 A.M. Private Spangler recalled that the oppressive heat and dust had made their first march even more strenuous. "The heat was still intense, and the suffocating dust more than ankle deep," he wrote.[13]

After a march of about three miles, the regiment encamped in a large grove of trees in an area referred to as Camp Defiance, which was the headquarters for sixty-five-year-old Major General Edwin V. Sumner, the oldest of all the corps commanders.[14] It was at this location and time that the 130th Pennsylvania Volunteer Infantry Regiment, along with the 108th New York Volunteer Infantry Regiment and the 14th Connecticut Volunteer Infantry Regiment, were brought together as the Second

---

10. Masonheimer Diary, September 7, 1862.
11. Spangler, 22.
12. Hemminger Diary, September 8, 1862.
13. Spangler, 22.
14. Masonheimer Diary, September 8, 1862; Walker, 128.

COLONEL DWIGHT MORRIS, COMMANDER,
14TH REGIMENT, CONNECTICUT VOLUNTEER INFANTRY
(National Archives and Records Administration, Brady Collection, College Park)

Brigade under the command of Colonel Dwight Morris, who commanded the 14th Connecticut Regiment.[15] This new brigade of green soldiers was assigned to the Second Army Corps' Third Division commanded by Brigadier General William H. French.

General French, a regular army officer and a veteran of the Mexican War, just before the outbreak of the Civil War was assigned a garrison in Texas.[16] When Texas seceded, he managed to lead his 300 men down the Rio Grande River to the Gulf of Mexico and eventually to the safety of the North. Red-faced and hot-tempered, his men called him "Old Blinky" because of his disturbing habit of frantically blinking his eyes as he spoke.[17]

Brigadier General Nathan Kimball commanded the Second Corps' First Brigade and Brigadier General Max Weber led its Third Brigade.[18] The other division commanders of the Second Corps were Major General

---

15. Hemminger Diary, September 8, 1862.
16. Stephen W. Sears, *Landscape Turned Red: The Battle of Antietam*, (Boston: Houghton Mifflin Company, 1983,) 237.
17. Ibid.
18. Walker, 87–98.

Israel B. Richardson, who commanded the First Division, and Major General John Sedgwick, who commanded the Second Division.[19]

General Robert E. Lee had soundly defeated the Union Army at what was to be known as the Battle of Second Bull Run and was continuing the momentum of his success by moving his forces onto Northern soil for the first time. He felt a push into Maryland would endanger the major Northern cities of Washington, Baltimore, and Philadelphia, and surely would demoralize the Northern population. The threat of Southern invaders bringing the devastations of war to their own doorsteps played heavy on the hearts and minds of Union soldiers, helpless to protect their own families. The 130th's Regimental Commander, Colonel Zinn, was no exception. In writing to his wife Mary on September 9, 1862, he warned, "I suppose the good people of Pennsylvania are in great ferment, fearing the approach of Jackson. If perchance he should, let me suggest that you go to Harrisburg, where I am confident the enemy can never get."[20] In this letter, Colonel Zinn described his recent experiences and personal concerns about what was to come:

> We have had a pretty rough time since we are out, and situated as I am, being the only field officer in the regiment, I do not feel so much like soldiering as formerly, but as a sense of duty, and the hope that things will soon go better, prevent me from becoming despondent. I often long for the comforts of home and the pleasure of your society; but that is useless, so I make the best of my situation and take things as they come.[21]

At 10:00 A.M. on September 9, the 130th formed into the Second Brigade and drilled the manual of arms for an hour.[22] Then began the day's march heading towards Frederick, Maryland, traveling through fields that paralleled the National Pike. Suffering with the intense heat and suffocating dust, the men of the 130th continued their strenuous seven-mile march.[23]

---

19. Ibid.
20. Henry I. Zinn to Mary, September 9, 1862.
21. Ibid.
22. Hardee, William Joseph (1855). *Rifle and Light Infantry Tactics, For the Instruction and Manoeuvres of Riflemen and Light Infantry*. J. O. Kane, Publisher, 126 Nassau Street, New York, 1862, 82.
23. Masonheimer Diary, September 9, 1862.

Wednesday September 10 brought more marching to the regiment, plus a possible confrontation with the Rebels and an unexpected surprise to the men of Company E from Newville. The order was given to go forward at 10:00 A.M. "with all speed."[24] Private Hemminger wrote of his experience: "Having gone a considerable distance the Brigade was formed into line of battle. No enemy appearing in view, we Stacked arms and from a cornfield near by secured a fine lot of roast ears for suppers."[25] The regiment continued its eight-mile march until about 10:00 P.M., camping in a woods belonging to a farm owned by the Reverend J. H. Henderson, who was a recently-retired Presbyterian minister ironically from Newville's Big Spring Congregation. Several of the minister's family, who were old neighbors and acquaintances, visited with the Newville men of Company E during that night.[26]

The following morning came early for the regiment. Awakened at 4:00 A.M., Private Hemminger noted the "word was passed to be ready to march as soon as possible."[27] After breakfast, the march resumed traveling through the village of Clarksville. Along the way, the regiment passed the tempting fruits of an apple orchard but was forbidden from helping themselves.[28] The regiment encamped about one mile past the north side of the town, after marching about six miles for the day. Shelling could be heard to the left of the regiment and the brigade was quickly formed into a line of battle expecting some action that, as usual, never came. After having supper, the regiment was given a call for regimental drill with many of the boys being tardy.[29] As punishment, Corporal Landis reported that he "was obliged to stand at 'Attention', for one hour for being late at dress parade."[30]

Early on Friday, September 12, the regiment continued its journey towards Frederick. After several miles of marching, the men halted temporarily at the town of Hyattstown, which Private Brehm referred to as, "a small place of no note situated in a hollow."[31] From there, they

---

24. Hemminger Diary, September 10, 1862.
25. Ibid.
26. Ibid.
27. Ibid.
28. Colonel Oliver C. Bosbyshell, *Pennsylvania at Antietam*, (Harrisburg Publishing Company, State Printer, Harrisburg, Pennsylvania, 1906), 160.
29. Masonheimer Diary, September 11, 1862; Hemminger Diary, September 11, 1862.
30. Landis Memoirs, 6–7.
31. Brehm Diary, September 12, 1862.

Seeing the Elephant: The Antietam Campaign

continued their eight-mile march, encamping at Urbana. Private Weiser found the opportunity to write his parents, telling them that he was on the march but to where he did not know: "We have marched more or less every day since we started, sometimes we was within one mile of the Enemy but could not overtake they being fast afoot and accustomed to running."[32] The men only knew that they were headed for Frederick, and nothing else.

They slept only a short time that night and were awakened by a roll call at 3:00 A.M. the next morning on September 13. [33] Ordered to eat a quick breakfast and be ready to march as soon as possible, the regiment was soon back on the road for another eight-mile march. On the way, after crossing over the Monocacy River and passing several deserted Rebel camps, they came to the Baltimore and Ohio Railroad where they found the bridge burned and wires cut by the fleeing Confederates.[34] As the regiment entered Frederick, Private Hemminger recalled, "Continuing our march, our ears were greeted with sounds of artillery fireing our front . . . Great cheering was heard in our rear, occasioned by the approach and passing of Major General George B. McClellan and Staff . . . passing along Main Street the Corps was reviewed by the general & his staff. amid much enthusiasm on the part of the troops."[35] This was the first glimpse most of the men had of their beloved General McClellan. Corporal Landis took special note of the commander: "The boys were very fond of him, calling him by the pet name of 'Little Mac', and his presence stimulated everyone."[36] Private Spangler remembered seeing General McClellan before entering Frederick: "Gen. McClellan with a brilliant staff rode up the turnpike through our corps, and was greeted with the most enthusiastic cheers."[37]

Unlike the unwelcomed reception the regiment received in Baltimore, this Maryland city welcomed the regiment in a much warmer fashion. Private Spangler recorded how the men of the 130th were so warmly greeted into the "church-spired" Frederick:

---

32. John S. Weiser to his parents, September 12, 1862.
33. Landis Memoirs, 7.
34. Hemminger Diary, September 13, 1862.
35. Ibid.
36. Landis Memoir, 7.
37. Spangler, 23.

MAJOR GENERAL GEORGE B. MCCLELLAN
(Library of Congress)

The streets resounding with applause [that] amounted to an ovation . . . Ladies, dressed in their best, waved their handkerchiefs and flags. The populace cheered to the echo, tokens of a most cordial welcome, and supplied water and refreshments to the thirsty and hungry men. Their smiles and tears of gratitude and joy, attested their loyalty to the Union in no uncertain degree.[38]

After experiencing such a welcomed display of patriotism, the regiment traveled to the northwest section of the city and bivouacked in a large field near the reservoir on the Liberty Turnpike.[39] Not long after the regiment arrived in camp, the men got a glimpse at another Union Corps Commander, Major General Ambrose E. Burnside, commander of the Ninth Corps, as he and his staff passed by traveling in the direction of

---
38. Ibid.
39. Hemminger Diary, September 13, 1862.

MAJOR GENERAL AMBROSE E. BURNSIDE
(Library of Congress)

South Mountain.[40] Private Hemminger recalled, "Burnside was riding a dark bey [sic] bob tail horse. His erect form, and large black side whiskers indicated the Ideal soldier . . ."[41]

Up at 7:00 A.M. the next morning, September 14, the regiment left Frederick on the Shooktown Road heading towards Middletown, crossing the Catoctin Mountain range at approximately 3:00 P.M.[42] As the regiment arrived on the other side of the mountain range Private Brehm recorded in his diary that it was met with the sounds of cannons: "When we arrived at the other side of the mountains and behold the beautiful valley in which Middletown is situated away over along the opposite mountains cannonading is going on briskly and a fine view we have of the conflict."[43] Ordered toward the field of battle, the regiment made a rapid advance in the direction of the cannonading. As they got closer, the ominous cannon sounds ceased. The weary men halted for a short time

---

40. Hemminger Diary, September 13, 1862; At that time Major General Burnside commanded the Union Ninth Corps.
41. Hemminger Diary, September 13, 1862
42. Hemminger Diary, September 14, 1862.
43. Brehm Diary, September 14, 1862.

in a plowed field on a hillside to cook coffee and make their suppers. "Too bad," recorded Private Brehm, "We are ordered off at a trot toward the scene of battle for the fight h[a]s resumed again."[44] They marched in six parallel columns in the direction of South Mountain where they knew that a battle was in progress.[45] "Up hill and down hill, across little streams, we marched, very tired," recalled Corporal Landis.[46] Private Masonheimer could not forget his first encounter with the shock of war: "Crossed the mountains . . . and seen the first horrors of wars. Dead men laying in the fields yet."[47] The regiment halted their march at midnight, for what they thought would be their night's camp. Suddenly, they were called to arms and ordered at the double-quick down the turnpike; and finally countermarching into a field of sod taking possession of a portion of the [South Mountain] battlefield "and lay down amongst the dead bodies for the night after an eighteen-mile grueling march."[48]

"At early dawn I awoke and found where I had lain [on] a human foot and fingers, that had been sacrificed for or against the Union cause. I could not tell which. Strolling over the field of Carnage, our eyes saw sights that told of the awful strife," noted Private Hemminger vividly describing the unpleasant scene early morning of Monday, September 15.[49] The morning was a gloomy one, with thick smoke hugging the mountaintops that marked the last evening's battle.[50] At sunrise, the regiment, along with the entire Union Second Corps, passed through the crest of South Mountain, marching through the aftermath of the South Mountain battle known as Turner's Gap. "Near the top I observed an old dwelling to which I hastened hoping to replenish my canteen with water," wrote Private Hemminger.[51] "A well was on the premises but to our horror was filled with confederate dead," recorded Private Hemminger.[52] As they reached the crest of the mountain near the "Mountain House,"

---

44. Ibid.
45. Landis Memoirs, 14.
46. Ibid.
47. Masonheimer Diary, September 14, 1862.
48. Landis Memoirs, 7. The men of the regiment were unaware of the strewn bodies throughout their bivouac site until early the next morning.
49. Hemminger Diary, September 15, 1862.
50. Brehm Diary, September 15, 1862.
51. Hemminger Diary, September 15, 1862.
52. Ibid.

Seeing the Elephant: The Antietam Campaign 51

they found hundreds of dead men littering the ground.[53] Both Union and Confederate dead and wounded were found along with guns and clothing scattered all about. Private Spangler's first encounter with the battlefield took him to a dead Confederate cavalryman:

> He was shot through the head, and his blood-covered face and glassy eyes made a ghastly sight. He was the first dead soldier I saw, and it was by no means a pleasing spectacle. As I reached the crest of the mountain near the "Mountain House," hundreds of dead Union and Confederate soldiers covered the ground.[54]

Rebel prisoners continually passed by the regiment throughout the day as Union artillery batteries and cavalry moved hurriedly in the direction of the enemy.[55]

Although spared from the battle of South Mountain, the men of the 130th saw first-hand the human carnage that war had brought, as they surely contemplated what would possibly soon lie ahead for themselves. From their position, the regiment saw the southern and northern ranges of the South Mountain. Westward could be seen the valley of the Antietam.[56]

About noon, the 130th began its march over the mountaintop down the National Pike on the western side of South Mountain, marching five miles down into the valley entering the small Maryland village of Boonsboro.[57] The road and town were full of prisoners captured at the battle of South Mountain.[58] As Colonel Zinn's men marched through the village, they were greeted by a group of local girls standing on the front stoop of a large brick house singing "Maryland, My Maryland."[59] The regiment continued on the turnpike to the gate above the village where they halted and rested until nightfall.[60]

After dark, the regiment struck out again heading southward on the Boonsboro Pike passing through the town of Keedysville, located on the

---

53. Spangler, 27.
54. Ibid.
55. Landis Memoirs, 8.
56. Hemminger Diary, September 15, 1862.
57. Ibid.
58. Ibid.
59. Ibid.
60. Brehm Diary, September 15, 1862.

road leading to Sharpsburg. A short distance beyond the town, the regiment set up camp bivouacking under the brow of a hill for the night, traveling a distance of about eight miles for the day.[61]

The entire next day, September 16, the regiment remained in camp a short distance south of Keedysville, off of the Boonsboro Pike, near the Pry House on the east side of Antietam Creek that was the location of General McClellan's headquarters.[62] The sounds of artillery fire could be heard in the distance from beyond Antietam Creek. Soon, the regiment experienced first-hand the effects of the Rebel artillery, when a battery began firing near their position, inflicting three casualties to a Union artillery battery positioned on their left.[63] Two soldiers in the artillery battery were killed and one was wounded. A nearby lieutenant viewing the shelling had his foot badly mashed.[64] "I remember how closely we hugged the bosom of mother earth, when we heard the screeching shells come," Corporal Landis recorded, "And what a relief it was finally, when the shelling ceased and we heard our band, off on a hilltop, play the Star Spangled Banner."[65] The Third Division was later ordered to move out of the range of the bursting artillery and formed en masse. Sometime after midnight, forty rounds of additional ammunition were distributed, giving each man eighty rounds to carry.[66] Forty rounds were carried in each soldier's cartridge box and the additional forty rounds were carried in his coat-pockets.[67]

The early morning weather on Wednesday, September 17, was overcast and described as "gloomy."[68] As the men rose early, cooked their coffee, and ate hardtack, they had no idea that this day would become one of the most prominent in the annals of American history. The true color of the regiment and each man would be shown on this monumental day.

With an order given to divest themselves of their blankets and any other items not needed, they rolled up their blankets, examined their cartridge boxes, and filled their canteens.[69] As the order to advance had

---

61. Landis Memoirs, 8; Hemminger Diary, September 15, 1862.
62. Hemminger Diary, September 15, 1862.
63. Hemminger Diary, September 16, 1862.
64. Masonheimer Diary, September 16, 1862.
65. Landis Memoirs, 8.
66. Hemminger Diary, September 16, 1862.
67. Spangler, 32.
68. Brehm Diary, September 17, 1862.
69. Spangler, 32.

been delayed at 7:00 A.M., Colonel Zinn took the opportunity to write his wife, perhaps out of fear that this would be his final letter to her:

> We are on the eve of a great battle and as I write cannonading in our front is tremendous . . . I anticipate getting into the fight soon. Do not be unnecessarily alarmed. The 130th is not in condition to go into a fight, but we will do the best we can, hoping that all will do their duty . . . A gentleman from Shippensburg is here who will put this note in the mail for me. I have not received any news from home since Camp Marcy, as we have had no mail since; but I hope that after the battle I shall hear from you. Give my love to all friends, and for yourself and the little ones accept my everlasting love.[70]

The delay to advance assuredly affected each soldier in a different manner. Some turned to God, as Private Spangler did as he took out his pocket Bible and read a chapter. He then handed his Bible to a fellow comrade, Private Christian Good, a small man like himself in the rear rank, instructing him, "read it, for it may be your last opportunity."[71] It was. Within an hour, Private Good would die on the battlefield.[72]

Promptly at 8:00 A.M., the regiment received orders to march, but not knowing where they were going. Major General Israel B. Richardson's First Division of the Second Corps joined the march, along with the other two brigades of their division. Marching westward, Private Spangler recounted how "passing through a hollow in the rear of a Union artillery battalion" in two separate columns, the two divisions reached the Antietam Creek at the Pry Ford a short distance south of the Upper Bridge.[73] Richardson's division halted on the east side of Antietam Creek, and did not cross until 9:30 A.M. It would later join in the attack on the Confederate center just east of the 130th's position.[74]

At approximately 8:00 A.M., Antietam Creek was crossed by the Third Division in three columns of brigades: General Max Weber's Third

---

70. Henry I. Zinn to Mary, September 17, 1862.
71. Spangler, 32.
72. Ibid.
73. Spangler, 33.
74. John M. Priest, *Antietam: The Soldiers' Battle* (New York: Oxford University Press, 1989), 159.

Brigade (1st Delaware, 5th Maryland, and 4th New York) on the left, Colonel Dwight Morris' Second Brigade (14th Connecticut, 108th New York, and 130th Pennsylvania) of new regiments in the center, and General Nathan Kimball's First Brigade (14th Indiana, 8th Ohio, 132nd Pennsylvania, and 7th West Virginia) on the right.[75] Corporal Landis vividly recalled the regiment's crossing:

> Heavy cannonading was in progress when our division forded the Antietam Creek. I was detailed as one of the Corporals in the rear guard. A great many ludicrous scenes occurred as the column crossed the stream. Not knowing that a battle was so imminent, some men stopped to take off their shoes and stockings.[76]

Years later, Private Weiser vividly remembered the event:

> Wading in the well-riled stream [two to three feet deep] your shoes become more or less occupied with sand and pebbles, and that some were fain to tarry long enough to remove these obstacles to comfort, but that the rear guard had imperative orders from Captain Henry I. Zinn to hurry up all laggards, and not to hesitate to use force if necessary.[77]

"Everyone finally got over in good order, and the column of our regiment put into shape again. Col. Henry I. Zinn led his regiment calmly on, whilst Major John Lee, who was most of the time with the rear guard, was galloping about swearing his hardest at the men," recalled Corporal Landis.[78] After crossing the ford and marching approximately a mile in three columns of brigades, the command was given, "By the left flank,"[79] forming three lines.[80] The entire Third Division abruptly changed direction and now headed southwest, not following General Sedgwick's First Division. Thirty minutes ahead of the regiment's departure and

---

75. OR, XIX, Series I, Part 1, No's 323–324.
76. Landis Memoirs, 8.
77. Bosbyshell, 161.
78. Landis Memoirs, 8.
79. Ibid.
80. OR, XIX, Series I, Part 1, No's. 323–324.

accompanied by General Sumner, General Sedgwick's First Division headed in a westward direction towards the Dunkard Church and West Woods.[81]

Upon being given the order, "By the left flank," the brigades in columns moved forward, entering the battlefield from the north along a ridge of the East Woods that separated the Roulette and Mumma farms.[82] Corporal Landis recounted, "Forward we went, bullets commenced to cut the leaves above our heads as we charged through the woods, over rocks, through bushes, weeds and thorns, until we soon emerged from the wood."[83] The sudden onslaught of artillery shelling and its effects unnerved the inexperienced Pennsylvanians and created confusion, causing them to stagger about. Within minutes, Brigadier General French arrived on the scene screaming, "For God's sake men, close up and go forward."[84] Corporal Landis recalled, "We moved on in the line of battle across the field, heading the southwest with the 'Mumma House' on our right, and came up to the 'Roulette' farm buildings."[85]

After progressing about a quarter of a mile while enduring a hot artillery fire, the rapidly advancing Third Division reached a meadow on the north side of the Roulette Farm at approximately 9:00 A.M. Here the brigades were re-aligned. General Weber's Third Brigade was positioned in front. Colonel Morris' Second Brigade was placed in the center. General Kimball's First Brigade was located in the rear. Both the Third and First Brigades were seasoned troops and were veterans of the Peninsula Campaign and Second Bull Run.[86] Conceivably, Colonel Morris' brigade was placed in the center since it was comprised of all new troops, unseasoned in battle.

This temporary pause to re-align the division finally gave Company K's Private Spangler time to catch up with his company despite given orders to stay back. A carbuncle that had developed on his right knee had left his leg inflamed and in severe pain that morning. After showing it to his captain, he was instructed to stay behind. Private Spangler vividly

---

81. OR, XIX, Series I, Part 1, No. 276.
82. Priest, 138.
83. Landis Memoirs, 8.
84. Priest, 138.
85. Landis Memoirs, 8.
86. Hemminger Diary, September 17, 1862.

ROULETTE FARM (Cumberland County Historical Society, Carlisle, Pennsylvania)

remembered that he did not wish to be considered a shirker by his comrades: "At this, a few of my comrades made invidious remarks that I was showing the white feather. This put me on my mettle, and I determined to go in, crippled as I was."[87]

After the brigades had realigned, Brigadier General Max Weber's Third Brigade was the first to advance, and promptly encountered Confederate skirmishers occupying the Roulette farm.[88] These were remnants from Brigadier General Samuel Garland's, and Colonel A. H. Colquitt's brigades, belonging to General D. H. Hill's Division.[89] The Rebels were well impressed with the magnitude of Brigadier General French's division as they saw them marching forward in a precise line with their new regimental colors in view. Federal soldiers three battle lines deep and at close interval extended the entire width of the Roulette farm. In the Sunken Lane, the Rebels were ordered to lie down and take cover behind the split rails they had piled as cover as the national colors of the Union units clearly came into view.[90] It was now 9:15 A.M.

In his official report, Brigadier General French recorded his division's initial encounter with Brigadier General D. H. Hill's troops: "The enemy, who was in a position in advance, opened his batteries, under which fire

---

87. Spangler, 32.
88. OR, XIX, Series I, Part 1, No's 323–324.
89. Priest, 136.
90. Priest, 139.

my lines steadily moved until the first line [Weber's Brigade] encountering the enemy's skirmishers, charged them briskly, and entering a group of houses on the Roulette farm, drove back the force, which had taken a strong position for defense."[91]

Brigadier General Weber's Brigade, which had led the attack, unsuccessfully routed all of the Confederate skirmishers from the Roulette's buildings and surrounding fields.[92] By that time, the Roulette outbuildings still hid over twenty Rebels.[93] The 130th Regiment, along with the 14th Connecticut and 108th New York, were to the immediate rear of Weber's Brigade.[94] After losing some momentum negotiating the post and rail fence along the pasture northwest of the Roulette farm, the 130th Regiment continued its advance behind Weber's brigade with the 14th Connecticut on its right and the 108th New York on its left.[95] The 14th Connecticut approached though the Mumma's Orchard and halted on the left to clear the Roulette's springhouse of Confederate sharpshooters while the 108th New York bypassed the farmhouse and outbuildings moving off to the left and east of the Roulette lane. The 130th Pennsylvania was directly in the sights of the awaiting Rebel skirmishers.[96]

The Roulette farm offered the unexpected presence of bee houses on the grounds that Private Hemminger noted in his diary, "Just beyond the garden a foe that greatly outnumbered both sides of the armies. In the line of our advance a number of bee hives were turned over and the little fellows resented the intrusion and did it most unceremoniously charge upon us, accelerating our speed through the orchard toward the entrenched position of the enemy."[97]

"The battle was now fairly upon us, although we were not yet in it," remarked Corporal Landis as his Company F approached the Roulette buildings, which were immediately in front of the 130th.[98] The area immediately surrounding the Roulette Farm house included a large bank barn, sheds, and a springhouse. Very near the house stood a garden

---

91. OR, XIX, Series I, Part1, No's 323–324.
92. Sears, 238.
93. Bosbyshell, 161.
94. Sears, 238.
95. Priest, 140.
96. Sears, 139.
97. Hemminger Diary, September 17, 1862.
98. Landis Memoirs, 9.

picket fence built upon a stone wall.[99] Within minutes, the shock of the battle would begin. Everything cumbersome the soldiers carried was discarded.[100] The time had now arrived for the men of the regiment to "see the elephant," as the soldiers called their first taste of battle. The Rebel skirmishers began targeting the untested men of the 130th. Corporal Landis carefully recorded the events:

> As our line moved on, we covered the distance from the spring house to the barn . . . Between the house and the spring-house fell our first man killed. In the charge I passed between the barn and wagon shed . . . Soon beyond the buildings, the line gradually arranged itself, and the charge went on in line. Everything cumbersome was now cast aside . . .[101]

During this advance into the Roulette's outbuildings the 130th, along with some soldiers from 14th Connecticut's Company B, took its first prisoners, capturing approximately twenty in the Roulette springhouse. The Rebels were sent to the rear in the charge of Sergeant Samuel Ilgenfritz from Company I.[102]

Company E, located in the center of the regiment, found the stone wall and picket fence that ran from the carriage house to the farm lane too high to scale and hastily cleared a path for the entire regiment.[103] Private Hemminger recorded, "The boys layed hold of the fence, and with a mighty pull the entire fence came down and fell on Theodore Boyl's [Private Theodore Boyle] o[f] our company. We all passed over, including the Colonel and his horse." Private Boyle was seriously injured with several crushed ribs.[104] The Pennsylvanians moved around the house, across the garden between the house and barn, around the barn and through the wagon shed in search of any Rebels foolishly remaining.[105]

Captain David Z. Seipe's Company K passed between the Roulette's barn and garden fence where it encountered the enemy and drove them

---

99. Hemminger Diary, September 17, 1862.
100. Landis Memoirs, 9.
101. Ibid.
102. Bosbyshell, 161.
103. Priest, 141.
104. Hemminger Diary, September 17, 1862.
105. Bosbyshell, 161.

Seeing the Elephant: The Antietam Campaign

CAPTAIN DAVID Z. SEIPE, COMMANDER, COMPANY K (Find-A-Grave)

out of the garden and orchard.[106] Here, several members of both Company K and the rest of the regiment made the decision that many make in battle, to run off. The term more often used was "skedaddle." Company E continued its push, passing over a deep gully in a plowed field, and was ordered to lie down on the eastern slope of a hill near a large elm tree. The Confederates on the crest of the hill fired volley after volley into their ranks. Private Spangler recounted years later:

The bullets flew thicker than bees, and the shells exploded with a deafening roar. I was seized with fear far greater than that of the day before. I hugged the ploughed ground so closely that I must have buried my nose in it. I thought of home and friends, and felt that I would surely be killed, and how I didn't want to be![107]

From their position on the hillside the men of Company K advanced headlong into the confronting Confederate infantry and artillery fire pouring into a cornfield, up through an orchard and over recently plowed fields, coming to rest in a field of clover. Corporal Landis remembered,

---
106. Spangler, 31.
107. Ibid.

"Bursting shells filled the air, showers of hissing bullets flew in our faces. Our thin blue line wavered . . . then it straightened and became taut."[108]

The men of Company F, as most others in the regiment, made it to the east side of the hill just south of the Roulette house taking on the blistering fire from the Confederates. "On and on into the cornfield plunged our right, up through the orchard under the laden apple trees swept our left, over the plowed field on to a stretch of clover. Bursting shells filled the air, showers of hissing bullets flew in our faces," recounted Corporal Landis.[109]

General D. H. Hill's Confederates had the strategic advantage with their position on the hill's crest. Corporal Landis recorded in his diary that day:

> From the crest of the hill our bullets were directed toward a thousand smoke-puffs that rose from the field of wavering corn . . . Above the corn and smoke waved the stars and bars of the confederacy . . . As the battle raged fiercer and fiercer I thought of my brother David, whom I had not seen since the early morning . . . I [was] determined to make my way . . . to the right where he was.[110]

The next morning Corporal Landis did find his brother, Private Daniel D. Landis, also of Company F, wounded in the right forearm with the bones splintered. After being treated at the field hospital, he was sent back to Harrisburg to recover.[111]

The regiment continued its rapid advance through open ground, coming on to a picket fence bordering the opposite side of the garden, smashing it with their rifle butts.[112]

Not far past the Roulette's outbuildings and the orchard south of the farmhouse, the regiment realigned with its left flank adjoining the Roulette farm lane.[113] While entering the orchard, the regiment captured

---

108. Landis Memoirs, 9.
109. Ibid.
110. Ibid.
111. Landis Memoirs, 10.
112. Hemminger Diary, September 17, 1862; Priest, 140.
113. Priest, 141.

more of the Rebel skirmishers while driving back the remaining ones into their own lines.[114]

With orders to take the hill to their front, occupied by Confederate skirmishers, the 130th continued its advance. The men moved up the slope with some passing through the cornfield on the right, while others negotiated a plowed field near the Clipp House located on Roulette Lane, finally reaching a clover field at the crest of the hill.[115] Here they were ordered to lie down.[116] Within minutes the Confederate bullets were "thicker than bees" and the artillery shells exploded all around them.[117]

The 5th Maryland from the Third Brigade was directly ahead of the 130th with the 1st Delaware ahead and to the right. "We finally drove the enemy from the corn-field, and going forward over a clover field we found him entrenched in a cut with piles of rails thrown up in front," recounted Corporal Landis.[118] The north side of the sunken lane was lined with several feet of fence rails.[119] The lane, which would become known as Antietam's infamous "Bloody Lane," would hold the crucial key to the Confederates.

The lane, located approximately 600 yards south of the Dunker church, was a little farm road that turned off of the Hagerstown turnpike to the east and ran southward connecting to the Boonsboro turnpike. Local farmers had used this lane to drive their loaded wagons to a gristmill on Antietam Creek for years. The continuous use, added to natural erosion, had worn down the road surface, sinking it several feet below the lane's original level, making it a natural military defensive position for the Rebels.[120] Another lane approximately 500 yards long ran south from the Roulette's farm and intercepted the sunken road.

The well-entrenched Rebels directly facing the 130th belonged to Brigadier General D. H. Hill's division. Opposing General French's Third Brigade front was Confederate Brigadier General Robert E. Rodes' Brigade made up of the 3rd, 5th, 6th, 12th, and 26th Alabama Regiments, and Brigadier General George B. Anderson's Brigade comprised

---

114. Hemminger Diary, September 17, 1862.
115. Ibid.
116. Bosbyshell, 174.
117. Ibid.
118. Landis Memoirs, 10.
119. Hemminger Diary, September 17, 1862.
120. Sears, 236.

of the 2nd, 4th, 14th, and 30th North Carolina Regiments. The 5th, 6th Alabama and the 2nd North Carolina regiments were positioned down and across the lane from the 130th Pennsylvania. The 6th Alabama, under the command of Colonel John B. Gordon, was positioned directly across from the 130th's position.

Earlier in the morning of September 17, General Gordon pledged to General Lee that his men would hold their position "'til the sun went down or victory is won."[121] Confederate artillery situated on the high ground directly behind the Rebel position posed an added danger to the 130th.

General Weber's Third Brigade was ordered forward, passing through the ranks of the 130th lying on the crest of the hill and a distance of about sixty feet from the awaiting Rodes' Alabamians. The Confederates in the sunken lane waited until General Weber's men crested the top of the hill, about sixty feet in the distance, before firing their first murderous volley into their ranks, taking a deadly toll of life; and within minutes, about one-third of the 1st Delaware and most their color guard were killed or wounded. The massed Rebel firepower hurled the Third Brigade rearward passing back through the 130th's ranks.[122]

About this time, the 14th Connecticut, located to the right of the 130th, reached the edge of the Mumma cornfield and began firing in the direction of the Rebel fire coming from the Sunken Road. In the process, they hit some men of the 1st Delaware as they fled back into their lines. A portion of General Weber's two regiments panicked, bolting from their position near the sunken road.[123]

In response, a combination of General French's Second and Third brigades began another frontal assault over the ridge, running headlong into the deadly Rebel fire from the sunken road. The intensive Rebel fire once again inflicted sudden death and chaos, causing this second assault to be repulsed with most of the two brigades being forced back about 200 yards into the Mumma cornfield.[124]

The 130th was then ordered to advance toward the Rebel line directly behind General Weber's 5th Maryland. The regiment continued to press steadily forward behind the Maryland regiment, over the open ridge void

---

121. Priest, 137.
122. Priest, 142.
123. Priest, 144.
124. Priest, 145.

of any protection from the Rebel fire coming from the sunken lane, until being stopped by an old worm fence bordering the southern end of the plowed field.[125] "Step by step we pressed toward the foe and were now up to an old [worm] fence. [T]his we lowered by pulling the under rails out until we could step over," recounted Private Hemminger.[126] When Company E's Corporal John H. Strickler stepped over the three of the four remaining rails, he was instantly struck in the shoulder by fragments from a bursting artillery shell. Falling backward, one his legs became entangled in the fence. Before he could be helped up, a Minié ball pierced his leg. Private Hemminger noted that "To help him off the fence Hamilton [Private William Hamilton, Co. E] and Woodrow [Corporal John B. Woodrow, Co. E] took hold of his shoulder, and I took his legs in my arms. Just as we raised him up his other leg was struc[k] by a ball. [L]aying him down we again took up out muskets to h[e]lp stay the furious onslaught."[127] Later, the three carried the wounded Strickler to the Roulette's springhouse for water. Just at that time his heel was struck and torn away by another round, his fourth hit. Corporal Strickler shouted, "My God must I be killed by inches?"[128] They carried him to a nearby field hospital only to find hundreds of other wounded soldiers awaiting the surgeon. Corporal Strickler would not survive, dying on October 4 as a result of his wounds.[129] After helping Corporal Strickler to the rear, the three men quickly returned to their original position to find that nothing had changed. The unshakable Rebels remained in the Pennsylvanians' front.[130]

At about the same time that Corporal Strickler had become entangled in the fence, twenty men from the 2nd North Carolina tried to flank the 130th's left by approaching them from the Roulette lane. Private Spangler clearly recalled the surprising Confederate flanking maneuver:

> The hill from which we delivered our fire descended abruptly to the fortified road filled with Confederates, and not more than three hundred feet distant. A score or more of venturesome ones came out of this road and advanced toward us along the rail fence

---

125. Ibid.
126. Hemminger Diary, September 17, 1862.
127. Ibid.
128. Ibid.
129. Bates, 214.
130. Hemminger Diary, September 17, 1862.

of a lane on our immediate left running from the sunken road to the Roulette buildings. All these brave men were killed.[131]

One poor Rebel was shot as he was crossing the fence, and hung there becoming riddled with bullets.[132] When the regiment buried him, they counted seventeen holes in his body.[133]

As the bloody struggle continued throughout the morning, the contest became one of attrition.[134] Casualties were quickly mounting on both sides. To help turn the tide, Major General Israel B. Richardson's First Division, that included the famous Irish Brigade, had crossed Antietam Creek at 9:30 A.M. and was ordered to join the attack on the Confederate center to the left of the 130th's position. They charged into a swale on the Roulette farm passing through portions of French's Division to the extreme left of the Roulette lane decimating Colonel Carnot Posey's advancing 16th Mississippians and driving the remaining Rebels back to safety behind the sunken road. The added strength of Brigadier General Richardson's Division gave the Union the advantage as the Rebels continued to fall in their positions in the sunken road. The Federals were gaining both in strength and momentum as the Confederate casualties continued to mount.[135]

General French's Third Division (less the 108th New York) continued its relentless fire into the Confederates across the lane mounting up casualties by the minute.[136] The 130th Pennsylvania was moved up and on line directly facing General Rodes' Alabamians only sixty yards away firing from their protected position of piled split rails on the southern side of the sunken road. Ammunition was beginning to run out. By this time

---

131. Spangler, 35.
132. Landis Memoirs, 10.
133. Spangler, 36.
134. Priest, 157.
135. Priest, 160, 162.
136. According to Michael Priest, the 108th New York Regiment remained protected on the northern slope of the first ridge east of the Roulette lane, where the 108th's regimental commander, Colonel Oliver H. Palmer, "was cowering on his belly behind the prone regiment." Lieutenant Frederick L. Hitchcock from the 132nd Pennsylvania Regiment yelled at Colonel Palmer "to get his soldiers to the front." General Nathan Kimball, witnessing the exchange between the two, ordered Lieutenant Hitchcock to "Get those cowards out of there or shoot them." Lieutenant Hitchcock unstrapped his holster flaps, grabbing his pistol. Yet, the 108th would still not budge. At that time, Major George B. Force of the 108th stood up, trying to rally the reluctant New Yorkers, when a cannon ball decapitated him. At that, all of the 108th's officers demanded the men in the 108th to get up and go forward. The men responded, moving to the right of the line as directed, leaving the cowardly Colonel Palmer behind. See Priest, 171–172, citing Ronald H. Bailey, Time-Life Books, *The Bloodiest Day, The Battle of Antietam, The Civil War* (Alexandria, Virginia: Time-Life Books, 1984), 97.

BLOODY LANE (U.S. Army Military History Institute)

BLOODY LANE (U.S. Army Military History Institute)

Company K's Private Spangler had used up his eighty rounds, "causing the barrel of my rifle to become so hot that it burnt me when I touched it."[137] With his ammunition finally used up Private Spangler recalled, "I turned over a soldier of the First Delaware, the top of whose skull was shot off, and took from his cartridge-box, ten Enfield rifle cartridges, which fortunately fitted the barrel of my Springfield rifle."[138]

Not long after Private Spangler had replenished his ammunition, Confederate Brigadier General Richard H. Anderson's Division arrived and with flags waving plunged into the sunken lane. A newly-arrived Confederate officer waving his sword to rally his men became an irresistible target for Private Spangler: "I was so anxious to get a shot at him that in the hurry I neglected to extract my ramrod and fired it with the charge."[139] Although disappointed that he missed his target, Private Spangler gleamed as he saw the Confederate officer felled by another member of the 130th.[140]

Despite the continuous rain of fire poured upon them, the men of the 130th pressed on towards the sunken lane to witness small white flags being hoisted along the Rebel lines. In wonderment, and assuming that the Rebels were surrendering, the 130th ceased firing and began to advance. Allowing the Union soldiers to approach to within mere yards, the Rebels dropped their white flags. "Suddenly they poured a deadly volley into our ranks . . . with many falling about us," recalled Private Hemminger.[141] Scores of unsuspecting Union soldiers fell at once as Rebel fire poured from the lane.

Once again, the Rebels hoisted their deceptive white flags, this time with only partial success. A third attempt proved fatal for many of them, giving Colonel Zinn's men time to reload. Private Hemminger recounted how "with deliberate aim we gave them the first volley which must have caused them greater loss than we had so far sustained."[142]

At that time one of the few Rebels trying to desert was spotted negotiating the fence on the south side of the road. Before he could make it over the fence, a soldier from the 130th had literally shot him in the rear.[143]

---

137. Spangler, 35–36.
138. Ibid.
139. Spangler, 36.
140. Priest, 170.
141. Hemminger Diary, September 17, 1862.
142. Ibid.
143. Priest, 170, citing James E. Marrill, ed., *Uncommon Valor* (New York: Rand McNally and Company, 1964), 202.

The time was now 11:30 A.M. and the stalemate continued with both sides taking on heavy losses. The sunken road was filling with the wounded, dead and the dying and the Union line seemed to be deteriorating.[144] "We were now within a short range of each other—the thinned ranks of our column was centering more and more on the colors but not dismayed," recalled Private Hemminger.[145] Private Spangler could not forget the conditions of the battlefield that day: "The battle field was mostly covered with an immense sheet of smoke . . . through which could be seen the flashes of infantry and artillery fire."[146]

The area near the intersection of the sunken road and the Roulette Lane began wavering, reaching a break point for the Union. At that time, due to a miscommunication between Lieutenant Colonel J. N. Lightfoot, commanding the 6th Alabama, and Brigadier General Rodes, the 6th Alabama moved from their position on the sunken lane to the rear rather than moving to another designated defensive position. Within minutes, after thinking a retreat had been ordered, Rodes' four other regiments began moving to the rear. According to author Edward A. Moore, "One by one, first in squads, then by platoons, Rodes' five regiments shattered and streamed rearward."[147] Before Rodes realized the mistake, it was too late for him to correct it. He had been wounded by a canister shot.[148]

At 1:00 P.M., a portion of Brigadier General Max Weber's veteran Third Brigade formed close to the rear of the 130th. Suddenly, the voice of their intrepid commander rang out, "Fix bayonets—ready forward double-quick—charge," Private Hemminger recorded.[149] The 130th was ordered to cease firing and stand fast. Weber's column charged through the 130th's depleted ranks to within a few feet of the sunken road where they were met with a furious and most deadly fire. "Many of those brave fellows were killed and wounded," wrote Private Hemminger.[150] Weber's men reeled and fell back to a position near the 130th. Within minutes, they reformed and were ready for another daring attempt. As they

---

144. Priest, 180.
145. Hemminger Diary, September 17, 1862.
146. Spangler, 38.
147. Priest, 190, citing Edward A. Moore, *The Story of a Cannoneer Under Stonewall Jackson* (Lynchburg, J. P. Bell, Inc., 1910), 157.
148. Ibid.
149. Hemminger Diary, September 17, 1862.
150. Ibid.

BRIGADIER GENERAL ROBERT E. RODES
(Library of Congress)

stepped forward, the center of the Union line joined, "in the advance with a tremendous shout."[151] Private Hemminger recounted, "The great excitement of the moment caused many of the 130th Regiment to join in the charge." The 130th's men pursued the Rebels into the lane.[152] The firing continued until guns became fouled, making it difficult to load them. Some of the men deliberately cleaned their guns and went on firing. Others threw their rifles away and supplied themselves with guns left by the killed and wounded.[153] The veteran Rebels, unable to withstand this onslaught, became pierced and broken, ultimately were driven from their once advantageous position on the sunken road.

By now the lane was packed with Confederate dead. Thirteen bodies were counted in one pile, and nearby some were piles some two, three, and five deep. In his address at the September 17, 1904 monument dedication, Edward Spangler intensely described the setting: "No battle of the war, of so such short duration, presented such a scene of carnage."[154]

At 1:30 P.M., after four hours of deadly and intense fighting, exhausted and out of ammunition, the remaining men of the 130th

---

151. Ibid.
152. Bosbyshell, 197.
153. Author Unknown, Personal Recollection, Newville Historical Society.
154. Bosbyshell, 175.

Pennsylvania were relieved.[155] They formed and waited on Roulette Lane approximately 200 yards north of the Sunken Road along with the 8th Ohio and 14th Indiana.[156] Their departure left a wide gap to the right of the regiment's former position, giving the Confederates an open opportunity. Confederate Brigadier General Howell Cobb's brigade, along with the 3rd Arkansas and 27th North Carolina Regiments pushed into the area to the immediate right of the 130th Pennsylvania's former position in the swale located on the Mumma farm.[157]

Intense firing began as the Confederates advanced to the hillcrest that had been occupied by the 130th only an hour earlier. Finding three massed Union regiments in the Roulette lane as easy targets, the Confederates opened their deadly fire. The unsuspecting 130th Pennsylvanians, along with the 14th Indiana and 8th Ohio in single file proceeded up the lane towards the Roulette house."[158] Lieutenant William H. Tomes of Company B, "a man of large statue, was struck in the groin by a bullet, and hurled fully two feet in the air," Private Spangler recounted.[159] Many of those in the 130th quickly responded by taking position in the Roulette orchard, holding the Confederates at bay until a battery of Union artillery with canister rounds slowed their advance.[160] Luckily, Colonel William Irwin's Brigade of the Union Army Sixth Corps had just arrived on the field from the north and quickly drove the advancing Confederates back across the Hagerstown Pike.[161] The 130th proceeded to a position north of the Roulette buildings "beyond the range of musketry but not from bursting shells" recorded Private Hemminger.[162]

The scenes behind the battlefield in some respects were more gruesome than on the battlefield itself, as Private Spangler witnessed, entering the house and barn where casualties from the Third Brigade were being collected:

> The house, barn and adjacent lawns were covered with wounded. The sight of hundreds of prostrate men with serious wounds of

---

155. Ibid.
156. Priest, 195.
157. Priest, 194.
158. Priest, 192.
159. Spangler, 37.
160. Bosbyshell, 175.
161. Priest, 202.
162. Hemminger Diary, September 17, 1862.

every description was appalling. Many to relieve their suffering were impatient for their turn upon the amputation tables, around which there were pyramids of severed arms and legs. Others screamed with excruciating pains. A few . . . ripped out a succession of oaths that must have required years of sedulous preparation. Many prayed aloud while others shrieked in the agony and throes of death.[163]

Here he found Private Adam Brown of his company shot in the abdomen. He implored Private Spangler to "put an end to his agony." Private Brown would not survive.[164]

Private Hemminger spent the night at the division hospital located northeast of the Roulette buildings with Private Thomas G. Gillespie from his company. Shot in the left breast and the surgeon unable to locate the ball, he was "unconscious and not expected to survive many hours," recalled Private Hemminger.[165] All through the night, Private Hemminger applied water to the wound as Private Gillespie beckoned, "water—water."[166] Private Gillespie would eventually recover from his wounds and be mustered out with his company in May 1863.[167] In his diary Corporal Landis recorded, "Surgeons were busy with knife and bandage, and comrades were rendering such assistance and comfort as they could."[168]

At sunset, the 130th Pennsylvania's companies gathered in their respective commands to identity those killed, wounded, or missing. Detailed to search the battlefield for his missing comrades, Corporal Landis recorded his experience:

> The scenes about the battlefield and especially about the Roulette buildings and spring were dreadful to behold, the dead and dying were seen on every hand. Many poor fellows were brought back to the spring, given a last drink of water to cool their parched lips, when they closed their eyes forever.[169]

---

163. Spangler, 38–39.
164. Spangler, 39.
165. Hemminger Diary, September 17, 1862.
166. Ibid.
167. Bates, 215.
168. Landis Memoirs, 10.
169. Landis Memoirs, 10; Author Unknown, Personal Recollection, Newville Historical Society.

Writing of the ordeal years later, Edward Spangler wrote, "With the close of the day ended the bloodiest single day of the war. Night afforded to the unharmed much needed slumber."[170]

The next morning, September 18, found the Confederates still entrenched in their second line where they had been driven the afternoon before.[171] The 130th Pennsylvania moved to about one mile to the rear of the battlefield.[172] During the day, Corporal Landis recalled how "We took to care for the wounded, fixing up our matters generally, and trying to get ourselves rested and in good soldierly shape again."[173] Later that day, rations were issued to the regiment for the first time in four days. "We had subsisted chiefly on green corn. which was now getting to hard," Private Hemminger recorded.[174]

From his vantage point at the division hospital, Private Hemminger saw two Confederate officers with a white flag ride to General McClellan's headquarters. Later, he learned that they had delivered a request from General Lee requesting a twelve-hour cessation of hostilities to bury his dead that was granted, but not to the approval of many rank-and-file of the Army of the Potomac.[175] Union Major General Fitz John Porter's Fifth Corps arrived that morning with 20,000 fresh Union troops. The granting of a temporary armistice by General McClellan would prevent another strike against the Confederates and would provide General Lee an opportunity to re-cross the Potomac into the safety of Virginia.[176]

Despite some occasional shots fired by skirmishers, many from both sides took the time to begin to gather the dead and care for the wounded. This was not the case for the 130th, as enemy sharpshooters all day prevented them access to the battlefield to bury their dead and locate their mortally wounded.[177]

Private Hemminger remained at the division hospital the entire day caring for the wounded, including Private Strickler. During the day, he

---

170. Spangler, 39.
171. Ibid.
172. Author Unknown, Personal Recollection, Newville Historical Society.
173. Landis Memoirs, 11.
174. Hemminger Diary, September 18, 1862.
175. Ibid.
176. Ibid.
177. Masonheimer Diary, September 18, 1862.

recalled that "many [wounded] were placed on straw along the fences. And for shelter we placed rails, one end on the fence and covered them with sheaves of wheat from a stack nearby affording protection from a heavy shower in the afternoon."[178] The wounded in this hospital totaled about 700 Union and 60 Confederates. The four tables used for amputations were in continual use for two full days.[179]

Corporal Landis was able to locate his wounded brother, Private Daniel D. Landis.[180] Private Brehm remained with wounded Private Jacob M. Leidigh and others in Company E who had been wounded, attending to their needs.[181]

Company G's Private Weiser wrote to his parents on September 18 describing his ordeal and letting them know that he survived his first battle:

> I take this opportunity . . . to let you know that I passed through the hardest fought battle that had been fought since the opening of this rebellion unharmed and without a scar although I took eighty three Rounds on the field with me it not being enough last until the Rebs kidadled I took twenty eight Rounds ouf [off] of a dead mans cartridge box . . . I had the pleasure of taking a Rebel second Lieutenant and two privates . . . We were under fire for five hours.[182]

On the morning of September 19, orders were given for a general attack only to find that the Confederates had already crossed the Potomac River back into Virginia. Major General McClellan had hesitated, losing an opportunity that perhaps could have ended the war. This failure would soon bring a new commander to the Army of the Potomac and two and a half more years of death, destruction, and deprivation on both sides of the Mason-Dixon.

Although still physically and emotionally exhausted from the horrors of combat, two days after the battle Colonel Zinn was able to find a spare

---

178. Hemminger Diary, September 18, 1862.
179. Ibid.
180. Landis Memoirs, 11.
181. Brehm Diary, September 18, 1862.
182. John S. Weiser to his parents, September 18, 1862.

moment to write his wife Mary a few lines describing his experiences in the battle and the regiment's losses:

> We have gone through our first fight and I am safe although many of our brave 130th have been sent to their long home. John Zinn and Emerson Zinn passed through untouched; but Rush Zinn was killed on the spot. A cannon shot took off his head while in the act of reloading his gun. We have lost about forty killed and one hundred and fifty to one hundred and sixty wounded. I hope it may never be our misfortune to get into a battle so terrible. My horse received two balls in the neck; one ball passed through the back part of the saddle and another through the blanket trapped behind the saddle. Lieutenant Givler, of Company F, was shot through the head in the beginning of the engagement and died soon after. He was insensible after being shot. Our regiment is reduced to four hundred and fifty men. A number of the men disappeared before the fight. They are probably among the skedaddlers. Remember me to all inquiring friends. I have not yet received any word from home. For yourself and the little ones accept my sincere love. Write often whether I get your letters or not.[183]

Early on the morning of September 19, young Private Hemminger returned to the pivotal ground on the crest of the hill opposite Bloody Lane, with S. W. Sharp of Newville, for a closer look at the carnage he would not forget:

> Early this morning I went out with S. W. Sharp of Newville to show him over the ground occupied by our Regiment on the day of the battle. Lee, as was expected had withdrawn all his forced across the Potomac leaving us free to go to any part of the field. The sight witnessed in and along the old sunken road was awful to behold. This place was literally covered with Confederate dead. Two. Three. and four deep most of whom received their death wound in the head. Showing the terrible execution of

---

183. Henry I. Zinn to his wife, September 19, 1862.

the shots fired from the rifles of the 130 Regiment who had concentrated . . . in this particular part of the lane for four jull [full] hours.[184]

In General Lee's hurried push to recross the Potomac River for the safety of Virginia, he left behind the horrid aftermath of conflict, the casualties of war. Thousands of Confederate wounded filled the hospitals, draining the already overworked Union surgeons, while thousands more remained unburied on the battlefield where they had paid their ultimate sacrifice to their cause.

Private Brehm began his September 19, 1862, diary entry with "this morning portents [sic] a fine day."[185] His prediction would fall short as he and his 130th Pennsylvania comrades were to learn early that morning. The burden of burying the dead for that particular part of the battlefield fell upon the 130th Pennsylvania "by reason of having incurred the displeasure of its Brigade Commander, was honored in the appointment as undertaker-chief."[186] By now, after three days, the decaying bodies were in a swollen and ghastly condition. "They were so greatly swollen that their clothing could hardly contain them, and they were of a livid blue-black color," wrote Corporal Landis, who partook in this unforgettable ordeal.[187] Large numbers of buzzards circled the air awaiting the opportunity to feast upon the now defenseless casualties of the battle. The weather became hotter as the day lagged on, only to intensify the stench from the maggoty bodies exposed to three days of torrid heat.[188] The men of the 130th used split rails to carry the bodies, placing them side by side in long rows in a trench deep enough to cover them well. Corporal Landis detailed his gruesome experience: "Where I was assisting we buried during this day and the next 75 of our Union men, and about 250 Confederates—or "Rebels" as we called them."[189] The bodies of the Union soldiers were buried singly, wrapped in a blanket with the grave marked by a wooden head board and inscribed with

---

184. Hemminger Diary, September 19, 1862.
185. Brehm Diary, September 19, 1862.
186. Bosbyshell, 164. No documentation explained the cause of the brigade commander's displeasure with the regiment. Of all of the brigade's regiments he should have been most displeased with the 108th New York.
187. Landis Memoirs, 11.
188. Spangler, 163.
189. Landis Memoirs, 11.

the soldier's name and command for later identification. Nearby in the Mumma field, 185 Confederates were buried in one trench one on top of the other.[190]

On Sunday, September 21, 1862 Colonel Zinn wrote home to his wife Mary:

> Dearest Mary: Our mail came from Washington to-day, bringing me three letters from you and one from Elsie. I am sorry to learn that George is growing so thin. You had better consult the doctor about him. The box you sent me by express will probably never be received as we are moving farther and farther from Washington. If received at this time it would do us little good as we would be obligated to eat it all at once or give it away. The 130th has been engaged three days burying the dead. The destruction of life on Wednesday's battle was enormous. We buried 400 rebels and 48 Union soldiers. Dead horses are

BLOODY LANE AFTERMATH (Library of Congress)

---

190. Spangler, 164.

THE ONE HUNDRED AND THIRTIETH PENNSYLVANIA REGIMENT OF VOLUNTEERS BURYING THE CONFEDERATE DEAD (*Frank Leslie's Illustrated*)

MOST LIKELY MEN OF THE 130TH WHO WERE ASSIGNED BURIAL DETAIL. PHOTO TAKEN ON SEPTEMBER 19, 1862.
(U.S. Army Military History Institute)

scattered around by the scores. Thousands of arms of every description lie scattered in all directions. These are being collected by the government . . . The horse purchased for me by Dr. Lenher came to-day, but he is not what I expected for the money, but I presume horses are high in price. The horse I bought last week for $115 is worth two of him.

No appointments for the regiment have as yet been made and I despair of any being made . . . I am sound as a dollar, but as dollars sometimes have holes punched in them, so I may one of these days; but never despair.

We left camp at Fort Marcy without a change of clothing. I have been wearing the same shirts for two weeks, and may have to wear them for two more. The money enclosed is for Elsie. I send much love to all.

Ever yours,
H. I. Z. [191]

Private Masonheimer noted in his diary on Sunday, September 21, "Found us burying the dead at what was called Burnt House and Barn. Their loss was numerous to ours. Quite a number of people visited from Carlisle and surrounding county. Drew three days ration."[192]

Before the bodies were buried, they were examined for identification and anything of value that could be sent home. Often, notes were found with specific instructions in case of their death. Corporal Landis discovered a note on the body of George N. McLure, from a Maryland Regiment, stating that he belonged to the Bible Society in Baltimore instructing that "If I should die on the battlefield or in the Hospital, for the sake of humanity, acquaint John McLure of Chesapeake City, Md. of the fact and where my remains may be found."[193] The men of the 130th fulfilled many such requests. The others would be placed in a nameless grave that would someday fill the endless rows found in our national cemeteries with the marker inscribed "unknown."

---

191. Henry I. Zinn to his wife, September 21, 1862.
192. Masonheimer Diary, September 21, 1862.
193. Landis Memoirs, 11.

GENERAL VIEW OF ANTIETAM BATTLEFIELD
(National Archives and Records Administration, Brady Collection, College Park)

The 130th had burials of its own, suffering with 32 killed and 146 wounded.[194] Fourteen of those listed as wounded later died of their wounds.[195] Second Lieutenant William A. Givler of Company F was the only officer killed.[196] Considering approximately 650 men of the 130th were engaged, the resulting casualty rate was 27 percent, placing the chances of being killed or wounded slightly over one-in-four.[197] The regiment's casualty rate slightly exceeded the 24 percent rate experienced by the Army of the Potomac, although was significantly less than the 38 percent rate suffered by the Army of Northern Virginia as documented by John M. Priest.[198]

Of the three regiments in the Second Brigade, the 130th Pennsylvania ranked first with the total number of killed and wounded at 178. Thirty-two were reported wounded and 146 killed. The 108th New York

---

194. OR, Series 1, Volume XIX, No. 5.
195. Bosbyshell, 184.
196. Bates, 216.
197. Spangler, 44.
198. Priest, 343.

ranked second with 148 casualties, numbering 26 killed and 122 wounded.[199] The 14th Connecticut experienced the least number of casualties at 108, with 20 killed and 88 wounded. The 130th had no men reported as "missing" in comparison with the 14th Connecticut of 48, and the 108th New York of 47.[200]

Henry I. Zinn was surely the wisest choice to be appointed the regiment's commander. He had clearly demonstrated his leadership ability to both his men and his doubting superiors. Although he had no prior formal military training, and his men were equally untrained and untested, they successfully overcame General Rodes' Alabamians, who were combat veterans positioned in a superior protected defensive position. In his official report, Brigadier General French remarked, "The conduct of the new regiments must take a prominent place in the history of this great battle. Un-drilled, but admirable armed and equipped, every regiment, either in advance or reserve, distinguished itself . . ."[201] Major General Edwin Sumner, the Second Corps Commander, in his official report commented, "Richardson's and French's divisions maintained a furious and successful fight from the time the entered the battle till the end of it, highly to the honor of the officers and soldiers."[202]

On Monday, September 22, the men of the 130th rose early at 3:00 A.M. to receive three days of rations, and were ordered to prepare for a march. At daybreak the regiment formed and began its march southward through Sharpsburg crossing the Potomac River in the direction of Harper's Ferry. Private Brehm recorded, "The scenery along the Potomac is wild and indeed delightful to the admirer of romance. Finally we come to Harper's Ferry which truly presents the hand work of the Creator as manifest in nature though sadly ruined by the ravages of war."[203] Since the Confederates had burned the railroad and pontoon bridges, the men waded across the Potomac River. Although not deep, the bottom was rocky, making wading difficult.[204] Private Landis vividly recounted the comical event that occurred during the regiment's crossing: "We passed

---

199. Charles D. Page, *History of the Fourteenth Regiment* (Meriden, Connecticut: Horton Publishing Company, 1906. Reprint, Salem Massachusetts: Higginson Book Company, 1998), 344.
200. OR Series I, Vol. XIX, Part 1, No. 5.
201. OR Series I, Vol. XIX, Part I, No's 70, 323.
202. OR Series , Vol XIX, Part I, No's 38, 275.
203. Brehm Diary, September 22, 1862.
204. Henry I. Zinn to Mary, September 24, 1862.

under the great overhanging rocks on the Maryland side, the band playing 'Yankee Doodle,' and on into the river, whose rocky bottom made fording rather difficult. This seemed to be the case with our band, for when just about in the middle of the river they suddenly stopped 'Yankee Doodle' and struck up 'Jordan am a hard road to trabble'; a song much in vogue at the time, which so amused and inspired us, that we passed over in a more cheerful mood."[205]

The now "veteran" regiment began its twelve-mile march, passing though Harper's Ferry, encamping on an area known as Bolivar Heights, located one mile west of Harper's Ferry, where, as described by Colonel Zinn, the "The scenery is beautiful, and if not marred by the ravages of war, would be the finest I ever saw."[206]

---

205. Landis Memoirs, 12.
206. Henry I. Zinn to Mary, September 24, 1862.

CHAPTER 4

A Respite at Harper's Ferry

THE HARDSHIPS endured by the battle-fatigued regiment upon their arrival at Bolivar Heights on September 22, 1862, showed no immediate signs of relief. The regiment now numbered only 583 enlisted men and officers, reduced significantly from its original strength of 986 when the regiment left Camp Simmons in August.[1] There were only sixteen officers available in the regiment fit for duty.[2] The men were wearing the same clothing since their departure from Camp Marcy for Rockville on September 7. Their regiment's camp equipment, officers' baggage, and men's personal belongings were still in storage in Washington.[3] The regiment had not received its Pennsylvania regimental flag and had been carrying only flank markers, and the officers' commissions had not yet arrived from Pennsylvania's Governor Curtin.[4] The men's advance pay and promised government bounties had not yet been paid.[5] Added to these mounting demoralizing deficiencies, a regimental chaplain had not yet arrived. Time was desperately needed for the regiment to reorganize, mend, and obtain all the clothing and equipment a Union infantry regiment required.

Ironically, the first two weeks at their new camp near Harper's Ferry brought more troubles than cures. Since Dr. Frederick L. Haupt, the 130th's chief surgeon, remained at Antietam caring for the wounded, the regiment had no medical staff until the arrival of the second assistant

---

1. John R. Turner to daughter Kittie, September 28, 1862.
2. Henry I. Zinn to Mary, September 24, 1862.
3. Ibid.
4. Author Unknown, Personal Recollection, Newville Historical Society; Henry I. Zinn, Letters to Mary, September 24, 1862.
5. Henry I. Zinn to Mary, October 5, 1862.

surgeon, J. H. Longenecker, around September 26. On October 5, Colonel Zinn related his increasing concerns to his wife:

> All is well with me. This cannot be said of the many poor fellows of the regiment who have been suffering for want of proper medical attendance since the battle. All our medical supplies were left behind with the exception of a small lot brought along by one of our surgeons, most of which was expended during and after the battle.[6]

The regiment was able to borrow some medications, although they lacked a supply of specialized drugs. The poor and scarce water led to diarrhea and dysentery, although there were a number of cases of ague (malaria) reported. By October 5, the regiment had 150 men reported as sick, about 100 had deserted and several officers were absent without leave.[7]

The remainder of September 1862 found the men occupied with the typical duties of camp life of drilling, inspections, dress parades and more drilling. On September 25, Brigadier General French ordered his units, including the 130th, to begin drilling twice a day.[8] The weather was often rainy, cold, and damp, which caused mold to be a problem. The most common complaint was diarrhea, a frequent ailment found throughout both armies.[9]

September 31 would be an eventful day in the Union encampment at Bolivar Heights. Unfortunately, the regiment would be away from camp. The entire regiment, ordered out on picket duty at 4 P.M. on September 30, was unable to get a glimpse of President Abraham Lincoln and his staff, who visited the camp and reviewed the troops. Although unfortunate, being struck like so many others with diarrhea and unable to go on picket duty with the regiment, Corporal Landis was one of the few who observed the grand event:

> The presence of that tall, pale, earnest man, always brought enthusiasm to the heart of the soldier. He felt that there was a

---

6. Henry I. Zinn to his wife, October 5, 1862.
7. Ibid.
8. Brehm Diary, September 25, 1862.
9. Ibid.

great serious soberness about the work he was engaged in. This was often dismissed from his mind; and it is well that it was so, or the strain would have been too great. But with the appearance of that great man, his patriotism struck deeper root into every fiber of his being.[10]

The regiment returned the evening of October 1 with some of the men spending a "sociable evening" in their large Sibley tents.[11]

Although the next day, Tuesday October 2, began with a thick mist, the day was to mark the beginning of a series of positive events for the regiment. After drilling, the regiment returned to "high living and delicacies in abundance" with such delights as light cakes, butter, pean [sic] butter, cheese, dry beef, jelly cake and pepper crackers issued. President Lincoln passed the rounds this afternoon and is saluted by the Batteries & cheered by the soldiery.[12] That same day overcoats, additional uniforms, and knapsacks were issued to the men.[13]

During the following two weeks the regiment's routine continued to be company and regimental drills, inspections, dress parades, and picket duty.[14] On October 6, Private Masonheimer was promoted to 4th Corporal "to date from the first of the month."[15] While on picket duty on October 7, the regiment encountered a flag of truce called by the Confederates to return four paroled prisoners.[16] "I accompanied the party that went to meet with them, and found the Rebels quite a fine looking gentlemanly set of fellows," Colonel Zinn wrote to his wife.[17] During the same week a new Union intelligence gathering technique was first seen by the regiment—balloon reconnaissance.[18]

The regiment was finally being adequately supplied by early October. Writing to his wife, Colonel Zinn conveyed his cautious optimism: "We have ample supplies of good living now. The good old days of Camp Curtin . . . have returned, but how long they will last I cannot tell."[19]

---

10. Landis Memoirs, 12.
11. Brehm Diary, October 1, 1862.
12. Brehm Diary, October 2, 1862.
13. Masonheimer Diary, October 2, 1862.
14. Masonheimer Diary, October 2–9, 1862.
15. Masonheimer Diary, October 6, 1862.
16. Henry I. Zinn to Mary, October 12, 1862.
17. Ibid.
18. Brehm Diary, October 8, 1862.
19. Henry I. Zinn to Mary, October 12, 1862.

During the same week, on October 9, a major shift in military leadership occurred in the Second Corps. Major General Edwin V. Sumner, the first commander who had organized the corps, was given a thirty-day leave of absence, vacating the Second Corps command. In his place, Major General Darius N. Couch, who had distinguished himself during the Peninsula Campaign, was named the Commander of the Second Corps. The oldest corps commander had been replaced by one of the youngest. Quite opposite in manner, style and demeanor off the battlefield, yet on the battlefield, they were much alike as "father and son."[20]

Sunday, October 11, brought an additional welcome enrichment to the regiment with the arrival of their long-awaited chaplain, Reverend George W. Chalfant. Colonel Zinn, elated, described him to his wife as "arriving last evening looking as fine as a new pin."[21] The regiment's

MAJOR GENERAL DARIUS N. COUCH,
COMMANDER, SECOND CORPS
(U.S. Army Military History Institute)

---

20. Walker, 128–130.
21. Henry I. Zinn to Mary, October 12, 1862.

chaplain from Cumberland, Pennsylvania, came from the O.S. Presbyterian Church of Cumberland.[22] Certified by six Pennsylvania clergymen, Reverend Chalfant received the unanimous vote of the regiment's company commanders and was subsequently appointed by Colonel Henry I. Zinn on September 27.[23]

In early October, the regiment's long-awaited officer appointments finally arrived. The Pennsylvania state document dated October 1, 1862 commissioned the regiment's staff and company officers retroactive to the date of their muster in August.[24] Relieved the appointments had finally arrived, officially now a colonel, Colonel Zinn told his wife, "The organization of the regiment is completed, the commissions have been received, and there is no danger that we will lose our pay. So tell the good people at home not to be uneasy about us, we expect to get money enough to pay our debts and to keep our families besides."[25]

The soldiers' everyday living conditions also began to improve since leaving Fort Marcy. Being on the march, the men had slept on the ground without a blanket (since those were left behind with their knapsacks), or found any means of protection that they could, rain or shine.[26] They now had the luxury of being quartered in Sibley tents sleeping on pine boughs.[27] While on the march it had been every man for himself for their meals. Sometimes while on the march they were able to "procure" some apples, corn, or potatoes to add to their ration of coffee and meat. Their daily rations while at Bolivar Heights "per man are ten crackers three & a half inches square half inch thick and as hard as a hickory chip three fourths of a pound of pork very good two tablespoons of coffee the same sugar once in a while a spoonful or two of molasses," wrote Private Weiser to his sisters and brothers.[28] He added that on occasion beans and rice were available but were considered "too much trouble to cook."[29] The men's appearance improved, with new uniforms being issued, and with

---

22. George G. Chalfant, Service Records, National Archives, Washington, DC.
23. George G. Chalfant, Service Record File, "Returns of the Chaplain," National Archives, Washington, DC.
24. Officer Commissions, 130th Regiment Pennsylvania Volunteer Infantry Regiment Records, Pennsylvania State Archives.
25. Henry I. Zinn to Mary, October 18, 1862.
26. John S. Weiser to his sisters and brothers, October 11, 1862.
27. Brehm Diary, October 18–19, 1862.
28. John S. Weiser to his sisters and brothers, October 11, 1862.
29. Ibid.

the nearby Shenandoah River quickly becoming a prized bathing spot for the regiment.[30]

Private Weiser, contented and rested, apprised his parents in his October 13 letter home, explaining that things had improved for him and describing his feelings after his first test in a battle:

> At present I am content and have plenty to eat and very good clothing we drew some new clothing on Saturday evening [October 11th] and we will get the balance this week. I would have not missed being in the Service of our Uncle Sam the past two months for all I that I ever did make or ever will if I live to get home[.] I will have something to talk about all my life and a Soldiers story never gets old. If I am killed or die through disease it is all the same to me as I am enlisted in a good cause and intend to do all for the old Flag that I can although when I went into the engagement at the Battle of Antietam I thought I was a coward but that fear left me in five minutes after we received the first fire from the Gray Backs and then I thought of nothing but loading and firing while my comrades were falling on my right and left Killed and wounded I never thought that I might be the next.[31]

Slowly, the regiment was beginning to regain the strength it had possessed before the desolation it had endured on the killing fields of Antietam.

Monday, October 13, 1862, was to be a most unforgettable day for the regiment with the formal presentation of the regiment's Pennsylvania Colors by Colonel Samuel B. Thomas representing Governor Curtin.[32] Corporal Landis recorded how this was "a day to be remembered as our colors were presented to our regiment . . . Col Zinn said that 'This flag shall never be disgraced.'"[33]

The remainder of the week passed with the normal routines of camp activities of target practice, company and regimental drills, dress parades, and their turn at picket duty. The only incident that interrupted the

---

30. John S. Weiser to his mother, October 13, 1862; Brehm Diary, October 4, 1862.
31. John S. Weiser to his mother, October 13, 1862.
32. Author Unknown, Personal Recollection, Newville Historical Society.
33. Landis Memoirs, 12.

A Respite at Harper's Ferry

130TH REGIMENTAL FLAG
(Capitol Preservation Committee)

regiment's tranquil interlude while at Bolivar Heights began during the night of October 15, with cannonading heard in the distance resulting in the regiment being kept in readiness until noon on the next day.[34] The newly-assigned Second Corps Commander, Major General D. N. Couch, ordered Brigadier General Winfield S. Hancock's First Division to conduct a reconnaissance into Charlestown to determine the Confederate strength. On October 16 the expedition found only a small contingent of Confederate cavalry and supporting artillery battery.[35]

On Thursday, October 17, the regiment participated in a division drill under the command of General French. The regiment's first death as a result from sickness occurred the next day when Private Charles A. Hitchcock of Company I died of a low form of typhoid fever brought on by a breast wound by a piece of shell he received at Antietam.[36]

Sunday, October 19, marked the regiment's first church service given by Chaplain Chalfant, whose sermon concerned "Matthew, 25th chapter and 1st clause of 28th verse—brief and practical," noted Private Brehm in his diary.[37]

---

34. Brehm Diary, October 16, 1862.
35. Walker, 131–132.
36. Henry I. Zinn to Mary, October 18, 1862.
37. Brehm Diary, October 19, 1862.

The typical rigors of camp life continued throughout the remaining days in October with the weather becoming rainy and turning colder as month came to an end. Colonel Zinn expressed concern about the effects of the oncoming winter in a letter to his wife: "The cold winds of winter are fast coming, and I must have clothing for myself and blankets for my horses and boys."[38] To everyone's relief, overcoats were drawn on October 23, which were a welcome addition to the uniform, particularly while detailed on picket duty.[39]

Picket duty was a dangerous duty that brought with it long, cold, and often wet nights. It also brought with it the possibility of capture as Private Weiser described in an unforgettable event that he witnessed on October 24th:

> There is hardly a day but what there is some of our men along the Picket line taken prisoner sometimes they are surrounded by the Rebs and cut their way out, yesterday there was twenty five men belonging to the fourteenth Connecticut taken (they belong to our Brigade) but our reserve was to close for the Gray Backs to hold them there was a nice little skirmish[.] [I]t lasted about ten minutes we had two men slightly wounded. I was looking through a Glass from the Heights.[40]

Camp rumor was beginning to circulate that the regiment may soon be on the move—somewhere.[41] Colonel Zinn, not intimidated by rumor, but faced with the realities of the war, conveyed his concerns to his wife: "From present indications, I presume it is intended that we shall remain here this winter; but as movements of the army are uncertain, a week hence may find us far from here."[42]

Colonel Zinn's intuition proved to be both accurate and timely. Late on Wednesday, October 29, the regiment was ordered to go on picket duty at 8:00 A.M. the next morning. Shortly thereafter, a second order was given, countermanding the first, directing the men to be ready to march the next morning.[43]

---

38. Henry I. Zinn to Mary, October 24, 1862.
39. Brehm Diary, October 23, 1862.
40. John S. Weiser to his parents, October 25, 1862.
41. Brehm Diary, October 25, 1862.
42. Henry I. Zinn to Mary, October 18, 1862.
43. Brehm Diary, October 29, 1862.

On October 26, Major General McClellan began putting his troops in motion, ordering his Army of the Potomac southward into the valley of the Shenandoah in pursuit of the Confederate forces that had encamped in the vicinity of Bunker Hill and Winchester after the Battle of Antietam.[44] In his work, the *History of the Second Army Corps*, Francis A. Walker recited Major General McClellan's intention:

> Upon reaching Ashby's, or any other pass, I found that the enemy was in force between it and the Potomac, in the valley of the Shenandoah, to move into the valley and endeavor to gain their rear . . . by striking in between Culpeper Court House and Little Washington I could either separate their army and beat them in detail.[45]

Major General McClellan was finally taking an offensive initiative that the Lincoln administration had been persuading him to do. The time to act was now. The Army of the Potomac now consisted of the First, Second, Third, Fifth, Sixth, and Ninth Corps.[46] The Twelfth Corps remained behind to guard that region of the upper Potomac. On October 30, the Second Corps would take the lead of the Army of the Potomac to begin the advance across the Shenandoah River, passing Loudon Heights into the valley of the Shenandoah in the direction of Ashby's Gap.[47]

The entire regiment was up before daylight on the morning of October 30, ate breakfast, and was given sixty rounds of ammunition.[48] Time continued to pass slowly with no orders to move. Finally, the regiment was ordered out on picket duty, where they remained until 4:30 P.M. when they were called back to camp. When they returned back to camp, Private Brehm recorded they found it "torn up and the troops almost gone."[49] After taking a "hasty" supper, the regiment left camp (they were the last regiment to depart from the heights) at dusk and marched down the pike and crossed over the Shenandoah River. They crossed the

---

44. Francis W. Palfrey, *The Antietam and Fredericksburg* (New York: Charles Scribner's Sons, 1882, Reprint, Harrisburg, The Archive Society, 1992), 131.
45. Walker, 131–132.
46. Walker, 131.
47. Ibid.
48. Brehm Diary, October 30, 1862.
49. Ibid.

pontoon bridge and continued their four-mile march down the river around the bluffs into Pleasant Valley until 9:00 P.M. when they caught up with their division. At the end of the march, Private Brehm remarked in his diary, "A little warm coffee, bread and butter, and then to 'bed.'"[50]

At 7:30 A.M on October 31, the regiment continued its march southward, halting around noon.[51] Soon after stopping after their five-mile march, the men heard cannonading in the direction that they would soon be headed early the next morning.[52]

At 9:00 A.M. on the following morning, November 1, the regiment continued its trek southward, knowing neither their ultimate destination nor purpose. As it marched along, the thunder of cannons continually rang out, reminding the men of their ordeal at Antietam and what fate could lie ahead for them. At 1:00 P M., they halted in a field for an hour of rest and quickly started off again around 2:00 P.M passing by a "fine" farmhouse where Private Brehm recorded that "the old lady and three fine looking ladies may be seen in the yard. They seem generous in giving apples and bread to the soldier but have 'secesh proclivities.'"[53] The regiment continued its march, halting in the "back of a wood on a hill facing sun rise."[54] The men received a most-welcomed treasure that day as their old knapsacks that had been in storage in Washington finally caught up with them.[55]

The following morning the regiment was up early, having breakfast of applesauce, bacon, and 'the tack'. As the sun rose that morning Private Brehm recorded that it caused a "beautiful landscape to the north east" with a mist that covered the valley, and the woods appearing like so many islands."[56] At 9:00 A.M., the regiment was ordered to receive three days' rations [which never came for some unknown reason] and move out.[57]

After maintaining a quick rate of march, the regiment arrived at the small village of Snickersville, Virginia, that Private Brehm referred to as "a little village of no admiration situated in the gap of two hills."[58]

---
50. Ibid.
51. Brehm Diary, October 31, 1862.
52. Masonheimer Diary, October 31, 1862.
53. Brehm Diary, November 1, 1862.
54. Ibid.
55. Masonheimer Diary, November 1, 1862.
56. Brehm Diary, November 2, 1862.
57. Ibid.
58. Ibid.

A Respite at Harper's Ferry

The men were ordered to stack arms where they had supper as they listened to the serenade of cannons not far off behind the hill.[59] Their camp that evening was located in an orchard where Private Spangler vividly recalled that they "found a half a dozen or more of swine which were quickly dispatched and filled our haversacks with juicy pork."[60] Brigadier General French's headquarters was located directly behind the regiment's camp. That evening Private Brehm recognized his division commander as he saw French having his supper sitting on the trunk of an old apple tree. The next few hours the men waited in anticipation, expecting to resume their march until they saw General French's tents go up. The regiment became relieved when Colonel Zinn passed the order to "lie down and sleep."[61]

Monday morning, November 3, brought news to the regiment that as the Confederates were retreating, they were to be ready to march at 9:00 A.M. Marching southward the remainder of the day, the regiment stopped a short time before sunset where the cannons were heard not too far in the distance. After a short rest, the regiment continued its advance until it finally halted at sunset in the village of Upperville, Virginia, on a hill directly opposite where Confederate General J. E. B. Stuart's Cavalry had encamped the night before.[62] The 84th Pennsylvania was encamped across the road.[63] Fatigued and hungry from the day's hard march, the men ate their supper and began settling in.[64] Anticipating a needed night's rest, Private Brehm recorded that this was not to be the case:

> Whisler, Crider & myself just nicely nestled under our blankets when the Colonel's voice sounds 'fall in every man' and soon we are off and stationed along a stone fence as out pickets. At 4 in the morning our post is relieved by reserves and we lie down. The next I see is the shining sun beautifully glimmering in the east—he betokens a fine day.[65]

---

59. Ibid.
60. Spangler, 56.
61. Brehm Diary, November 2, 1862.
62. Brehm Diary, November 4–5, 1862.
63. Masonheimer Diary, November 4, 1862.
64. Brehm Diary, November 3, 1862.
65. Ibid.

By November 4, the entire Second Corps had reached Upperville, with Union cavalry in front that brought on an artillery duel with General Stuart's artillery. The contest slowed the Union advance that allowed the Confederate cavalry to slip through Ashby's Gap.[66]

The regiment remained encamped near Upperville during November 4, with no orders and little to keep them occupied.[67] During the day the encampment was a hub of senior leader activity with Generals McClellan, Burnside, French, and Whipple passing up and down the main camp road.[68] Later, General Burnside, Commander of the Union Ninth Corps, passed the regiment with his entire corps. The evening ended with the insistent roar of constant cannonading heard well into the night.[69]

The men breakfasted on crackers and pork the next morning, which arrived with a heavy frost.[70] The Army of the Potomac had begun to move that morning "with a considerable force" that passed through their camp near the Virginia town of Upperville. Later in the afternoon Brigadier General Winfield S. Hancock's First Division of the Second Corps marched past the regiment, joining those already on the move as the men of the 130th awaited their orders.[71]

With some precious idle time, Colonel Zinn was able to write a few lines home informing his family of his whereabouts the best he could:

> The whole Army is in motion, and moving in the same direction. The enemy has been falling back before our advancing columns, keeping only a few hours ahead of us. Night before last we could plainly see the Confederate campfires. With the force we now have in the field, we should be able to whip them easily.[72]

By November 10, 1862, the total number present for duty in the Army of the Potomac totaled 127,574 officers and men.[73] Although the total force in the field may have been sufficient, the 130th Pennsylvania

---

66. Walker, 133.
67. Brehm Diary, November 4, 1862.
68. Masonheimer Diary, November 4, 1862.
69. Brehm Diary, November 4, 1862.
70. Brehm Diary, November 5, 1862.
71. Ibid.
72. Henry I. Zinn to Mary, November 5, 1862.
73. Palfrey, 138.

was now reduced to 350 men "with but a sprinkling of officers," roughly one-third of the regiment's original strength.[74]

The order to move finally came at 8:00 A.M. on the morning of November 6 and the regiment moved out with "our haversacks replenished with beef for the boys were out confiscating beef yesterday," noted Private Brehm.[75] Marching through Upperville, enduring the cold and threatening snow, the regiment encamped near the small Virginia town of Rectortown for the night.[76]

The regiment remained in camp the next day enduring the decreasing cold temperatures.[77] Snow began falling early in the morning and continued throughout the day with blankets providing the men's only shelter.[78]

At 8:30 A.M. on the following morning, November 8, the regiment received orders to march. Promptly at 9:00 A.M., it joined the rest of the Army of the Potomac traveling southward deeper into Virginia, marching through Rectortown and Salem in view of the Rattlesnake Mountains.[79] After crossing the Manassas Railroad, the long blue column changed direction to a southeastwardly direction, stopping at 3:00 p.m. for the night.[80]

Rested and ready to resume the march at 7:30 A.M. the following morning, Sunday, November 9, the regiment trekked eight miles further into Virginia, finally reaching Warrenton.[81] Corporal Masonheimer thought Warrenton "The nicest looking town I seen in Virginia," although he found the regiment's welcoming reception to be less than hospitable when a girl made a face at him.[82] After marching through the town, the regiment was ordered to countermarch, encamping approximately one mile southeast of town. That evening many of the Pennsylvanians attended a short religious service.[83]

---

74. Henry I. Zinn to Mary, November 5, 1862.
75. Brehm Diary, November 6, 1862.
76. Ibid.
77. Brehm Diary, November 7, 1862.
78. Ibid.
79. Masonheimer Diary, November 8, 1862. The Virginia town of Salem that Corporal Masonheimer referred to was renamed "Marshall" during the late nineteenth century due to confusion with another Virginia town named "Salem" near Roanoke.
80. Brehm Diary, November 8, 1862.
81. Masonheimer Diary, November 9, 1862.
82. Ibid.
83. Brehm Diary, November 9, 1862.

HEADQUARTERS, SECOND CORPS, WARRENTON, VIRGINIA, NOVEMBER 1862. L TO R: CAPT. W. G. JONES, MAJOR L. KIP, LT. COL. J. H. TAYLOR, GEN. SUMNER, CAPT. GARLAND, CAPT. S. S. SUMNER, CAPT. A. CUSHING, LT. COL. W. W. TEALL (U.S. Army Military History Institute)

HEADQUARTERS, ARMY OF THE POTOMAC, WARRENTON, VIRGINIA, NOVEMBER 1862. L TO R SITTING: GEN. H. J. HUNT, GEN. W. S. HANCOCK, GEN D. N. COUCH, GEN. O. B. WILLCOX, GEN. J. BURFORD.
L TO R STANDING: GEN. M. R. PATRICK, GEN. E. FERRERO, GEN. J. G. PARK, GEN. A.E. BURNSIDE, GEN. J. COCHRANE, GEN. S. D. STURGIS.
(U.S. Army Military History Institute)

A Respite at Harper's Ferry

The overall health of the regiment was beginning to improve with the number of men available for duty increasing daily. Yet, serious cases of jaundice were taking its toll among the regiments. Colonel Zinn had himself come down with the ailment.[84] "My skin and the whites of my eyes are yellow as saffron. I have the jaundice. You can perhaps imagine how I feel camping in this cold, snowy weather . . . There are quite a number of cases of jaundice in the regiment," he informed his wife on November 9. Both of the regiment's surgeons were ill. Dr. Haupt, who was left in charge of the regiment's sick who remained at Bolivar Heights, had returned to Pennsylvania.[85] Dr. Longenecker, although sick himself, remained with the regiment. Both the commander and chaplain of the 14th Connecticut were also ill with the jaundice.[86]

The following day, November 10, would be one of the more memorable days for the men of 130th. Awakened early with orders to fall in at 6:00 A.M., the men marched about three-fourths of a mile to find almost the entire Army of the Potomac positioned on both sides of the road.[87] Three days prior, on November 7, orders were sent from Washington to General McClellan relieving him of his command of the Army of the Potomac.[88] Major General Ambrose E. Burnside, formally the commander of the Union Army's Ninth Corps, was appointed its new commander.

It was not until that morning in Warrenton that the troops become aware of the fate of their esteemed Major General McClellan. The Second and Fifth Corps of the Army of the Potomac were drawn up on both sides of the Centerville Pike in columns, by regiment, to bid a final farewell to beloved commander.[89] Corporal Masonheimer, like most soldiers in the Army of the Potomac, was moved by his sudden departure: "As General [McClellan] passed the line he bid us farewell with tears in his eyes. The most beautiful sight I ever saw."[90] History would later record that no other Union commander would be held in the same high regard to the common soldier in the Army of the Potomac. Private Brehm recounted that at the conclusion of the momentous event the regiment returned

---

84. Henry I. Zinn to Mary, November 9, 1862.
85. Henry I. Zinn to Mary, November 9, 1862.
86. Ibid.
87. Brehm Diary, November 10, 1862.
88. Walker, 136.
89. Ibid.
90. Masonheimer Diary, November 10, 1862.

to its camp later to "sit around the camp fire" until roll call when they retired to the "frail little shelters made of oil-cloth and gum blankets for the crowed accommodation of four."[91]

One of Major General Burnside's first acts was to reorganize the Army of the Potomac into the formation of three Grand Divisions made up of the Right, Centre, and Left Grand Divisions. Major General E. V. Sumner commanded the Right Grand Division that included the Second and Ninth Corps. The Centre Grand Division was commanded by Major General Joseph Hooker that included that Third and Fifth Corps. The Left Grand Division made up of the Sixth and First Corps was commanded by Major General William B. Franklin.[92]

For the next four days, the regiment remained encamped near Warrenton with the time being taken up with the normal routines of daily camp life. Some in the regiment had the opportunity to locate friends in the 126th, 131st, and 133rd Pennsylvania Regiments that were camped nearby. On Wednesday, November 12, a thirteen-gun [cannon] salute was heard in honor of Major General Burnside.[93]

On November 13, the entire Third Division was called out for an inspection after rumors were heard that it would soon be on the move.[94] A rumor that the entire Second Corps would be sent to Texas was also circulating the camp.[95] The rumor concerning moving was given credibility when the men were given eight days' rations later that evening.[96] Although expecting to be on the march early on the 14th, the day's activities were back to company drill and "brightening up the guns."[97] Late that evening the regiment received orders to be ready to march the next morning.[98]

Not long after General Burnside assumed command, he submitted his plan of operations to Washington, to Major General Henry W. Halleck, the General-in-Chief, who disapproved his plan. After two days of face-to-face consultations in Warrenton on November 12 and 13,

---

91. Brehm Diary, November 10, 1862.
92. Walker, 138–139.
93. Brehm Diary, November 11–12, 1862.
94. Brehm Diary, November 13, 1862.
95. Henry I. Zinn to his wife, November 11, 1862.
96. Masonheimer Diary, November 13, 1862.
97. Brehm Diary, November 14, 1862.
98. Masonheimer Diary, November 14, 1862.

both generals were at an impasse, leaving the final decision to President Lincoln who ultimately sided with Major General Burnside. In brief, General Burnside's plan was to deceive the Confederates into believing that he would be attacking either Culpeper or Gordonsville, while accumulating four to five days of supplies in order to make a rapid drive into Fredericksburg. Once Fredericksburg was taken, Richmond would then be within his grasp.[99]

At 11:00 A.M., November 14, 1862, the same day that he received President Lincoln's telegraph approving his plan, General Burnside issued orders for his three Grand Division commanders to begin their move towards Fredericksburg with the Second Division taking the lead at daybreak the next day.[100]

Early on the morning of November 15, the regiment packed up with three days rations, taking its place in line with the Second Corps to begin its march deeper into Virginia, according to General Burnside's plan.[101] Although many knew they were headed in the direction of Richmond, the destination of Fredericksburg would not be conveyed to them until the following day.[102] They marched through the streets of Warrenton, down the railway towards the station, turning left, passing over the Orange & Alexandria Railroad.[103] They continued their eleven-mile march into Stafford County and encamped for the night.[104] "Up early and off" the next morning, November 16, wrote Private Brehm.[105] Their march took them through mostly areas of barren pine passing occasional log houses with wooded chimneys.[106] Not impressed with what he saw, Private Brehm called the landscape, "A poorly cultivated and thinly settled country."[107] At sunset, after marching a grueling seventeen miles, the regiment halted for the night.[108] Rain that night would make getting a decent night's rest a challenging one.[109]

---

99. Palfrey, 136–137.
100. Palfrey, 138.
101. Brehm Diary, November 15, 1862.
102. Brehm Diary, November 16, 1862.
103. Ibid.
104. Masonheimer Diary, November 15, 1862.
105. Brehm Diary, November 16, 1862.
106. Masonheimer Diary, November 16, 1862.
107. Brehm Diary, November 16, 1862.
108. Masonheimer Diary, November 16, 1862.
109. Brehm Diary, November 17, 1862.

Orders were received the next morning, Monday, November 17, to move at 7:00 A.M. Burdened with the detail to guard an ammunition train, the regiment still managed to march another ten miles. Private Brehm made the march "tolerable well sore feet excepted."[110] Corporal Masonheimer "almost gave out" only to become sick later and fall out of ranks.[111] As the day ended, the regiment found itself near the banks of the Rappahannock River, about four miles from Fredericksburg where cannonading could be heard to their front.[112] Two Union artillery batteries quickly responded to quiet the Confederate artillery poised on the outskirts of Fredericksburg, awaiting the coming Union onslaught.[113]

That day Colonel Zinn was able to find a few precious minutes to write home to comfort his family, "As you will perceive we have been once more on the march toward Richmond, the goal of every northern soldier." He finally was able to ward off jaundice; however, "owing to the quality of our living," he was "troubled with diarrhea. I am however, nearly well."[114]

With Fredericksburg a short distance away, the men assuredly wondered what direction they would soon be headed in the morning. At noon, orders were given for hourly roll calls and for everyone to be prepared to fall in under arms on a moment's notice. Within a short time, the men took down their tents, packed their equipment, drew three days rations, and marched through the small town of Falmouth to await the remainder of the brigade.[115] Once the Second Brigade arrived, it marched three miles further eastward and encamped for the night unaware of its destination.[116]

The next morning, November 18, would offer more confusion, rather than answers. The day would be a miserable one; however, by evening the regiment's role for the next few weeks would begin to emerge. "Off at 8 o'clock and lose the way. It begins to rain. March and countermarch with making but little progress," wrote Private Brehm.[117] "We got on

---

110. Ibid.
111. Masonheimer Diary, November 17, 1862.
112. Ibid.
113. Brehm Diary, November 17, 1862.
114. Henry I. Zinn to his wife, November 17, 1862.
115. Brehm Diary, November 18, 1862.
116. Masonheimer Diary, November 18, 1862.
117. Brehm Diary, November 19, 1862.

[the] wrong road, marched through woods and mud . . . a gloomy day," echoed Corporal Masonheimer in his daily diary entry.[118] Initially, most likely due to being on the wrong road, it seemed to the men that they were headed to Aquia Station [Aquia Landing], located about nine miles north of Falmouth. Later, it became evident that they were headed to Belle Plain Landing, an inlet of the Potomac River located approximately ten miles east of Falmouth which was one of two Union supply bases on the Potomac River. Supplies arrived there by ship and were transported by wagon to the troops in Falmouth. By 4:00 P.M. on November 19, the regiment finally arrived at Belle Plain Landing after marching nine miles through pouring rains, camping in a meadow along Potomac Creek.[119]

BELLE PLAIN LANDING (U.S. Army Military History Institute)

---

118. Masonheimer Diary, November 19, 1862.
119. Ibid.

BELLE PLAIN LANDING (U.S. Army Military History Institute)

BELLE PLAIN LANDING (U.S. Army Military History Institute)

CHAPTER 5

Death Comes to a Commander: The Fredericksburg Campaign

WITH THE UNION Army's Second Corps approaching Falmouth, General Robert E. Lee correctly concluded that Fredericksburg was the objective of the new commander of the Army of the Potomac.[1] Quickly he would need to formulate a strategy, once again, to guard the gates to Richmond.

After Antietam Lee had divided his army in half, placing Major General James Longstreet's First Corps at Culpepper. Lieutenant General "Stonewall" Jackson's Second Corps was ordered to occupy the Shenandoah Valley in an area between Berryville and Charlestown. The Confederate cavalry led by Major General J. E. B. Stuart was dispersed on the Rappahannock and in the Shenandoah Valley supporting General Jackson.[2]

On November 18, Major General Longstreet's First Corps began its march towards Fredericksburg, arriving in the city on November 23. Fredericksburg is situated south and directly across from Falmouth, separated by the Rappahannock River. On November 26, a week after the Army of the Potomac arrived at Falmouth, Lee directed Jackson to march his Second Corps east to Fredericksburg, arriving on December 1.[3]

Lee positioned Longstreet's corps of 38,000 along a seven-mile line, from a position above Fredericksburg on the Rappahannock River to an area known as Hamilton's Crossing below the city. Confederate General

---

1. Edward J. Stackpole, *Drama on the Rappahannock: The Fredericksburg Campaign*, (New York: Bonanza Books, 1957), 74.
2. Ibid.
3. Edward J. Stackpole, *The Battle of Fredericksburg*, (Harrisburg: Eastern Acorn Press, 1965; Reprint, 1981), 7. Hereinafter cited as Stackpole, *The Battle of Fredericksburg*.

Jackson's Second Corps were dispersed over a wide area from Hamilton's Crossing to Port Royal, Virginia. The Confederate cavalry protected the army's flanks.[4]

While on the march to Fredericksburg, Burnside, anticipating the need to cross the Rappahannock River quickly, requested from Washington that pontoons be delivered to Falmouth to meet his Army when it arrived. Because of "garbled orders, botched assignments, and misplaced documents," the pontoons were delayed, arriving ten days late.[5] Undoubtedly, this mistake changed the outcome of Fredericksburg Campaign, by providing Lee the necessary time to mass his forces in anticipation of Burnside's expected offensive that he anticipated to come from somewhere between an area north of Falmouth to Port Royal.

In an effort to move the Army of the Potomac, the first task given the 130th after arriving at Belle Plain was to repair a corduroy bridge and assist with the construction of corduroy roads.[6] These details, in addition to picket duty and the other demands of camp life, became more burdensome with the continual soaking rains that left the men and their clothing and blankets constantly wet.[7]

The regiment was additionally tasked with loading and unloading commissary and quartermaster supplies from a fleet of Federal transports and canal boats arriving at Belle Plain.[8] This was a temporary measure until repairs could be made to the railroad running from Aquia Creek to Falmouth.[9] Company E's Private Brehm, ordered to report at noon for a detail on Sunday, November 23 noted, "Get along finely as I am acting clerk on the canal boat. This is the depot from which the Army receives [its] supplies and is consequently a throng place. The 'Song Branch' and another boat bring in our supplies."[10]

As the Confederates were massing their forces on the ridges above Fredericksburg, the men of the 130th were enduring soaking rains and chilly mornings with little protection, using their gum blankets for shelter

---

4. Stackpole, *The Battle of Fredericksburg*, 2–8.
5. Victor D. Brooks, *Marye's Heights: Fredericksburg* (Conshohocken, Pennsylvania: Combined Publishing, 2001), 18.
6. Brehm Diary, November 21, 1862. Corduroy roads were roads built by laying logs horizontally.
7. Masonheimer Diary, November 6, 1862.
8. Spangler, 58.
9. Henry I. Zinn to Mary, November 24, 1862.
10. Brehm Diary, November 23, 1862.

from the elements.¹¹ The questionable absence of adequate shelter during these first weeks in Falmouth continued well after the war ended, in the form of disability pension requests. Private Spangler later recounted, "The weather was cold and it rained a great deal, often mingled with snow. As we had no tents or shelter of any kind, and the plain being low, flat and impervious, causing water to stand inches deep, we suffered intensely."¹² In a November 20 letter to his wife, Colonel Zinn reported a somewhat different account:

> It has been raining nearly all the time since we came here, which makes it very unpleasant for the men, as they are without shelter except for their gum blankets. The government furnishes the men no shelter save that of shelter tents, consisting of three pieces carried by them and affording shelter for two men. Poles for the tents are procured by the men upon arriving in the new camp. Up until within a few day[s], the men have demanded 'A' tents, refusing their shelter tents; and now that they have consented to accept them, they should not murmur at delay as there may not be opportunity to get them immediately.¹³

Private Spangler decided to take on the issue in his own way:

> With an air of authority, I went upon one of a score or more of canal boats filled with tents, and asked the soldier on guard duty whether this was one of Quarter-master Captain Pitkin's boats, and upon receiving an affirmative reply, I stated that I was commanded to secure one of his tents. Believing me, he allowed me to take a large one which I had the greatest difficulty in carrying to the company.¹⁴

The final weeks of November 1862 found the regiment still encamped near Belle Plain with their days filled with duty on the wharfs, company

---

11. Brehm Diary, November 21, 1862.
12. Spangler, 56.
13. Henry I. Zinn to Mary, November 20, 1862.
14. Spangler, 58.

and regimental drills, dress parades and the dreaded guard detail.[15] The regiment received its principal surgeon, John S. Ramsey, on November 20.[16] The new surgeon had been promoted from Assistant Surgeon with the 55th Pennsylvania Volunteer Regiment.[17] Colonel Zinn assessed his new surgeon as "quite a young man, but as an army surgeon, he has had considerable experience, and that is a great consideration with us, as our assistant surgeons have no experience in military surgery.[18]

The winter weather improved as the week progressed, with Sunday, November 30, beginning as "A beautiful morning like spring," observed Corporal Masonheimer.[19] No religious services were held due to the absence of the regimental chaplain; however, later that afternoon, the regiment was called out for a dress parade and heard the Articles of War read by the regimental Adjutant, H. Clay Marshall, as cannonading was heard in the direction of Fredericksburg.[20]

The regiment remained encamped at Belle Plain, performing fatigue duty and unloading supplies from transports and canal boats the first week of December. The first days of December were noted as being "rough and cold."[21] On December 2, 1862, Private Andrew Mitzell of Company C died of an unknown cause while at Belle Plain.[22] In the evening of Wednesday, December 3, "the President's message was read at our camp fire," recounted Private Brehm.[23] The repairs on the railroad from Aquia Creek to Falmouth had been completed to allow the supplies to be transported by rail, rather than by ships arriving at Belle Plain.[24] Colonel Zinn penned a hint of the forthcoming battle in a December 2 letter: "The mail carrier informed us this evening that we will not receive any mail for two weeks to come. If this be true, then there must be something important going on. We will see."[25]

---

15. Masonheimer Diary, November 24–30, 1862.
16. Henry I. Zinn to Mary, November 24, 1862.
17. Bates, 207.
18. Henry I. Zinn to Mary, November 24, 1862.
19. Masonheimer Diary, November 30, 1862.
20. Brehm Diary, November 30, 1862.
21. Brehm Diary, December 3, 1862.
22. Henry I. Zinn to his wife, December 2, 1862; Bates, 212.
23. Brehm Diary, December 3, 1862. Although the diarist did not document the content of President Lincoln's speech, it most likely concerned Lincoln's request for a constitutional amendment that would provide for the emancipation of slavery.
24. Henry I. Zinn to his wife, December 2, 1862.
25. Ibid.

Death Comes to a Commander: The Fredericksburg Campaign

PONTOON BRIDGES, FREDERICKSBURG (Library of Congress)

Something was indeed "going on" on both sides of the Rappahannock River. On November 27, the long-awaited pontoons arrived at the Lacy House directly across from Fredericksburg. Although Union engineers could have built two pontoon bridges that night, General Burnside did not permit it. On the opposite side of the Rappahannock River Jackson's corps arrived on December 1, adding the second wing to Lee's forces.[26]

A campaign that was originally based upon speed had lost its momentum, shifting to one based upon mere numbers.[27] The Federal forces numbered 127,574 on November 10, compared to the 78,288 Confederates present for duty on December 10.[28] Initially, General Burnside considered moving his army across the Rappahannock River, a far distance below Fredericksburg in the area between Skinker's Neck and Port Royal; however, reports from Federal scouts and Professor Thaddeus S. Lowe's balloon reconnaissance indicated significant Confederate forces in those areas. Contrary to military doctrine and sound reasoning, on December 8 Burnside made the decision to cross the Rappahannock directly into the city in the face of the Confederates lining the ridges behind the town.[29]

---

26. Stackpole, 98.
27. Brooks, 39.
28. Palfrey, 138–141.
29. Brooks, 38.

PROFESSOR THADDEUS S. LOWE,
AERONAUTIC INVENTOR OF BALLOON GAS GENERATOR
(National Archives and Records Administration, Brady Collection, College Park)

On Friday, December 5, the regiment received orders to leave Belle Plain and return to its first camp with the Third Division near Falmouth.[30] The sudden onslaught of three inches of snow that day delayed the movement until the following morning.[31] Several companies, including Company E, remained at Belle Plain, not making the nine-mile march until December 11.[32]

On December 8, 1862, Colonel Zinn would write to his wife:

> Dearest Mary: As you will observe, we have returned to Falmouth and are within a mile or two of the camp we occupied before going to Belle Plain. We got orders on Friday to be prepared to march that day, but as it snowed all day we did not leave until Saturday Morning. The roads were in a horrible condition. Saturday night, yesterday and last night, the cold was intense. To-day the weather has moderated, but it is still uncomfortably cold. Since our arrival we have received orders to prepare winter quarters and the men are busy putting up huts. I hardly think they will be permitted to occupy them long.

---

30. Henry I. Zinn to Mary, December 8, 1862.
31. Masonheimer Diary, December 6, 1862.
32. Brehm, December 11, 1862.

Death Comes to a Commander: The Fredericksburg Campaign

WAGONS AND EQUIPMENT, CAPITOL IN THE BACKGROUND
(National Archives and Records Administration, Brady Collection, College Park)

I got your letter of the 30th ultimo, and was glad to learn that Georgie is so much improved in health. If we remain here any considerable length of time, I shall try to get home for a few days to see you.

To-day I am twenty-eight years of age, and a very disagreeable birthday it is to me. I think I could enjoy it much better at home than in this inhospitable climate. Brother John was left at Belle Plain sick. He is very ill, but I was informed to-day that he is improving. Wesley Leidig is also improving slowly. Quite a large number of men who had been absent sick, returned to the regiment yesterday. Re-introduction into camp life was pretty severe on them, but I hope most of them can stand it. Mr. Turner, the Q. M. has not yet returned, but we expect him shortly. If you had thought of sending me the gloves presented by Dr. Lenher, it would have been a happy thought. Who sent the one fingered mittens, and for whom were they intended?

Enclosed you will find ten dollars which will contribute to your comfort until I can send more.

As it is very cold, and being without fire, writing is hard to do so will you please pardon me for making my letter short. I shall write again in a few days. Tell Elsie that I am obliged to her for her letter.

Affectionally,
Z.[33]

---

33. Henry I. Zinn to Mary, December 8, 1862. His final letter.

POST OFFICE TENT AND STAFF
(U.S. Army Military History Institute)

U. S. MAIL WAGON, SECOND CORPS
(U.S. Army Military History Institute)

Death Comes to a Commander: The Fredericksburg Campaign

Late on the evening of December 10, 1862, Brigadier General Henry Hunt, the Union's artillery chief, positioned over 147 artillery pieces on the left bank of the Rappahannock River opposite the city. These pieces would offer protective fire to the Union engineers and soldiers erecting the pontoons, who quickly became easy targets for Brigadier General William E. Barksdale's sharpshooters from the 13th Mississippi positioned safely in houses and outbuildings in the city.[34]

At around 2:00 A.M., December 11, the Union engineers began dragging the pontoons down to the frigid shoreline of the Rappahannock River and began to lay two pontoon bridges opposite Hawk Street across the river.[35] After allowing the 50th New York Engineers to lay approximately two-thirds of the span, the Confederate artillery found its mark, clearing the engineers. The deadly and accurate barrage continued as the Union engineers made nine desperate attempts to complete their work fully.[36]

PONTOON BRIDGES ON THE MARCH TO FREDERICKSBURG
(Frank Leslie's Illustrated)

---

34. Walker, 146.
35. Brooks, 42.
36. Page, 78.

At 7:00 A.M., Thursday morning, December 11, the regiment began its march towards Fredericksburg from Falmouth. After a two-hour halt, while listening to the constant thundering of Union cannonading, it was ordered to continue marching to the Lacy House (also known as Chatham), Union General Sumner's Headquarters, located across the river from Fredericksburg. The regiment camped that evening on the banks of the Rappahannock just below the Lacy House. Private Spangler vividly recalled that day:

> No troops were ever more delighted when . . . we received orders to break camp on this snow-covered and inhospitable spot. On our way through the forest, wild turkeys flew over our heads, and all the time being wished for shot guns. As we reached the large plain opposite Fredericksburg, we beheld a hundred or more guns on the north bank of the river bombing the city. That night we bivouacked at a stately mansion, the Lacy House, opposite the city. It was very cold, and the ground being snow-covered, I was singularly fortunate in being able to sleep on a wet plank.[37]

Later that evening, details were assigned to the critical task of assisting the engineers laying the pontoons. As the Pennsylvanians went about their risky work, they witnessed the city of Fredericksburg being devastated by Union artillery.[38] Private Brehm described the unforgettable events in his diary:

> About midnight orders to march next morning arrive. Consequently an early breakfast and off. Cannoning begins early in the directions of the city. We march slowly until within ¼ mile from the river and halt. The engineers with great difficulty lay one bridge at the city on account of the enemy's sharp shooters stationed in the houses on the opposite bank. The most terrific cannoning is kept up by our artillery to which the enemy's guns are silent. At evening 3 Regts. cross and a severe fight in the city takes place and continues until some time after night. Howard's

---

37. Spangler, 61.
38. Masonheimer Diary, December 11, 1862.

LACY HOUSE, ALSO KNOWN AS CHATHAM MANOR AND SERVED AS A UNION HEADQUARTERS AND LATER AS A HOSPITAL, (U.S. National Park Service)

FREDERICKSBURG FROM THE LACY HOUSE
(National Archives and Records Administration, Brady Collection, College Park)

UNION ARTILLERY. UNION ARTILLERY, FREDERICKSBURG
(National Archives and Records Administration, Brady Collection, College Park)

division gets over. During the night our Regt. assists in laying another pontoon bridge.[39]

The morning of December 12 began "clear, calm and beautiful," as the regiment marched across the upper pontoon bridge that led into Hawkes Street on the opposite bank of the Rappahannock.[40] General French's Third Division took the lead.[41] With a feeling of relief upon reaching the banks of the city, the band stuck up the tune "Dixie," that was promptly terminated by a staff officer. From Hawkes Street the regiment turned left onto Sophia Street that ran parallel to the Rappahannock River.[42]

As they marched into the city at daybreak, the Union troops first noticed the seriously damaged houses hit by their artillery. The town appeared unoccupied. The townspeople had either left the city to flee the Union bombardment or were hiding in their cellars.

When Company K marched into the city, their first encounter was with a group of Union soldiers breaking into whiskey barrels. Not to pass up such an opportunity, Private Spangler recounted that he and

---

39. Brehm Diary, December 11, 1862.
40. Page, 79.
41. Brehm Diary, December 12, 1862.
42. Page, 79.

FREDERICKSBURG AFTER BURNSIDE'S BOMBARDMENT
(National Archives and Records Administration, Brady Collection, College Park)

his comrades "secured a tub which they partly filled with the tonic, and brought it to our company." He admitted that "On account of the intense cold, I was prevailed upon to take a drink—the first in my life—and it produced a warmth that was congenial, to say the least."[43]

Union soldiers, no doubt, felt the sensation of conquest as they marched into the once prestigious Southern city. Refusing a formal demand to surrender, the town became subject to the soldiers' emotions that quickly escalated into looting, pillaging, and destruction of property. Stragglers had broken into some of the houses and stores and emerged wearing women's hats or wearing a "plume of peacock feathers." Some pillagers were seen carrying gilded mirrors, while another straggler was seen carrying a pulpit Bible.[44] Clothing, furniture, books, antiques and virtually anything they could lay their hands on became either a personal prize or was destroyed by being tossed in bonfires, perhaps as a symbol of triumph.[45] The town, now a smoky ruin, was littered with Confederate dead. "One dead Confederate especially attracted my attention," recalled Private Spangler. "He was in a standing position leaning against

---

43. Spangler, 42.
44. Page, 79–80.
45. Brooks, 56.

the corner of a block-house with his gun in his hands, and all of the head above the mouth was taken off by a shell."[46]

Sophia Street was literally lined with both Union and Confederate dead. One Confederate dead soldier was found lying in the middle of the street with both arms gone, pierced by a shell. "The glassy eyes and agonies of death pictured on the countenances of the dead made a ghastly sight," recalled Private Spangler years later.[47]

The regiment stayed in the city the remainder of the day near the upper pontoon bridge, awaiting the rest of the Right Grand Division to cross over the pontoons. Since most of the houses had been evacuated, some of the soldiers began taking the provisions that were stored in them.[48]

Some of the 130th's soldiers helped themselves to chewing tobacco while Private Spangler emptied a jar of pickles, replacing the contents with eggs. After purchasing a cleaned chicken from a fellow soldier for fifteen cents, he was now contented since his haversack, "was filled to repletion."[49] By nightfall, members of the regiment took refuge in whatever shelter was available. The soldiers of Company A took quarters in a three-story brick house while those in Company K took refuge in the Methodist Church.[50]

As the regiment made its way across the pontoons into the city, everyone believed that they were taking part in a well-planned and calculated military offensive operation. In fact, at the time Burnside had no plan at all, other than throwing division after division across the Rappahannock River to take a town that had been evacuated.[51]

Sometime on December 12, Major General Couch passed on to Burnside that he had intelligence from Confederate deserters, contrabands, and local citizens that a deep trench ran through the town and would be an obstacle for troops should they assault the hills now occupied by the Confederates. Burnside brushed the issue aside and told

---

46. Spangler, 62.
47. Spangler, 63.
48. Francis O'Reilly, *The Fredericksburg Campaign: Winter War on the Rappahannock* (Baton Rouge: Louisiana State University Press, 2003), 248; Spangler, 63.
49. Spangler, 63.
50. Masonheimer Diary, December 12, 1862; Spangler, 63.
51. Walker, 154.

Couch that he was mistaken. He had occupied the city earlier with the Ninth Corps and no such trench existed.[52]

Finally, on December 13, at 6:00 A.M., Burnside forwarded orders to Major General Sumner, to extend his corps to the left and connect his forces with that of Major General Franklin's Left Grand Division who would extend his forces to the right. Major General Burnside also directed Major General Sumner to send a division or more along the Plank and Telegraph roads in the direction of the heights in the rear of the city.[53] Later in the morning, at 8:15 A.M., Sumner ordered Couch to send one division into the heights with the column advancing in three lines.[54] One division would be held in reserve.[55] The remainder of the Second Corps would safeguard the upper section of the city.[56] In effect, Burnside had directed that 5,000 to 10,000 Union soldiers advance against Longstreet's Corps of 40,000 veterans solidly entrenched on high ground overlooking a large flat plain spanning about 3,000 yards to the edge of the city.[57]

Major General Couch, in turn, assigned French to ready his Third Division in columns by brigades with intervals of two hundred yards apart. They would be the first in. Hancock's First Division would be the reserve division. At 11:30 A.M. General Couch received orders to begin his advance. Exactly at 12:00 P.M., French's skirmishers came upon the first Confederate pickets. French's First Brigade, commanded by Brigadier General Nathan Kimball, was ordered to lead the advance. Shortly after General Kimball's brigade began their advance, they came upon the obstacle that their corps commander had warned Burnside about. From the western edge of town, the open ground fell slightly into a waste water canal approximately fifteen feet wide and four to six feet deep, and six hundred yards from the entrenched Confederates. Had Burnside heeded the warning and conducted a thorough reconnaissance, countless Union soldiers' lives would have been spared.[58]

---

52. Walker, 156.
53. Ibid.
54. O'Reilly, 246.
55. Walker, 156.
56. O'Reilly, 246.
57. Walker, 158–159.
58. Walker, 159–162.

COLONEL OLIVER PALMER, COMMANDER,
108TH REGIMENT, NEW YORK VOLUNTEER INFANTRY
(National Archives and Records Administration, Brady Collection, College Park)

Brigadier General French's Third Brigade, commanded by Colonel John W. Andrews, was the second brigade to advance followed by the Second Brigade, now commanded by Colonel Oliver H. Palmer of the 108th New York.[59]

Up at daybreak, December 13, the men of the 130th took breakfast followed by a roll call, while hearing firing down river.[60] Fog hung over the city, removing from view both the enemy position and the Union artillery on the opposite of the Rappahannock.[61]

The regiment began its eastward march in the left column along Sophia Street, the street that ran closest and parallel to the river.[62] Once the regiment reached Frederick Street, which ran parallel to the railroad, it turned right heading southward and advanced a short distance to a location north of the railroad where the Third Division assembled for its

---

59. Walker, 166–167. This is the same Colonel Oliver H. Palmer who shamed himself and his regiment during the battle of Antietam. See footnote #135, chapter 3.
60. Masonheimer Diary, December 13, 1862.
61. Page, 246.
62. Spangler, 64.

Death Comes to a Commander: The Fredericksburg Campaign 117

assault. It was now 10:00 A.M.[63] French positioned the Second Brigade on Princess Anne Street, north of Hanover Street, where it aligned with Colonel John W. Andrew's Brigade. The Third Brigade was aligned with the 14th Connecticut on the left close to the courthouse, with the 130th Pennsylvania in the center, and the 108th New York on the right, ending on George Street.[64]

Brigadier General Nathan Kimball's First Brigade prepared themselves to make the initial assault. At 11:00 A.M., Couch received the orders to begin the attack and ordered Kimball's brigade to move out. Brigadier General Kimball's Brigade first encountered Confederate sharpshooters followed by murderous and accurate artillery shelling from the Confederate Washington Artillery positioned at the top of Marye's Heights. Men began to fall as they were open easy targets for the skilled Southern artillerists. Some took refuge in the canal while others used portions of the wooden fence that encircled the fairgrounds as cover. Moving forward, Kimball's Brigade advanced nine hundred yards to the

THE OPEN GROUND THE 130TH PROGRESSED THROUGH
ON THEIR ASSAULT ON MARYRE'S HEIGHTS.
(National Archives and Records Administration, Brady Collection, College Park)

---

63. O'Reilly, 247
64. O'Reilly, 248.

THE STONE WALL BELOW MARYE'S HEIGHTS AFTER THE BATTLE
(National Archives and Records Administration, Brady Collection, College Park)

Southerners directly to their front. Waiting until General Kimball's men reached within one hundred yards, Brigadier General Thomas R. Cobb's Georgians, hidden behind the three and one-half foot stone wall, stood up and virtually annihilated Kimball's on-rushing skirmishers. The first Union wave stalled, suffering over a 25 percent casualty rate. Brigadier General French requested that Colonels Andrew's and Palmer's Brigades, the second wave, to make themselves ready. It was now noon.[65]

Colonel Andrew's Third Brigade was the first to move followed by Colonel Palmer's Second Brigade.[66] Once entering Princess Anne Street, Andrew's brigade began to receive Confederate artillery fire from Marye's Heights that intensified when it entered into Prussia Street.[67] After receiving the order to fix bayonets, the Second Brigade followed Andrew's brigade's route out of the city, with the 14th Connecticut in the lead, followed by the 130th Pennsylvania and 108th New York.[68]

Colonel Zinn left his horse behind and mingled with his men on the march, urging them in a "firm clear voice, 'Forward men.'"[69] After progressing only a short distance, "we saw on our right the concentrated fire of the Confederate artillery tearing through and silencing the five batteries brought across the river and stationed at the edge of the city," wrote Private Spangler.[70] As they continued their march, artillery shells shattered rooftops, spreading debris over their heads. Confederate

---

65. O'Reilly, 261.
66. O'Reilly, 261–263.
67. O'Reilly, 262.
68. O'Reilly, 261.
69. Bosbyshell, 166.
70. Spangler, 64.

artillery zeroed in on the advancing division creating gaps throughout its ranks.[71] The artillery onslaught that came from both Marye's Heights and Willis' Hill were too much for some men who sought shelter behind a nearby brick warehouse.[72] Pushing forward and emerging into the open plain when the regiment was about to deploy in a line of battle, it came under a deadly artillery fire about the time it reached the canal Major General Burnside had refused to acknowledge existed.[73] Private Spangler wrote the canal was "a most serious and embarrassing obstacle, and very distressing under a raking storm of projectiles."[74] The canal was impassable with the exception of several damaged street bridges, many with only the stringers intact, that left only room enough for soldiers to negotiate in a single file.

This delay provided Confederate artillery the time to adjust its aim accurately and pour its devastating fire into the oncoming Union columns. After negotiating the canal, the regiment continued by columns of four for a considerable distance to be met once again by massive Confederate artillery bombardment.[75] Private Spangler recalled that, "while in this formation a shower of missiles created havoc in our ranks, one of which took off the head of Captain McLaughlin of Company E, scattering the brains over our company.[76] Lieutenant Franklin G. Torbert from Company I was also killed.[77] "When in line going up the field, a battery opened on our right flank killing two men," wrote Corporal Masonheimer.[78]

The regiment was ordered to lay down, with no other orders. Private Spangler took this opportunity to rid himself of his haversack, which was "filled to repletion," that was hindering his advance.[79] On his left was Private Eli W. Myers with Private William Clemmens to his right, both of Company K. Private Spangler remembered:

> A bullet knocked off Clement[']s [sic] cap and a moment later a shell exploded over us, a piece of which violently struck Myers in

---
71. Ibid.
72. Ibid.
73. Ibid.
74. Spangler, 65.
75. Ibid.
76. Ibid.
77. Bosbyshell, 166.
78. Masonheimer Diary, December 13, 1862.
79. Spangler, 65.

the back. I got up to assist in carrying him off the field, but being small, was pushed aside by others equally anxious to get beyond the range of fire for we all felt that success was a forlorn hope. The wound would prove fatal.[80]

The devastating artillery fire and its deadly results caused a few men of the regiment to take momentary cover behind the depot on the nearby brickyard.[81] The 130th and remainder of the Second Brigade quickly reformed behind the canal as the Confederate artillery continued to pour out its accurate and devastating shelling.[82]

The Third Brigade made the first assault, losing half of its ranks within the first fifteen minutes.[83] Within the next five minutes, after seeing the Third Brigade's attempt fail, the men of the 130th formed a line of battle that was 150 yards behind Colonel Andrew's Brigade.[84] The men slipped and fell as they clawed their way out of the murky waste water canal and "tramped forward in neat ranks and measured steps" while Confederate artillery tried to slow their progress. Colonel Zinn jumped to his feet and shouted, "Stand up to it boys!"[85] "Shot shell and bullets were pouring around us," noted Corporal Masonheimer.[86] Pouring rifle fire into the protected Confederates as the regiment moved forward, the 130th came under a terrific storm of bullets from the tested veteran Confederates of the 18th Georgia, 24th Georgia, and Phillips Legion, belonging to Brigadier General Howell Cobb's Georgia Brigade, assigned to Brigadier General Robert Ransom's Division.[87] As they moved closer to the stone wall, the Confederate artillery changed its munitions from shell to canister, taking an immediate heavy toll of casualties by the hundreds.[88] The 130th returned fire while charging across the ground that had been the Fredericksburg Fairgrounds, stopping half way.[89] Here Major John Lee was hit.[90]

---

80. Spangler, 66.
81. O'Reilly, 264.
82. O'Reilly, 265.
83. O'Reilly, 266.
84. O'Reilly, 267.
85. Masonheimer Diary, December 13, 1862.
86. Ibid.
87. O'Reilly, 267.
88. Ibid.
89. Ibid, 268.
90. Ibid.

Death Comes to a Commander: The Fredericksburg Campaign

ASSAULT OF THE UNION RIGHT GRAND DIVISION ON MARYE'S HEIGHTS. THE 130TH REGIMENT WAS ASSIGNED TO THE RIGHT GRAND DIVISION AND IS MOST LIKELY DEPICTED IN THIS SKETCH
(Frank Leslie's Illustrated)

As the regiment's color bearer fell, Colonel Zinn, waving his sword in his right hand, grasped the falling regimental colors in his left hand lifted them in the air and shouted, "Stick to your standard, boys! The One Hundred and Thirtieth never abandons its colors; give them another volley!"[91] These were the beloved Colonel's final words. Within seconds, a Rebel bullet ball struck him beneath his left eye. Within the hour, he succumbed to his mortal wound in the presence of the regimental Chaplain, George W. Chalfant. The chaplain later accompanied the colonel's body to his home to Churchtown.[92] Company A's Commander, Captain William A. Porter, immediately assumed command of the regiment.[93]

Within a short time, the regiment was swept back by musketry, and canister "rising tier after tier, which no troops could withstand," recalled

---

91. Spangler, 66.
92. John D. Hemminger, *Cumberland County Pennsylvania in the Civil War: 1861–1865*, 1926, (Harrisburg, Pennsylvania: State Library of Pennsylvania), 35; Pennsylvania Antietam Battlefield Commission. *One Hundred and Thirtieth Regiment Pennsylvania Volunteer Infantry: Ceremonies and Addresses at Dedication of the Monument at Bloody Lane, Antietam Battlefield, September 1904*. n.p., 1904. USAMHI, Carlisle Barracks, Pennsylvania.
93. Masonheimer Diary, December 14, 1862. In John Hemminger's *Cumberland County Pennsylvania in the Civil War*: 35, First Lieutenant Sharp of Company E was noted as being in charge of the regiment.

Private Spangler.[94] While the regiment was about to renew the attack, the Confederates leaped over the wall charging the Pennsylvanians, but quickly returned to the safety of the stone wall.[95] Unable to withstand the massive Confederate artillery and musketry firepower, the regiment turned about and returned to the edge of the fairgrounds joining the 14th Connecticut.[96] Within minutes, Captain Porter saw Union artillery to the rear begin firing, with its first rounds striking the regiment.[97] The men of the regiment began to run, but regained their composure as best they could. The open area of the fairgrounds left no cover from the friendly artillery fire decimating the ranks.[98]

The Second Brigade's ranks had dwindled significantly, losing its cohesion. The regiment remained on the field, with little effect, as long as possible to the point that its ammunition had been almost exhausted. Finally, acknowledging their desperation, some of the men returned to the canal while others left the field in small groups and headed back into the city. Brigadier General French gave the order for his division to make their way back to Fredericksburg.[99]

As General Winfield S. Hancock came upon the field meeting the returning regiment, he greeted them with his personal orders to advance back to the heights with his newly-arrived division.[100] Shattered and broken, the men of the 130th retired past him. Private Spangler later recalled that "he must have felt sorry for upbraiding us" since he was not aware that French had ordered the Third Division off the battlefield.[101]

The regiment, along with French's entire Third Division, made their way back into the city, still suffering casualties from the Confederate artillery poised on Marye's Heights.[102] Confused and unorganized, the Pennsylvanians found whatever shelter available.

Many of the men from Company K found refuge in a house on Sophia Street owned by a Mrs. Mills. Private Spangler later recalled that "At nightfall the boys began to bake 'slapjacks' in the yard" but quickly gave up the endeavor since the fire became a target for Confederate artillery.

---

94. Spangler, 66.
95. Ibid.
96. O'Reilly, 269.
97. Ibid.
98. Ibid.
99. O'Reilly, 272–274.
100. O'Reilly, 274.
101. Spangler, 67.
102. Hemminger, 35.

MEN FROM COMPANY K WOULD TAKE REFUGE IN
THE MILLS HOUSE AFTER THE BATTLE
(*My Little War Experience*, Edward Spangler)

Around 7:00 P.M., as the men were sleeping "as a result of shear exhaustion on the first floor . . . a spherical shell penetrated the brick wall . . . scattering bricks and mortar debris all over the room." Fortunately for those nearby, the fuse was spent, causing no injury or loss of life.[103]

The following day, Sunday December 14, the regiment assembled and marched along the shore of the Rappahannock River, stopping near a general hospital where the men remained under arms throughout that day and night. As the Confederates continued to pelt the town, Union troops recrossed the pontoon bridge back into Falmouth.[104] "A sad day" penned Corporal Masonheimer in his diary.[105] At 6:15 P.M. that evening, both Union and Confederate soldiers witnessed the night sky coming alive with a dazzling illumination known as an aurora borealis, or northern lights.[106] On Monday December 22, 1862, The *Richmond Dispatch* reported, "A magnificent aurora borealis made its appearance just at sunset, tinging the heavens blood red, as it were with the blood of the martyrs who had offered their lives as a sacrifice to their native land.[107] Assuredly, both sides considered this rare occurrence a heavenly sign.

---

103. Spangler, 68.
104. Masonheimer Diary, December 14, 1862.
105. Ibid.
106. O'Reilly, 441.
107. *Richmond Dispatch*, Richmond, Virginia, December 22, 1862, 1.

Later in the evening on the night of December 15, "in the midst of a violent storm," the army recrossed the pontoon bridge to return to their old camp near Falmouth.[108] Company E's Lieutenant Joshua Sharpe led the orderly withdrawal of the regiment, both exhausted from the strain and emotions of battle and grief-stricken over the loss of their commander.[109] Around noon, on December 16, the regiment arrived at its former camp.[110] "A tired boy I was when I landed," lamented Corporal Masonheimer.[111]

On December 16, Lee gave permission to the Union Army to bury its dead on the battlefield.[112] Captain William Laughlin's body was found, stripped of his uniform."[113] The following week, Captain Laughlin's brother, John, returned his body to his home in Newville, Pennsylvania.[114] The regiment's seventy-nine casualties included five killed, seventy-one wounded, and three captured or missing.[115]

Not unlike most men in the Army of the Potomac after the battle, those in the 130th were wrought with despair, desperation, and low morale. In a letter to his parents, Private Weiser described his feelings after the recent debacle: "I consider the move a perfect failure for the loss of life in killed and wounded . . ."[116] Private Spangler placed the blame squarely on the Army of the Potomac's commander, claiming that he was "Utterly incapable of commanding so large an Army. Burnside lost his head the moment he confronted so able and formidable an adversary as Lee."[117]

From December 16 through 24, the regiment remained in its Falmouth camp recovering from the effects of battle while carrying out necessary military duties as drill, picket duty, guard duty, and inspections. A detail of eighteen men from the regiment's Company A performed guard duty at Major General Darius N. Couch's headquarters on December 16.[118] After returning from a sleepless night taking his turn guarding Couch's headquarters on December 19, Company E's Private Brehm complained

---

108. Hemminger, 35.
109. Bosbyshell, 166.
110. Hemminger, 35.
111. Masonheimer Diary, December 15, 1862.
112. O'Reilly, 458.
113. Hemminger, 35.
114. Ibid.
115. OR Series I, Vol. XXI, 131.
116. John S. Weiser to his parents, December 17, 1862.
117. Spangler, 80.
118. Masonheimer Diary, December 16, 1862.

of the personal demands of military life: "There is truly no rest for the soldier and now he realizes the severity & hardships of an outdoor life."[119]

Christmas Day 1862 found most of the men in the regiment longing for the company of their families and the comforts of home. Being away from friends and family during the Christmas holiday undoubtedly played heavy on everyone's hearts. In a letter to his daughter, Kittie, Quartermaster Officer Turner described his holiday away from home: "Today I hope will be the last Christmas I will spend in such a place as this. I had to day a big dinner fried onions and potatoes & pork boiled together hard crackers & coffee (but I cannot drink the coffee we get here)."[120] Company E's Private Brehm's diary day clearly revealed his frame of mind:

> Thurs. 25. Christmas. Can this be Christmas day. Indeed it seems anything else. How the soldier could relish a slice of good bread spread with butter just from the home cupboard. Well the day passes off dryly, but stop I believe we draw potatoes and onions, well this is a dainty in itself.[121]

Corporal Masonheimer's account of his Christmas Day was much the same: "nothing in our stockings. No Christmas gifts, no turkey for dinner; but a big piece of fat pork . . . A very dull Christmas to me.[122]

The closing days of 1862 passed with little significance. On Sunday, December 28, the 130th's men who were hospitalized as sick or wounded were sent to Washington.[123] An evening sermon was given from the text "today if ye will hear his voice, harden not your hearts."[124]

On the last day of 1862, "A cold bluster day," the regiment was serenaded by the 14th Connecticut's Band as the "band played its ear out."[125] Private Brehm's final 1862 diary entry noted, "These Holidays have been rather dry and long to be remembered."[126]

---

119. Brehm Diary, December 20, 1862.
120. John R. Turner to daughter Kittie, December 25, 1862.
121. Brehm Diary, December 25, 1862.
122. Masonheimer Diary, December 25, 1862.
123. Masonheimer Diary, December 28, 1862.
124. Brehm Diary, December 28, 1862.
125. Masonheimer Diary, December 31, 1862.
126. Brehm Diary, December 31, 1862.

CHAPTER 6

A Camp Near Falmouth

"All hail: to the New Year's morn. It is clear & cold this morning. During the day it becomes more pleasant where the wind is broken and I notice a few warbles from the Blue birds happy voice," noted Private Brehm on the first day of the new year 1863.[1] The positive tone of Private Brehm's notation is perhaps one of hope—hope to never have to see the needless wholesale slaughter of his fellow soldiers, the loss of his regimental commander, and the feeling of disgust, despair, and shame. Within a short span of four months, this regiment of raw Pennsylvania recruits and inexperienced officers had fought two fierce battles in the most treacherous positions in the eastern theater. In both clashes, the Army of the Potomac could not claim victory. To the Federal government, the War Department, the Lincoln administration, and perhaps most important, to the individual soldier, a victory must be attained in order to turn the tide of war and return pride and dignity to the North.

Falmouth would become the winter home for the 130th Pennsylvania Regiment along with the entire Army of the Potomac. The first days of January 1863 were taken up preparing for the effects of the oncoming Virginia winter. A genuine concern was adequate long-term shelter for the soldiers. Shelter tents would not suffice for the harsh winter. Permanent log huts provided a quick and simple solution. Rectangular holes were dug approximately two and a half feet deep and lined with logs that projected about three feet above the ground.[2] Mud and plaster was placed between the gaps of the logs to keep out the wind and cold air.[3]

---

1. Brehm Diary, January 1, 1863.
2. Spangler, 87.
3. Harman R. Miller to his sister, January 15, 1863, Antietam National Park Collection, U.S. Department of the Interior, Sharpsburg, Maryland.

A Camp Near Falmouth

WINTER QUARTERS, POSSIBLE LOCATION AT FALMOUTH
(National Archives and Records Administration, Brady Collection, College Park)

Private Masonheimer's hut measured thirteen-by-five feet.[4] Uprights and a cross piece were placed on the top with the shelter tents stretched over the structure making the roof.[5] At the exterior of one end there was a three foot square chimney built with empty commissary barrels stacked about eight feet high, completing the chimney.[6] Generally, these winter huts could house four men although "it required tight squeezing."[7]

The first two weeks were uneventful for the men of 130th giving them time to slowly recover from battle and prepare for winter. Considering battle casualties, sick, discharged, and those recovering from battle wounds, the regiment's effective strength was at approximately 175 men in mid-January 1863.[8] Drawing rations, fixing their huts, dress parades, guard duty and drill occupied the majority of their time. Picket duty on the banks of the Rappahannock River directly across from Fredericksburg was tasked to the regiment.[9] Company C's Private Harman R.

---

4. Masonheimer Diary, January 5, 1863.
5. Spangler, 87.
6. Ibid.
7. Ibid.
8. Harman R. Miller to his sister, January 15, 1863.
9. Spangler, 88.

WINTER QUARTERS POSSIBLE LOCATION AT FALMOUTH,
HORACE REELEY MAY BE PICTURED WEARING THE TOP HAT
(National Archives and Records Administration, Brady Collection, College Park)

Miller wrote his sister that things were now going well: "We have good times since the battle get plenty to eat each one does his own cooking we set down at the fire and make a tin cup of coffee and, fry crackers when we get fresh beef make rice soup and cook beans."[10] On occasion, tiny sail boats filled with coffee were sent across the river to the Confederates in trade for Southern tobacco.[11] In the spare time available, some soldiers would be found reading a copy of the local newspaper, *The Observer*, sent from home, or visiting friends in nearby regiments.[12]

On Saturday morning, January 17, the regiment received orders to be ready for a review. Permanently joining the Second Brigade was the 12th New Jersey commanded by Colonel R. C. Johnson.[13] They marched two miles to Major General Sumner's headquarters where Major General Burnside reviewed the corps while the men stood in the cold for an hour.[14] As Burnside rode through the lines, he received little applause

---

10. Harman R. Miller to his sister, January 15, 1863.
11. Spangler, 88.
12. Brehm Diary, January 5–15, 1863.
13. Walker, 196.
14. Masonheimer Diary, January 17, 1863.

BRIGADIER GENERAL WILLIAM HAYES,
(U.S. Army Military History Institute)

or cheering, which clearly demonstrated the men's lack of confidence in their commander.[15]

About the same time in January, the Second Brigade command was given to Brigadier General William Hayes, who was transferred from the Reserve Artillery within the Second Corps.[16] General Hayes replaced Colonel Oliver H. Palmer who was discharged from the service.[17]

Fortunately for the regiment, as well as the entire Second Corps, it was spared from the fiasco of Burnside's infamous "Mud March," which took place between January 20 and 24. The Second Corps may have won a reprieve due to the lead role they took in the assault on Marye's Heights.[18] In response to pressure from Washington, and perhaps in an attempt to redeem himself as the Commander of the Army of the

---

15. Brehm Diary, January 17, 1863.
16. Walker, 206.
17. Walker, 210.
18. Walker, 199.

Potomac, General Burnside planned to cross the Rappahannock River several miles above Falmouth, at Banks Ford turning southward, and attack the flank of Confederate forces at Fredericksburg.

Although the regiment did not actively participate in General Burnside's ill-fated effort, since the Third Division was to be the reserve for this action, they would be drawn into it.[19] Tuesday morning, January 20, began as a cloudy morning with a hint of oncoming snow. After division drill in the morning and a dinner of bean soup, orders were received to be ready to march the next day. Private Brehm recorded that "Cheering of troops on the surrounding hills on hearing the orders to march the next morning. Battery after battery pass to the right of our camp over the hills and to the left a column of infantry has been passing since noon."[20] Later that evening, after the regiment went to bed, it began raining and blowing, continuing all night.[21]

When the regiment awakened the next morning, it witnessed pontoon wagons "sticking about the hillsides" and "supply wagons stalling in the hollows;" despite the rain and wind the troops kept coming throughout the day.[22] Wagons were in the mud almost to the hubs of the wheels.[23] "Things look disparaging upon the whole," Private Brehm recorded in his diary.[24] The saturated ground acted as a sponge, causing doubled and quadrupled teams pulling the heavy guns to sink in the mud, blocking the way for those that followed.[25] Private Masonheimer recalled, "This is the day to try my patriotism" as water ran though his hut, while waiting for orders to move that never came.[26]

Orders were given for the regiment to remain in camp the next day, January 22.[27] The day started out cloudy, but later turned to a constant drizzle.[28] Realizing that any attempt to hit the Confederates now would prove fatal, Burnside ordered the troops to march back to their camps.

---

19. Masonheimer Diary, January 21, 1863.
20. Brehm Diary, January 20, 1863.
21. Masonheimer Diary, January 20, 1863.
22. Brehm Diary, January 21, 1863.
23. Masonheimer Diary, January 21, 1863.
24. Brehm Diary, January 21, 1863.
25. Samuel P. Bates, *The Battle of Chancellorsville*, (Meadville, Pennsylvania: Edward T. Bates, 1882. Reprint, Gaithersburg, Maryland: Ron R. VanSickle Military Books, 1987), 14.
26. Masonheimer Diary, January 21, 1863.
27. Masonheimer Diary, January 22, 1863.
28. Masonheimer Diary, January 22, 1863; Brehm Diary, January 22, 1863.

The delays robbed him of any semblance of surprise.[29] Some of the stray soldiers attempting to locate their camps wandered into the 130th's camp seeking shelter for the day.[30] A few of the men in Company A helped pull stuck caissons and wagons out of the mud with the aid of ten mules. Later, they had to dig the mules out.[31] In a letter to his daughter, Lieutenant Turner offered a vivid description of the tragic yet comical ordeal: "The mud is awful some chuck holes big enough to bury two mules and very often we can see horses and mules fall in and sink into the mudd [sic] and then the tuggs [sic] begin. The teamsters must get right into the mud knee deep sometimes."[32]

Private Brehm comically noted the events of January 23: "A most novel sight to stand on the brow of our hill and see the swarms of our troops crossing the hollows through deep mire and trudging up the eastern hills. Next ambulances & wagons horses splashing away & drivers bawling & shouting & whooping."[33]

In a January 23 letter Private Weiser described the ordeal to his parents:

> The troops was passing our camp all day Tuesday and Wednesday it commenced raining on Tuesday evening and rained up until yesterday evening it has put a stop to the whole move and the troops are going back to their old camps. We did not move out of our Shanties as we are laying close to the river while others are laying fourteen miles back. I suppose if it had not have rained there would have been by this time another hard battle fought.[34]

On January 22, Burnside departed his Falmouth Headquarters and headed for Washington.[35] Before he left, he drew up what was later to be referred to as Order No. 8, calling for the dismissal of certain officers from the service and the removal of others from the Army of the Potomac. When he arrived in Washington, he handed the order to President

---

29. Bates, 14.
30. Brehm Diary, January 22, 1863.
31. Masonheimer Diary, January 22, 1863.
32. John R. Turner to his daughter, Kittie, January 31, 1863.
33. Brehm Diary, January 23, 1863.
34. John S. Weiser to his parents, January 23, 1863.
35. Masonheimer Diary, January 21, 1863.

Lincoln along with his own resignation. If President Lincoln would approve his order, he would see that it was carried out and he would withdraw his resignation. President Lincoln chose to accept neither the order nor his resignation. Instead, he relieved him of command of the Army of the Potomac and returned Burnside to his previous command.[36]

In his place, Lincoln placed Major General Joseph Hooker who had been with the Army of the Potomac from the beginning of the war and had earned the nickname of "Fighting Joe Hooker."[37] Almost immediately, the new commander of the Army of the Potomac did away with the grand division plan, returning to the previous corps organization, and focused the army's attention on drilling and instruction.[38] The new commander also introduced the concept of Corps badges, to easily identify units down to the division level by design and color. The third division's assigned badge was a blue trefoil, or cloverleaf, often made of cloth and worn on the top of the soldier's hat or kepi.[39] Later, other cloth and medal badges appeared that were pinned on the soldier's uniform. The next two months, General Hooker spent reorganizing, re-equipping, and improving the overall welfare of the men of the Army of the Potomac. which had fallen into a state of depression.

Six months had now passed since the men of the 130th had boarded the train in Harrisburg bound for Washington. With only three more months remaining, most in the regiment, as Private John Weiser, were contemplating what could happen in the meantime: "We have only three months to serve from Saturday evening next and if I stand it and slip through the battles if any there are fought I think I will be none the worse for having served nine months as I have learned many a thing in the Army that a man never would notice any other place."[40]

Just as Private Weiser counted his remaining days, so did the new commander of the Army of The Potomac. The terms of service for approximately 400,000 Union soldiers who had enlisted for nine months would soon expire.[41] General Hooker needed to act soon; or otherwise,

---

36. Bates, 15.
37. Bates, 16.
38. George H. Washburn, *A Complete Military History and Record of the 108th Regiment N. Y. Vols.* (Rochester, New York, 1894. Reprint, Salem, Massachusetts: Higginson Book Company, 1998), 39.
39. Spangler, 89.
40. John S. Weiser to his parents, January 23, 1863.
41. Washburn, 39.

MAJOR GENERAL JOSEPH HOOKER
(Library of Congress)

later, face his formidable opponent with a tremendous loss in his military strength.

The remaining days in January 1863 found the regiment occupied with the normal duties of army life, policing their quarters, doing laundry, gathering firewood, inspections, picket duty, and dress parades. They were able to find time to have fun playing ball. On Sunday, January 25 wrote Private Brehm, "Rained some last night. Clears off and the sun shines at noon. Some of the boys play ball. Pontoons pulled up on to the hill today.[42] And on the following Monday, an eleven-inch snowfall occurred that "drifted our hut almost shut" wrote Corporal Masonheimer.[43] Time seemed to stand still for the men during January, with little to keep them busy other than their military duties and trying to keep warm in their crude huts. Private Brehm ended his diary "we all hail the last day of a long month."[44]

---

42. Brehm Diary, January 25, 1863.
43. Masonheimer Diary, January 29, 1863.
44. Brehm Diary, January 31, 1863.

The first day of February 1863 was appropriately the Sabbath, which found many in the regiment attending church services with the 14th Connecticut Regiment. The chaplain's service pertained to Chapters Mark 12th & 17th: "Render to C[a]esar . . . The discourse was edifying," wrote Private Brehm.[45] After church service, the men had the day to do as they pleased followed by a dress parade later in the day.[46]

Private Brehm recorded on February 2 that it "is Candlemas day, as the sunshines I guess the 'Ground Hog' made a hasty retreat to his winter quarters."[47] As the ground hog may have retreated to his winter quarters during those cold blistery days of February 1863, so did the men of the 130th. Cold nights, snowfalls to twelve inches, sleet, rain, and strong winds were common descriptions recorded during the month of February 1863.[48]

The command of the regiment had been vacant since the death of Colonel Zinn, and the duties of the position had been taken on temporarily at varying times by both Captain William M. Porter from Company A and Major John Lee from the regiment's staff. At a regiment's officer meeting on January 12, 1863, the officers nominated Major Lee for the position since Lieutenant Colonel Maish had not yet returned to the regiment.[49]

Lieutenant Colonel Maish had been recovering in the U.S. General Hospital in York from a gunshot wound in his right lung that he had received during the battle of Antietam.[50] Twenty-six-year-old Lieutenant Colonel Maish, a lawyer from York, Pennsylvania, had recruited the company of volunteers from York that became Company K of the 130th regiment. While at Camp Simmons, he was promoted to the Lieutenant Colonel of the regiment on August 17, 1862.[51] By order of the Union Army Adjutant General's Office, Maish was promoted to Colonel on February 3, 1863, to replace the fallen Colonel Henry Zinn.[52] He would command the regiment until its term of service expired on May 21, 1863.[53]

---

45. Brehm Diary, February 1, 1863.
46. Masonheimer Diary, February 1, 1863.
47. Brehm Diary, February 2, 1863.
48. Brehm Diary, February 1–28, 1863; Masonheimer Diary, February 1–28, 1863.
49. John Lee, Document, Nomination of Major John Lee, Regimental Records.
50. Levi Maish, Service Record, Medical document from the U.S. General Hospital, York, Pennsylvania, National Archives, Washington, DC.
51. Bates, 222.
52. Levi Maish, Promotion document from Adjutant General's Office.
53. Bates, 222.

COLONEL LEVI MAISH
(Courtesy of Roger Hunt)

On Saturday, February 14, the regiment sent twenty men and a sergeant to the Lacy House for picket duty, for the first time, along the Rappahannock River opposite Fredericksburg. Within a short time, the Rebel pickets began to yell over to them although their orders were not to reply.[54] Two hundred and fifty men of the regiment were sent back to the picket line on February 26, not to be relieved until 3:00 P.M. on the following day.[55]

Two men of the regiment succumbed during the month of February while in camp near Falmouth. Private D. T. Raffensberger of Company K died on February 11, followed by Private Peter T. Knisley from Company F on February 16.[56]

For many in the regiment, the most significant day in February was the last, the 28, when they were mustered with the entire Second Brigade by the commander, Brigadier General William Hayes, for an inspection, and to be finally paid for their military service from August 5, 1862 to January 1, 1863.[57] Corporal Masonheimer received the handsome sum

---

54. Brehm Diary, February 14, 1863.
55. Masonheimer Diary, February 26–27, 1863.
56. Bates, 223, 217.
57. Masonheimer Diary, February 28, 1863.

of $63.70.⁵⁸ Many of the men sent money home, while others spent it quickly and foolishly, moving from one sutler's tent to another purchasing such delicacies as "wooden" ginger cakes, brandy, peaches, and "cast-iron" pies.⁵⁹

The first day of March began as most other days with rain in the morning and one hundred of the regiment's men being sent off for their turn at picket duty.⁶⁰ On that day, the 130th received its second chaplain, George M. Slaysman, a minister from Huntington County, Pennsylvania, who replaced the regiment's chaplain, George H. Chalfant.⁶¹

In a letter to the regiment's acting commander, Major John Lee on January 3, 1863, Chaplain Chalfant tendered his resignation:

> Recent events have transpired in my pastoral charge impairing and threatening to destroy its prosperity and making it my duty to return at once if possible. My family is without any male person to care

CHAPLAIN GEORGE M. SLAYSMAN
(Courtesy of Penny Lydic Daughtry)

---

58. Ibid.
59. Page, 111.
60. Masonheimer Diary, March 1, 1863.
61. Ibid. The officers of the regiment elected the Reverend G. M. Slaysman on January 24, 1863. See Regimental Records.

for it and owing to the exigencies of the times and the prevalence in the community of a fearful epidemic [of] smallpox—as now . . . many necessary attentions but is greatly in danger of being left helpless These considerations led me to offer this my resignation of the position of chaplain of the regiment and to respectfully urge its acceptance. This resignation to be . . . immediate.[62]

Chaplain Chalfant was officially dishonorably dismissed from the army on January 7, 1863.[63] On April 25, 1863, by Special Order No. 185, the War Department amended the discharge to "honorable" retroactive to January 7, 1863.[64]

In the remaining days of March 1863, the men of the regiment's experiences typified the routine army camp life of boredom, idleness, and general military duties. The cold and windy "disagreeable" weather continued with alternating rains and snow. Dress parades, reviews, inspections, picket duty, maintaining their huts and frequent drilling took up the majority of the daylight hours, leaving the evening hours for socializing with friends assigned to nearby regiments and preparing for the next day's duties.[65]

At 3:00 A.M. on April 1, the regiment was ordered out "under arms," due to Confederate cavalry being reported in the vicinity on the Warrenton Road. The well-planned incident turned out to be a bit of "Aprils Fools" trickery ushering in another month "in a camp near Falmouth."[66]

The first week of April was uneventful for the regiment, with company and regimental drill on April 3 and brigade drill the following day. Later, on April 3, a portion of the regiment went on picket duty where it endured the continuance of winter with snow falling on April 5. Brigade drill and dress parades were repeated on April 6 and 7.[67]

---

62. Chaplain George H. Chalfant to Major John Lee, January 3, 1863, George H. Chalfant Service Record, National Archives, Washington, DC.
63. George H. Chalfant, Service Record, Resignation Letter, National Archives, Washington, DC. The circumstances behind his dismissal remains a mystery. A portion of the lower left-hand section of the original document in the National Archives that included approvals/comments by the chain of command had been obviously intentionally ripped out. Perhaps the missing comment would have explained the original dishonorable discharge.
64. George H. Chalfant, Service Record, SO #185, War Dept., Washington, April 25, 1863, National Archives, Washington, DC.
65. Masonheimer Diary, March 1–31, 1863.
66. Brehm Diary, April 1, 1863; Masonheimer Diary, April 1, 1863.
67. Masonheimer Diary, April 3–7, 1863.

On April 8, the regiment came to understand fully the reason for the recent repeated drilling and dress parades. This momentous spring day would surely be one that would be long remembered by the men of the regiment as they began a four-mile march at 8:00 A.M. that morning.[68] In a large parade ground carved out in an area not far from the Lacy House, they would join 60,000 other soldiers from the Army of the Potomac to participate in a review by President Lincoln, who would be accompanied on his trip by his wife and young son Tad.[69] Sergeant John Hirst, from the regiment's sister regiment, the 14th Connecticut Regiment's Company D, carefully recorded the memorable event that took place on Sunday, April 5:

> The whole Army of the Potomac was there, dressed in its best bib and tucker, with their arms shining like burnished silver, while we were dirty, sleepy and ragged. Just look at us with our overcoats and knapsacks on, our blankets in a coil around our shoulders, a canteen filled with water, a haversack containing bits of beef, crackers and pork, three or four cooking utensils, such as frying pans, tin cups, old tomato cans, etc., hitched to various parts of our body. Of course we were all armed and some of us had axes besides.[70]

"The most beautiful sight ever I seen," wrote Private Brehm, obviously excited over such a most unforgettable day. This colossal review not only awed the presidential party and high-ranking generals, but it instilled a sense of confidence in the ranks to be a part of such a huge military force capable of great victories yet to come.[71]

The following week brought the warmer weather of springtime, yet little to do for the men of the regiment other than picket duty, guard duty, company and regimental drill, and a dress parade on Sunday, April 13.[72] On that same day, the regiment noticed that Union cavalry and infantry units were beginning to move.[73] What they were witnessing was

---

68. Brehm Diary, April 8, 1863.
69. Ernest B. Ferguson, *Chancellorsville 1863* (New York: Vintage Books, 1993), 61.
70. Page, 114.
71. Ferguson, 62.
72. Masonheimer Diary, April 8–15, 1863; Brehm Diary, April 8–15, 1863.
73. Masonheimer Diary, April 13, 1863.

A Camp Near Falmouth 139

the initial stage of Major General Hooker's later aborted plan to send Brigadier General George Stoneman's newly-organized cavalry corps upstream above Fredericksburg to attack the communication and transportation assets in the Confederate rear.[74] Word was circulating that the regiment would soon be on the move although it had not yet received orders.[75]

On the following day orders did arrive, requiring the men to draw five days' rations to put into their knapsacks, and another three days rations to carry in their haversacks. Expecting to move at any time, the regiment remained in camp ready to march once the order would arrive. After almost two weeks had passed, the order finally arrived on Monday, April 27. The regiment was to be ready to move out at 3:00 A.M. the following morning. At 5:00 P.M. that evening, the regiment stood for an inspection to insure that they had adequate ammunition and rations.[76] With less than a month before their nine-month term would expire, the regiment would soon be taking part in perhaps one of the most remarkable and most tactically-studied campaigns of the entire war.

---

74. Gary W. Gallagher, *The Battle of Chancellorsville*, (Washington, Pennsylvania: Eastern Acorn Press, 1995), 9–10.
75. Brehm Diary, April 14–15, 1863.
76. Masonheimer Diary, April 27, 1863.

CHAPTER 7

Holding the Line: The Chancellorsville Campaign

OVER FOUR MONTHS had passed since the Union Army's disastrous strike against General Lee's Army of Northern Virginia at Fredericksburg. The long cold winter had given way to spring and both armies remained facing one another across the Rappahannock. The North was beginning to become impatient.[1] During this time, the Army of the Potomac had improved by great expense both logistically and in strength.[2] It was now time for its commander to act.

After months of preparation, General Hooker formulated a plan to move the majority of his army northward secretly, and then to swing back southward and assault Lee's left flank in two directions.[3] In a ruse, he would send the remainder of his army, made up of the First and Sixth Corps, in plain view below Fredericksburg crossing the Rappahannock River with the appearances of a concentrated attack.[4] Simultaneously, he would send two much larger wings northward to approach Lee's forces in their left flank and rear for the actual attack. On April 29 and 30, the Eleventh, Twelfth, and Fifth Corps crossed the Rappahannock River in hopes of engaging the Confederates in the vicinity of the Wilderness.[5] Anticipating that Lee, in turn, would move his forces to the right, they would be met by Hooker's second wing of First and Third Divisions of the Second Corps that crossed over the Rappahannock River on two pontoon bridges at the

---

1. Bates, 36.
2. Ibid.
3. Ibid.
4. Ibid, 44.
5. Ibid, 49.

Holding the Line: The Chancellorsville Campaign

United States Ford.[6] Among these troops on that rainy Thursday morning of April 30, 1863, were the men of the 130th Pennsylvania.[7]

Around noon of April 30, the regiment arrived at United States Ford which was designated as their crossing point over the Rappahannock River located about six miles northwest of Fredericksburg.[8] At that time, General Hooker's order was read to the troops that held that "General Lee was outgeneraled and his army compelled to either ingloriously fly or give him battle on his own ground, where certain destruction awaited it."[9] After crossing the river over the pontoon bridge, the regiment rested until 6:00 P.M. They marched westward by moonlight another five miles, passing deserted unfinished Confederate earthworks left in haste by the fleeing Rebels.[10] The regiment encountered the Confederate's rear guard "at the White House on the muddy road to Chancellorsville" where the weary regiment encamped for the night.[11]

The following morning, May 1, while the regiment heard cannonading, the Fifth Corps passed by.[12] At around 10:30 A.M., the regiment, along with the entire Second Brigade, was ordered out to the front.[13] Heavy firing was heard around noon.[14] Here the brigade passed the area of Chancellorsville, which consisted of a large brick mansion situated in a clearing of about fifty acres.[15] Later, the order was countermanded and the Second Brigade was ordered back. They marched to a ridge located approximately one-quarter mile north of the Chancellor house, located immediately on the western side of Plank Road. Here the men camped for the night, with the exception of Companies A, F, and D of the 130th that were the unlucky recipients of picket duty.[16]

The next morning the Companies A, F, and D were relieved from their picket duty and immediately ordered, along with the remainder of the regiment, to guard General French's headquarters.[17] Heavy musketry

---

6. Walker, 216.
7. Brehm Diary, April 30, 1863.
8. Spangler, 90.
9. Ibid.
10. Brehm Diary, April 30, 1863.
11. Spangler, 90.
12. Brehm Diary, May 1, 1863.
13. Masonheimer Diary, May 1, 1863.
14. Ibid.
15. Spangler, 90.
16. Masonheimer Diary, May 1, 1863.
17. Masonheimer Diary, May 2, 1863.

CHANCELLOR HOUSE (U.S. Army Military History Institute)

fire from both sides was heard throughout the morning.[18] Artillery fire continued all day.[19] The 130th was told to expect orders to move at any moment. The orders finally came down at 5:00 P.M., moving the regiment approximately five hundred yards south to the Orange Turnpike, about three hundred yards west of the Chancellor house, with their front facing westward in a defensive position.[20]

The intersection of Bullock Road and the Orange turnpike lay approximately one thousand yards west of their position. Directly across the Orange Turnpike approximately one hundred and fifty yards were artillery batteries from the 1st New York Light Artillery and the 4th United States Artillery. The 130th was on the brigade's extreme left closest to the Orange Turnpike, with the 108th New York on its left followed by the 12th New Jersey and the 14th Connecticut on its right flank. To their front were regiments of the First and Second Brigade, Second Division, Third Corps. The 11th New Jersey and 16th Massachusetts were positioned to immediate front of the 130th. The troops were poised in wait

---

18. Ibid.
19. Brehm Diary, May 3, 1863.
20. John Dove, *Battle of Chancellorsville*, (National Park Service, n.p., 1998). Historical research by Frank A. O'Reilly and illustrated by John Dove. Map 5 of 12. Hereinafter cited as Chancellorsville NPS Maps with corresponding map number.

Holding the Line: The Chancellorsville Campaign   143

for what would become one of the most noted strategic ruses during the entire war.[21]

By now, since there had not been any further Union activity, Lee realized that the prior movement and current position in his front at Fredericksburg of Hooker's First and Sixth Corps was merely a feint, and that "the main attack would be made upon our flank and rear."[22]

The Army of Northern Virginia's available strength of 60,892 was about half of that of the entire Union forces placed at 133,868.[23] The Confederate commander's intent was to continue to protect his lines at Fredericksburg while still meeting Hooker's main thrust on his right flank and his rear near Chancellorsville. Contrary to military doctrine, Lee divided his forces by leaving a division from Jackson's Corps, a brigade from Brigadier General Lafayette McLaws' division, and a portion of a reserve artillery unit to defend their entire Fredericksburg position.[24] By 8:00 A.M. on May 1, the majority of Confederate forces were marching in the direction of Chancellorsville.[25]

Late that evening the famous meeting took place at Lee's field headquarters, at the point where his line crossed the plank road. There, under the shadow of a pine tree seated on some cast-away cracker boxes, Lee and Jackson discussed the tactical situation and planned their next day's actions.[26]

Lee was convinced that that the majority of the Army of the Potomac was concentrated near Chancellorsville. Furthermore, intelligence from Lee's cavalry commander, General J. E. B. Stuart, indicated that the right flank of the Union Eleventh Corps "was defenseless and easily assailable."[27] It was at this point that Jackson proposed to march his entire corps quietly southward. This would give the appearance that he was marching away from the Army of the Potomac.[28] Jackson would then detour his 28,000 men via a little-known rural road leading through

---

21. Chancellorsville NPS Maps, Map 5.
22. Bates, 66.
23. Ferguson, Appendix 2.
24. Bates, 66.
25. Ibid.
26. Bates, 82.
27. Abner Doubleday, *Chancellorsville and Gettysburg*, (New York: Charles Scribner's Sons, 1882; Reprint, New York: Da Capo Press, 1994), 20.
28. Bates, 82.

the woods, turning in a northwestwardly direction.[29] He would march his men in total silence around the Union front positioning his troops, unobserved, in the rear and flank of the unsuspecting Eleventh Corps.[30]

Lee agreed, split his army into two small forces for the second time, again disregarding sound military strategy, relying on the potential of shock and resulting confusion. Jackson's Corps was in place by 5:00 P.M.[31]

As cited in Samuel P. Bates' *The Battle of Chancellorsville*, General Hooker was notified of Confederate movements to the west of the Eleventh Corps' position. General Howard, the Eleventh Corps commander, sent a dispatch to General Hooker at 10:00 A.M. on May 2: "From General Devens' headquarters we can observe a column of infantry moving westward on a road parallel with this on a ridge about one and a half to two miles south of this. I am taking measures to resist an attack from the west."[32] Assuming that the Eleventh Corps were taking appropriate defensive measures, General Hooker did not provide them support, although he did move portions of the Second and Third Corps near the Chancellor house to be held in reserve that could be sent in any direction.[33] This was the movement taken by the 130th on May 2, around 5:00 P.M., shifting their position approximately three hundred yards south to a wooded position that was only a short distance north of the Orange Turnpike.[34] There was a dense forest to their front and right, and a large open clearing located to their extreme left across and south of the Orange Turnpike.[35]

At approximately 5:15 P.M., Jackson gave his corps the order to advance on the unsuspecting Union Eleventh Corps.[36] Both Lee and Jackson's assumptions were remarkably accurate, and their brilliant plan was shrewdly executed. The Eleventh Corps had neglected to post pickets, and the soldiers were engaged in cooking supper when rushing hordes of yelling Confederates emerged from the dense thickets.[37] The result was a total rout and stampede of the vulnerable Eleventh Corps, whose

---

29. Gallagher, 22.
30. Ibid, 22–23.
31. Ibid, 27.
32. Bates, 89–90.
33. Ibid.
34. Chancellorsville NPS Map, Map 4.
35. Ibid.
36. Bates, 100.
37. Page, 119.

soldiers offered some pocket resistance, but largely fled eastward, running in terror through the ranks of the 130th Pennsylvania.

"When the disaster began our division was a short distance . . . from the Chancellor house . . . east of Howard. Shortly after, we encountered stampeded wagons, ambulances, packmules, cannon and caissons, with men and horses running for their lives," recorded Private Spangler.[38] The entire Second Brigade, along with General Berry's First Division of the Third Corps, was ordered to stand fast and to stop the mass of fleeing Union Eleventh Corps soldiers and then meet the pursuing enemy close behind them. Efforts were taken in vain to stop the thousands of fleeing Eleventh Corps Germans who were later referred to as the "Flying Dutchmen." The only soldiers who stopped were those who were either "knocked down by the swords of staff officers, or the sponge staffs used for the artillery."[39] The only reply given by the fleeing Germans was *"All ist veloren; vere ist der pontoon?"*[40]

As cited by Charles D. Page in *History of the Fourteenth Regiment*, during this incident, a rather extraordinary response surprisingly came from the 14th Connecticut's band during this fiasco. According to Page, in an effort to put a stop to the fleeing Eleventh Corps soldiers, the band: "went right into the open space between our new line and the Rebels, with shot and shell crashing about them, and played 'The Star Spangled Banner', 'The Red, White and Blue' and 'Yankee Doodle' and repeated them for fully twenty minutes."[41]

It was now dusk. "The Confederate shells came in showers, the fuses making streaks of fire like blazing meteors of huge rockets and burst over our heads with a defending roar," noted Private Spangler.[42] The threatening Confederate onslaught was quickly "checked."[43] Confederate rifle and artillery action lasted about a half hour along their line and temporarily paused. The enemy lines that ran in the heavy-thicketed woods were now in total darkness. Years after the battle Edward Spangler recollected that during the intervals between the rifle and artillery volley "the cries

---

38. Spangler, 90.
39. Page, 119–120.
40. Page, 120.
41. Page, 121.
42. Spangler, 92.
43. Ibid.

COUCH'S CORPS FORMING LINE OF BATTLE TO COVER THE
RETREAT OF THE 11TH CORPS (*Harper's Weekly*)

and groans of the wounded and the shouting and swearing of the more profane" could be heard.[44]

After a temporary pause, the chaos returned, recounted Private Spangler:

> At first like pattering drops upon a roof; then a roll, crash, roar and rush—with deep and heavy explosions like the crashing of thunderbolts. Our artillery battalions were massed on the Chancellorsville plateau, Fairfax . . . where guns double shotted with grape and canister, in continuous roar thundered volleys over our heads, causing the ground to convulsively quake and tremble . . . It was the most frightful and terrible night I ever experienced and the horror of the scenes defies even an approximate description.[45]

Late on May 2, around 9:00 P.M., unknowingly the men of 130th lay within a very short distance from the site of an unfortunate, yet epic

---

44. Ibid.
45. Ibid.

Holding the Line: The Chancellorsville Campaign

event that would undoubtedly change the course of the war.[46] Approximately six hundred yards to their front, Jackson and a portion of his staff rode outside of his lines to reconnoiter, when newly-posted Confederate pickets mistook the party as General Alfred Pleasanton's Union cavalry.[47] Most of Jackson's escort were either killed or wounded and the general received three bullets that "shattered both arms."[48] General Jackson would succumb to his wounds on May 10.[49]

Varying versions describing the circumstances of that historic event have surfaced over the years. One plausible version involved an officer assigned to the 130th who may have been within twenty feet of the infamous incident, and may well have been, indirectly, the cause of it.[50] On Saturday, May 2, around 7:00 P.M., a Second Corps staff officer approached Adjutant John Hays, the regiment's adjutant, and conveyed General Couch's order to move the Second Brigade west on the Orange Turnpike, to support Major General Hiram G. Berry's Second Division, which was assigned to the Third Corps. Within a short time, Brigadier General French arrived, protested that Major General Couch was not using proper command channels, and ordered Brigadier General William Hayes not to move. In response, according to Adjutant Hays, the Second Corps staff officer turned to him and exclaimed, "General Hayes! You have heard the order from General Couch, and the responsibility of obeying or disobeying it rests upon you."[51] General Hayes took little time moving the brigade, leaving General French shouting profanities.

The brigade passed by the Chancellor house, marching through the orchard on the way to the Orange Turnpike, dodging falling branches that were struck by Confederate artillery, and finally stopping by a Union artillery battery located close to the road. Since no one knew the whereabouts of General Berry, Adjutant Hays was selected to locate General Couch to ascertain where the regiment should position itself. Upon finding General Couch and hearing his reply, "Damn it! Go where

---

46. Bosbyshell, 167.
47. Doubleday, 39.
48. Ibid.
49. Ibid, 40.
50. Hays, 61.
51. Raphael S. Hays II, *John Hays, Civil War Soldier, Lawyer, Businessman*, self-published for the 250th Anniversary of Cumberland County, 2000, 59. Raphael S. Hays, II (John Hay's great-grandson) interviewed by author, at Hays' office, (President) Frog and Switch Company, Carlisle, Pennsylvania, October 26, 2006.

the fighting is," Adjutant Hays returned to the spot where he had left the brigade to find them gone. In search of the brigade, Adjutant Hays arrived close to a position recently evacuated by a Confederate artillery battery when he saw a group of horsemen on the road. "They appeared to be standing there perfectly quiet," recalled Adjutant Hays. It was now approximately 8:00 P.M. "I had gone but a little way beyond when a heavy volley of musketry was fired so close to me that the guns seemed to flash in my face. My horse—never under fire before—wheeled around and started to run down the hill. As he turned he could see quite a commotion in the group of horsemen on the road and the thought instantly occurred to me that the volley of musketry had taken effect upon the horsemen . . ." Contemplating becoming a prisoner, Adjutant Hays galloped off in the opposite direction a short distance, tying his horse to a tree and proceeded on foot until reaching the Union lines where he was quickly cautioned not to speak "above a whisper" since the Confederates were so close.

Adjutant Hays contended the noise made by his horse only twenty to thirty feet away may have drawn the attention of the Confederate pickets, who were fearful that Union cavalry was in the vicinity. The Confederate order to fire and resulting volleys struck General Jackson and his entourage, and undoubtedly changed the course of the war, passing closely over the head of Adjutant Hays.[52]

At approximately 2:00 A.M. on May 3, the fierce fighting had finally given way, leaving the forest "strewn with dead and wounded" in its aftermath.[53] The 130th had heroically "held the line" once again. At 5:00 A.M., enemy firing recommenced.[54] The entire Confederate line assaulted the Union front beginning at 5:15 A.M. and continuing all through the early morning.[55] Confederate Major General William D. Pender's Brigade (13th, 16th, 22nd, 28th, and 34th North Carolina Regiments) of Jackson's Second Corps occupied the ground opposing

---

52. Hays, 61. John Hays returned to the Chancellorsville battlefield on September 29, 1910, and located this position. Upon finding the spot only twenty feet away was the monument marking the location where General Jackson fell. Supporting correspondence from Union General Joseph Revere, Lt. Col. Kyd Douglass who was assigned to General Jackson's staff, and Randolph Barton, who was assigned to Confederate General Paxton's staff, adds creditability to John Hays' accounts. A significant difference between the versions recorded involve whether Jackson and his men were either moving, or at rest as John Hays contended.
53. Spangler, 92.
54. Masonheimer Diary, May 3, 1863.
55. Walker, 241.

the 130th and remainder of the Second Brigade. Crossing Bullock Road, Pender's Brigade made those early assaults into the area of the battlefield occupied by the 130th Pennsylvania and remainder of the Second Brigade. Brigadier General Joseph W. Revere's Second Brigade (assigned to the Second Division, Third Corps) and two regiments (11th New Jersey and 11th Massachusetts) from Brigadier General Joseph B. Carr's First Brigade, from the same division as General Revere, occupied the position to the immediate front of the 130th.[56]

The 130th held the position approximately 300 yards from the Confederate's original position, remaining steadfast throughout the morning over the contest for ground.[57] Several Union brigades assaulted into the Confederate lines being repulsed each time.[58] Between 6:00 A.M. and 7:00 A.M., the 130th moved up to become first in line directly opposing Pender's Brigade.[59]

Sometime between 7:00 A.M. and 8:00 A.M. on May 3, Major General Berry's Second Division of the Third Corps moved up to the front

GENERAL HOOKER'S REPULSING ATTACK (*Frank Leslie's Illustrated*)

---

56. Chancellorsville NPS Map, Map 8.
57. Spangler, 110.
58. Ibid.
59. Chancellorsville NPS Map, Map 8.

of the 130th.⁶⁰ The intensity of fighting increased along the entire line and the Confederates gained ground on the right of the regiment. About fifty yards in front of Company K stood a Federal 12-pounder Napoleon cannon that had been used intensively the night prior.⁶¹ It was eyed as a prize by the oncoming Confederates. The fight for the cannon resulted into a "hand to hand contest" for its possession, with the Confederates being repulsed and the gun recovered by the blue-clad troops.⁶²

Around 7:30 A.M., Pender's regiments pushed an assault through the first Union line, reaching the second line held by Hay's Second Brigade.⁶³ The 13th North Carolina turned to the right and flanked the 12th New Jersey, catching most of the nearby Second Brigade staff by surprise, capturing Brigadier General Hayes and his entire staff with the exception of one officer.⁶⁴ The attack was smartly repulsed. Being the senior regimental commander, Colonel Charles J. Powers immediately took command of the Second Brigade.⁶⁵ Colonel Powers had replaced Colonel O. H. Palmer, who had resigned as the commander of the 108th New York after the Battle of Fredericksburg.⁶⁶

At approximately 7:30 A.M., Major General Berry personally delivered an order and checked on his brigades located near the 130th.⁶⁷ He dismounted his horse, that was shaken by the terror of battle, and ventured into Company K's position to view the ongoing attack through his field glasses, when an enemy bullet fatally struck him.⁶⁸ Four soldiers from the 130th's Company E carried his body to the rear.⁶⁹

Brigadier General Joseph W. Revere succeeded the fallen Berry and immediately ordered an orderly retreat of Berry's division, along with the 130th and the remainder of its Second Brigade sister regiments. Not only did this unauthorized order cause Revere to be later dismissed from the army, it provided the Confederates the opportunity to take possession of

---

60. Spangler, 110.
61. Ibid.
62. Ibid.
63. Stephen W. Sears, *Chancellorsville* (Boston and New York: Houghton Mifflin Company, 1996), 323.
64. Ibid.
65. Washburn, 190.
66. Ibid.
67. Sears, 323.
68. Spangler, 110–111.
69. Spangler, 111.

Holding the Line: The Chancellorsville Campaign

COLONEL CHARLES J. POWERS, COMMANDER
2ND BRIGADE, 3RD DIVISION, SECOND CORPS
(U.S. Army Military History Institute)

important ground "at the edge of the Chancellorsville plateau." About this time, the center and the right of the battlefield had fallen.[70]

By 9:00 A.M., most of the Union troops and artillery batteries were exhausted and out of ammunition.[71] The resupply requests and calls for reinforcements brought no response. Although thousands had fallen on the field, the Union had remained positioned on the same ground, and all of the engaged units remained organized and effective. Sometime after 9:00 A.M., the pivotal point in the battle arrived when Major General J. E. B. Stuart, who had taken command for the fallen Lieutenant General Jackson, brought together the two wings of his corps for a final assault en masse. Literally every piece of Confederate artillery opened up with a "fearful fire over the plain, which fairly shrieks with the flying, purging shells." Then the entire Confederate line advanced.

---

70. Walker, 243.
71. Walker, 241-242.

The Army of the Potomac was again in retreat and the field was lost. The area around the Chancellor house was now a "hell of fire" as Bates described, with "shots screaming over it from every direction . . . the house itself was in flames." To add more to the horrors of war, the forest caught fire and quickly spread. In its path were the helpless wounded and dying soldiers who would soon perish in the conflagration. Bates further described that "Of the more than 20,000 who went down . . . by far the larger part fell on this little belt of forest . . . unquenched by the blazing tide that swept over it."[72]

Under orders from Brigadier General Revere, the 130th and its division fell back into a clearing near Bullock Road.[73] Later that morning the 130th and the entire Second Brigade's position would move to a location approximately five hundred feet northeast of the intersection of Bullock and Plank Roads on the north side of Mineral Springs Road.[74]

Private Spangler later vividly described the horrifying scene after arriving in the regiment's new position: "The forest where the battle raged the fiercest was now on fire, and many of the severely wounded were burnt to death. One of the nerviest things I saw in our new position was a tall soldier, with his right arm shot off, walking off the field apparently unconcerned."[75]

The regiment remained in its position near the Bullock Clearing inactive throughout the day. At 5:00 P.M., skirmishers to the right of the regiment drew some Confederate soldiers from the woods, whereupon several nearby Union artillery batteries opened up. While the artillery was "piling them up" the infantry captured one of their colors. The thunder of constant cannonading was heard on the regiment's left throughout the daylight hours of May 4 and into the night.[76]

Early on the morning May 5, Confederate infantry fire awakened the regiment early and continued throughout the entire day.[77] At noon, the weather took a dramatic change with thick clouds, thunder, heavy wind gusts, and rains that continued all that night.[78] Exhausted and fatigued,

---

72. Bates, 128–129.
73. Spangler, 110.
74. Chancellorsville NPS Map, Map 11.
75. Spangler 112.
76. Masonheimer Diary, May 4, 1863.
77. Ibid, May 5, 1863.
78. Brehm Diary, May 5, 1863.

the regiment's men were permitted to lie down for a short rest in the afternoon, when suddenly an unexpected "tremendous crash of lightning" abruptly roused the entire brigade with most of the men grabbing their rifles, believing that the battle had resumed.[79]

With no other orders, the regiment laid down for the night, only to be awakened and told to pack up and be ready to leave.[80] After several hours of waiting for their turn, around 2:00 A.M. on the morning of May 6, the regiment took its place in line with the rest of the Army of the Potomac and headed in the direction of the same pontoons at the United States Ford, which it had crossed over only five days before.[81] The retreat route included a new road that had just been hastily cut the day before, leaving exposed stubs and small stumps resulting in already tired soldiers tripping and falling "headlong into the mud."[82] The new "so-called" road took the regiment through brooks, mud holes, and anything else that stood in the way leading to the pontoons to the United States Ford and across the Rappahannock River and back to their previous Falmouth winter camp.[83] Private Spangler recorded the details of his ordeal: "I became so tired and exhausted trampling through mud and thickets and stumbling over stumps that I was compelled twice to fall out of ranks and lie down and take brief rests. The thought, however, of becoming a prisoner and confined to horrible Rebels prisons nerved me to renewed efforts . . ."[84] Making matters even worse, as a result of the heavy rains the day before, the pontoon crossing was made difficult by an unexpected rise in the river, turning the approaches to the pontoons into a mire.[85]

Along with the entire Army of the Potomac, the regiment crossed over the pontoons at daybreak on May 6, finally reaching its old campsite around noon after a miserable muddy twelve-mile march and no breakfast.[86] In the rain, the men put back their shelter tents over their old huts and began to settle back into their familiar quarters, most likely saying little, for no words could express their disgust and disappointment.

---

79. Spangler, 115.
80. Masonheimer Diary, May 5, 1863.
81. Brehm Diary, May 5, 1863.
82. Page, 123.
83. Ibid.
84. Spangler, 118.
85. Walker, 251.
86. Masonheimer Diary, May 6, 1863.

TROOPS CROSSING US FORD (Library of Congress)

The regiment suffered only light casualties at Chancellorsville, compared to Fredericksburg and Antietam, with only four officers and twenty-five enlisted men listed as wounded.[87] The regiment's staff suffered several casualties. Colonel Maish was hit in his thigh, after only recently recovering from his lung wound received at Antietam.[88] The regiment's adjutant, Adjutant Hays, was hit seven times, with four of the bullets tearing through his uniform and three into his body, with one bullet striking his leg.[89] The regiment's Sergeant Major, William H. Eisenhart, was struck in the abdomen.[90]

The overwhelming sentiment, from the lowest private to the Army of the Potomac's corps commanders, clearly placed the blame on their new commander, Major General Joseph Hooker. "The troops engaged never fought more gallantly, the disaster being alone due to the indefensible errors and blunders of the commander. The most costly blunders of General Hooker followed in rapid succession and lost us the battle. The whole affair was unrelated and disjointed," claimed W. Spangler years later.[91]

On May 3, the regiment's adjutant, Adjutant John Hays, encountered Major General Hooker on the front porch of the Chancellor house.

---

87. OR. Series I, Vol. XXXV/1.
88. Levi Maish, Service Record, Casualty Sheet, National Archives, Washington, DC, Folder 11, #274.
89. Hays, 22.
90. William H. Eisenhart, Service Record, Casualty Sheet, National Archives, Washington, DC, Folder 11, #274.
91. Spangler, 116.

When questioned as to what brigade Adjutant Hays belonged, upon Adjutant Hays' response, Major General Hooker replied, "My god! Is he driven in! I haven't a man I can send in there!" Adjutant Hays contended that Major General Hooker was "wild with excitement—not with liquor as some had charged—and did not seem to have a grasp upon affairs. He lacked the dignity, calmness, and full knowledge of affairs that seem essential to the command of the army."[92] Major General Couch had become so outraged "in every nerve and fiber of his body" by the shear ineptness of his superior General Hooker that, in a meeting with President Lincoln on May 22 acting as a spokesman for the majority of his fellow commanders, he recommended that Major General George G. Meade be given the command. While his recommendation was not adopted, at least for the time being, and General Couch deferring the position, the respected Commander of the Second Corps asked to be relieved. On June 10, the command of the Second Corps devolved to the distinguished and battle-proven Major General Winfield S. Hancock who had so competently commanded the Second Corps' First Division.[93]

---

92. Hays, 63.
93. Walker, 253–255.

CHAPTER 8

Home Again

THURSDAY, MAY 7, was not unlike any other day in their camp in Falmouth with a morning inspection of arms and ammunitions.[1] Some men were unlucky enough to be ordered to report for picket duty while others were afforded the opportunity to rest and recuperate from the previous day's grueling march.[2] The next two days brought much the same routine with picket duty along the Rappahannock River and little else to keep the regiment occupied. Sunday the 10th brought with it the warmth of summer and was considered "almost scorching" by Private Masonheimer.[3] Being Sunday, the men were given time to themselves with the exception of a dress parade. Time was assuredly passing slowly, with the anticipation that soon their term of service would be over, although no order had yet arrived.

On Monday May 11, 1863, Private Lewis Masonheimer penned his last diary entry that revealed not only his thoughts, but those of the entire regiment: "A very warm day. Detail made from the Regt for Picket. Great excitement about going home. Dress parade. Received two months pay. Very unexpected," noted Private Masonheimer in his diary that day.[4] The following day, the long-awaited orders were published—the regiment was going home! (See Appendix B—May 12, 1863, Special Orders #122.)

On Tuesday May 12, 1863, the men of the 130th Pennsylvania had served their required term of enlistment and were ordered back to Harrisburg, Pennsylvania, to be officially mustered out of service. Passing

---

1. Masonheimer Diary, May 7, 1863.
2. Brehm Diary, May 7, 1863.
3. Masonheimer Diary, May 10, 1863.
4. Ibid, May 11, 1863.

through York, they arrived in Harrisburg on May 21 and were officially mustered out of Federal service, turning over their rifles and cartridge boxes to the state.[5]

A special town meeting, held in York, took place on May 15 to plan an official reception "in a manner befitting their gallantry and distinguished service" for those members of the regiment from York and surrounding areas. After receiving a dispatch from Harrisburg at 2:00 P.M. on Saturday, May 23, the York church bells were rung, announcing their Harrisburg departure, signaling that all the stores were to close and that everyone prepare for the regiment's arrival. The church bells rang out once again at 4:00 P.M. announcing their arrival on North George Street, where the Patapeco Guards met the York veterans and led the procession to the Barracks "where a handsome collation provided by the Ladies Aid Society was furnished to the war-worn veterans. "All the flags were thrown to the breeze, and the town was filled with people, which gave it a lively and animated appearance."[6] Later in the day, the regiment's York veterans were given a banquet under an open canvas in the United States Hospital enclosure that was located on the city commons.[7]

A week later, the residents of Carlisle welcomed their veterans of the 130th in a similar fashion. Carlisle's church bells also rang out when the train arrived where the town's reception committee met the distinguished veterans. They were escorted to the town square for a celebratory reception dinner.[8]

Newville's Company E arrived home on May 22. After arriving at the Newville depot, the company was led through the streets by a fife and drum. On May 28, Professor John Leidigh, Captain Sharp, and Ex-Governor Joseph Ritner hosted them at a formal dinner at Liberty Hall where addresses were given.[9]

As the returning soldiers of the 130th marched through their hometown streets overwhelmed with jubilation, now reunited with their families and friends, assuredly their thoughts turned to those who were now not with them, never to return, who gave the supreme sacrifice.

---

5. Spangler, 122.
6. *The York Gazette*, May 26, 1863.
7. Spangler, 122.
8. *The Evening Sentinel*, December 28, 1929.
9. *The Valley Star*, June 18, 1863.

CONCLUSION

"Manhood Shall Be the Best of Citizenship"

THE REGIMENT suffered its greatest number killed at the battle of Antietam at thirty-two, compared with eight at Fredericksburg and two at Chancellorsville.[1] The 4.1 percent of those killed in action was only slightly higher than the 4.0 percent overall average of Civil War battle deaths.[2] A soldier in the 130th had approximately a one-in-five chance that he would be either killed or wounded, with the same odds of being discharged due to either wounds or sickness. Wounds, disease, accidents, and imprisonment resulted in 92 deaths during the nine-month term of service.[3]

Fortunately, the 130th endured only 1.6 percent of those assigned who succumbed to disease.[4] In comparison with the overall 7.2 percent for all who served, this statistic speaks well of the regiment's concern with adequate sanitation practices and the quality of its surgeons. These figures cannot include the unknown actual number of casualties considering the untold numbers of these veterans who continued to die as a direct result of wounds, disease, and exposure long after the war. (Refer to Annex D for detailed casualty statistics.)

While compiling statistical data, several trends became quickly apparent. Soldiers' interpersonal relationships often developed with a soldier

---

1. Bates, 207–223.
2. Frederick H. Dyer, *A Compendium of the War of the Rebellion* (Des Moines: The Dyer Publishing Company, 1908.); The Civil War CD-ROM: The War of the Rebellion: A Compilation of the Official Records of the Union and Confederate Armies (Carmel Indiana: Guild Press of Indiana, Inc., 1996), Part 1, 11–12.
3. Dyer, 524.
4. Bates, 207–223.

with the next name in the alphabet. In many instances, these soldiers would share similar war experiences, some fatal. For instance, two privates from Company H obviously influenced one another. On August 17, 1862, Private John Miller deserted from Harrisburg before leaving on the train bound for Washington. The next day, Private Charles A. Morgan deserted when he arrived in Washington. Company B's Privates Thomas Toben and John Tray were killed at Antietam on September 17, 1862; the same day that the Kennedy brothers, Alexander and Cyrus, from Company E, were wounded. Company E's Privates Thaddeus McKeehan and William A. McCune were killed at Antietam. These are just a few examples demonstrating that a soldier's fate was often a matter of the spelling of his last name.[5]

Throughout the regiment's nine-month term of service, the official records indicate that the regiment was a well-disciplined one, with only two general courts martial proceedings. In general courts martial proceedings in Alexandria, Virginia, on December 30, 1864, Private Abraham Lowkart from Company B was found guilty of deserting the regiment on September 18, 1863, the day after the battle of Antietam. Although Private Lowkart pleaded "not guilty" to the charge, he was unable to provide the officers convening the board any plausible explanation of his disappearance. He was found "guilty" by the board and sentenced to serve out his nine months assigned to another regiment without pay.[6]

The regiment's other general courts martial charged Major Joseph S. Jenkins on the count "Absent Without Leave" during the period of January 29, 1863, to February 9, 1863. The proceedings took place on at 10:00 A.M., on February 25, 1863, and were conducted at the 108th New York Regiment's headquarters under the guide of its Judge Advocate officer, Major F. E. Pierce. The convening board consisted of five officers detailed from other regiments. Major Jenkins pleaded "guilty" to both the specifications and charges offering the board a sincere explanation that led to his action.[7]

---

5. Bates, 207–223.

6. Abraham Lowkart Courts Martial File, National Archives Record Group 153: Records of the Judge Advocate General's Office (Army), Court-martial case file, LL2963.

7. Joseph S. Jenkins Courts Martial File, National Archives Record Group 153: Records of the Judge Advocate General's Office (Army), Court-martial case file, file LL223. Hereinafter referred as Jenkins Court Martial File.

> At the time I raised my company [Company C] last summer, I had expected to be able to return home from Harrisburg and make some provisions for my family (as by reason of some misfortunes my means were very limited and all that I had that was available I expended in raising my company) . . . All this time & up to the present the Government has failed to pay me any money, and my family was in need. I was led to take this step which I know was contrary to orders, in order to relieve them.[8]

Further, Major Jenkins informed the court that during this time away he traveled back to Fort Marcy to secure the company books that were left behind when the regiment departed in September 1863. Major Jenkins ended his statement claiming that there were mitigating and extenuating circumstances and, "that a man may owe a higher duty to his family under certain circumstances than he does to his country, particularly when his country might spare his services for a few days without injury of or loss and his suffering family require his protection."[9]

The courts martial board found Major Jenkins "guilty" on both the specifications and charges, sentenced him to forfeit one month's pay, and he received an official reprimand. Major General French approved the board's action, although he felt the board "too lenient for an officer who occupies so conspicuous position as does a field officer."[10]

In 1888, the surviving veterans of the regiment formed an association, holding annual reunions over the next forty years in Harrisburg, Antietam, Carlisle, Shippensburg, Mechanicsburg, Newville, New Cumberland, and Frederick.[11] Only on four occasions were reunions not held. John Hays and J. D. Hemminger were strong supporters of the association, credited with the success of many of the regiment's reunions. Appropriately, the 130th's final reunion took place on the sixty-fifth anniversary of the Battle of Antietam, September 17, 1927, which was celebrated by eight veterans: Washington L. Stoey, Company A; Ephriam Lease, Company A; Josiah Hovetter, Company E; J. D. Hemminger, Company E; J. R. Maxwell, Company F; M. H. McCall, Company I; Adam Wiseman, Company I; and Henry Horn, Company K. Exactly

---

8. Ibid.
9. Ibid.
10. Ibid.
11. *The Evening Sentinel*, December 28, 1929.

one year later to the day, the association's secretary and regimental diarist, J. D. Hemminger, passed away.

In April 1903, at the request of the Antietam Battlefield Commission of Pennsylvania, the Honorable Samuel W. Pennypacker approved the funding of the commissioning of granite and bronze monuments to mark the position of 130th Pennsylvania Regiment, along with the twelve other Pennsylvania commands engaged in the Battle of Antietam.[12] Committees of three survivors from each command were selected to meet with the commission and select the site and design of their respective memorial.[13] Dr. Samuel M. Whistler from Company E, John Kirk from Company H, and Michael W. French from Company F served on the 130th's committee.[14]

The memorials were officially dedicated and transferred to the Federal government on the forty-second anniversary of the battle, at 2:00 P.M. September 17, 1903. Attending the formal dedication ceremonies were the Governor of Pennsylvania and his staff, the Assistant Secretary of State, the Commander-In-Chief of the Grand Army of the Republic, the Carlisle Industrial School Band, veterans representing each of the thirteen Pennsylvania Commands, and thousands of guests. Ceremonies were conducted at each monument in the morning.[15]

At 10:30 A.M., a group of between one hundred fifty and two hundred of the regiment's survivors, wives and families, and guests gathered around the gray granite monument near the regiment's position at Bloody Lane.[16] "'At Ease' was the subject chosen by the . . . committee that depicts a manly American Volunteer . . . in half dress uniform resting easily on his musket ready at a moments notice to resume the firing that has for the time ceased."[17] A bronze life-like portrait medallion of Colonel Zinn was placed on the front of the pedestal of the monument.[18] The 7 foot 4 inch statue rests upon a large rectangular pedestal, giving the monument a total height of 14 feet 9 inches.[19]

---
12. Bosbyshell, 5–10.
13. Ibid.
14. Ibid, 233.
15. Ibid, 5–10.
16. *The Valley Star*, September 22, 1904.
17. Bosbyshell, 183.
18. Ibid, 184.
19. Ibid, 183.

PENNSYLVANIA DAY AT ANTIETAM, SEPTEMBER 17, 1904. THE DAY THAT ALL OF THE PENNSYLVANIA MONUMENTS WERE DEDICATED. PICTURED ARE SURVIVORS OF THE 130TH REGIMENT AND SPOUSES. PRIVATE JOHN D. HEMMINGER IS IN THE BACK ROW, FAR RIGHT AND CAPTAIN WILLIAM MILLER IS FIFTH FROM THE RIGHT WEARING TALL TOP HAT.
(Cumberland County Historical Society, Carlisle, Pennsylvania)

John D. Hemminger then introduced the first regiment's chaplain, Reverend George W. Chalfant, D.D., to give an opening prayer, and called the 130th's ceremony to order. The "Star Spangled Banner" was sung, followed by the unveiling of the monument.[20] John Hemminger provided a report that explained the role of Antietam Battlefield Commission, and how the monuments were funded and selected. He ended his comments by honoring the regiment's first commander: "As we think of Colonel Zinn as the man who made the One Hundred and Thirtieth Regiment what it was. Surely no noble an officer as he was, fearless in battle, a good disciplinarian, affable and courteous, and yet dignified, is worthy of this recognition in which you, my comrades, may take pride from the consciousness of the fact that in response to our Secretary's appeal for funds with which to do it, you liberally contributed."[21]

Dedication addresses followed by S. M. Whistler and Edward W. Spangler, who gave tribute to Colonel Zinn and provided a full history of the regiment that vividly detailed the regiment's sacrifices and hardships

---

20. *The Valley Star*, September 22, 1904.
21. Bosbyshell, 153–156.

throughout its nine months of hard campaigning.[22] Upon the conclusion of the services, the survivors retraced their steps through the Roulette House and Bloody Lane.[23] At 2:00 P.M. that afternoon many of the survivors attended the general dedication ceremony that took place later in the National Cemetery in Sharpsburg.[24]

As volunteers they came, knowing full well that many would pay the supreme sacrifice, while others would carry the wounds and scars of battle for the remainder of their lives. Civil dissension jeopardized their government that called upon them to defend the principals of its founding fathers. In his closing remarks at the dedication service Simon M. Whistler spoke for all of his comrades who served in the 130th Pennsylvania Regiment: "It was for the good of the people of the South as well as for the people of the North that the Union should be preserved. To those who follow you must be entrusted the sacred duty of defending the principals for which you stood—that the American government must ever be upheld as the highest form of organic democracy in which manhood shall be the test of citizenship."[25]

---

22. Bosbyshell, 156–182.
23. *The Valley Star*, September 22, 1904.
24. Ibid.
25. Bosbyshell, 168.

130TH REGIMENT REUNION TAKEN AT THE
CUMBERLAND COUNTY COURT HOUSE STEPS ON SEPTEMBER 17, 1890.
(Cumberland County Historical Society, Carlisle, Pennsylvania)

COMPANY B, 130TH REGIMENT, REUNION, SEPTEMBER 17, 1900.
(From the collection of the York County History Center, York, Pennsylvania)

"Manhood Shall Be the Best of Citizenship" 165

COMPANY D, 130TH REGIMENT, REUNION TAKEN IN SHIPPENSBURG ON SEPTEMBER 17, 1900 (Flickr)

130TH REGIMENT (MOST LIKELY MEMBERS OF COMPANY E) REUNION TAKEN ON SEPTEMBER 17, 1903 AT THE BIG SPRINGS PRESBYTERIAN CHURCH CEMETERY (Newville Historical Society)

AFTERWORD

May 21, 1863 saw the mustering out of federal service for the courageous men of the 130th that occurred in Harrisburg, Pennsylvania. Surely, a day of the mixed emotions of sorrow for the loss and injuries of their comrades, gratefulness that they returned safely, considerations to reenlist and the anticipation of their futures.

Many of the men of the 130th reenlisted and diligently served their country while others returned to their homes, some to marry, some to advance their careers and some who were unable to return to their normal lives due to their now permanent disabilities.

The final death toll from our nation's Civil War will never be determined as many, long after discharge, would succumb to their lingering injuries and physical deprivations throughout their military service.

Sadness and despair came to the multitude of the widows and their children of those men who made the ultimate sacrifice. Typically, a private's widow received $8 per month, along with another $2 for each child under the age of sixteen. Widows' pensions were based upon the widow's husband's military rank. Typically, if the widow's husband held the rank of colonel, she received $30 per month as did the widow of Colonel Zinn.

Mary A. Clark married **Henry I. Zinn** on September 18, 1855, in Carlisle, Cumberland County. She was the daughter of James Clark of Monroe Township, Cumberland County. By 1860, Henry and Mary had two children, Elsie Myra (born 1856) and James Henry (born 1858) with a third child, George Arthur, who was born in January 1861.[1] At that time the family was residing in Monroe Township, Cumberland County, where Henry was a teacher. Sadly, son James Henry succumbed to

---

1. 1860 US Census, Monroe, Cumberland County, Pennsylvania, Record Group 29; Series Number M563; Roll: M653_1101; Page 486; Washington, DC; National Archives and Records Administration.

diphtheria sometime before August of 1862, and daughter Elsie Myra died of measles on December 26, 1862, just weeks after her father's death. Not long after the tragic death of her husband, Mary began receiving a widow's pension of $30 per month, plus $2 for her young son George.[2] By 1870, Mary and son George relocated to Shippensburg, Pennsylvania, where Mary operated a millinery store.[3] She remained active throughout her life as a member of the Presbyterian Church, the Women's Relief Corps, the Auxiliary of the H. I. Zinn Post G.A.R., the Woman's Club, and the Shakespeare Club of Mechanicsburg.[4] Mary passed away on September 25, 1920, at the age of eighty-four. She is buried beside her husband Henry in the Mount Zion Cemetery, Churchtown, Cumberland County, Pennsylvania.[5]

COLONEL HENRY I. ZINN
(Library of Congress)

Levi Maish, who became the next commander of the 130th, became a US Congressman for Pennsylvania, and provided an appointment for Zinn's son, George, to attend the U.S. Academy at West Point. Upon graduation, George was commissioned a second lieutenant, making the Army a career, and retiring at the rank of colonel.[6]

As readers, it is only natural to want "more," as I do. With that, I have included short biographies of just a few of the soldiers of the 130th to provide a glimpse into their life's stories.

Levi Maish, a York County native, began his studies at the York Academy, although later in 1855 he learned the machinist trade. Wanting to pursue a more professional career, he taught school several years and later studied

---

2. US Civil War "Widows Pensions", 1861–1910, Henry I. Zinn, widow's pension application no. 12825, Record Group 15, Roll no. 485, National Archives and Records Administration, Washington, DC.
3. 1870 US Census, Shippensburg, Cumberland County, Pennsylvania, Roll: M593_1333; Page 371b; Washington, DC.; National Archives and Records Administration.
4. *The Chronicle*, Shippensburg, Pennsylvania, October 7, 1920, Page 1.
5. "Mary Clark Zinn," Mary Ann Clark Zinn, Find-A-Grave, Memorial ID: 34957563, viewed at https://www.findagrave.com/memorial/34957563/mary-ann-zinn.
6. "George Arthur Zinn," Find-A-Grave, Memorial 28099515, viewed at https://www.findagrave.com/memorial/280995515/georgearthur-zinn.

law under D. J. Williams, Esq.⁷ In response to President Lincoln's call for additional troops in 1862, at the age of twenty-four he raised and organized a company of volunteers which became Company K, 130th Regiment.⁸ Upon the regiment's organization, he was elected Lieutenant Colonel.⁹ During the battle of Antietam, he was struck in the right lung by a Minié ball, and took leave to recuperate, missing the Battle of Fredericksburg. With the killing of Colonel Zinn during the Battle of Fredericksburg, Levi was appointed the regimental commander upon his return to duty. Wounded again during the Battle of Chancellorsville, this time he was struck in the hip, which affected him the

COLONEL LEVI MAISH, POST-WAR IMAGE
(From the collection of the York County History Center, York, Pennsylvania)

remainder of his life. Upon his recovery and mustering out of service on May 21,1863, he resumed the study of law, passing the bar in 1864. Soon after, in 1866, he was elected to the lower house of the state legislature of Pennsylvania. He later served several terms as a US Congressman representing the Pennsylvania Nineteenth Congressional District.¹⁰ After his tenure in the US Congress, he returned to his legal practice. Levi Maish married Louise L. Miller, and they had one son, Alexander William Maish, who joined the Army, retiring at the rank of colonel. Levi Maish passed away on February 26, 1899, at the age of sixty-one, and is buried in Arlington National Cemetery, Arlington, Virginia.¹¹

John Lee, from Carlisle, Cumberland County, studied law under A. B. Sharpe in 1854, and was admitted to the Cumberland County Courts in 1856. In response to the call for additional troops in the summer of 1862, at the age of thirty-five he raised a company of men for military service

---

7. Gibson, John, ed., *History of York County Pennsylvania*, Chicago, IL: F. A. Battey Publishing Co., 1886.
8. "Levi Maish," Find-A-Grave, Memorial 7189097, viewed at https://www.findagrave.com/memorial/7189097/levi-maish.
9. Bates, 207.
10. *Lancaster Intelligencer*, Lancaster, Pennsylvania, March 1,1899, Page 2.
11. Levi Maish," Find-A-Grave, Memorial ID 7189097, viewed at https://www.findagrave.com/memorial/7189097/levi-maish.

which became Company G, where he was captain.[12] He was later promoted to the rank of major, and in December 1862 was promoted to lieutenant colonel of the regiment. After the 130th Regiment was mustered out due to the expiration of its nine-month service, John returned home to Carlisle and resumed his law practice, focusing upon military pensions and claims. Sometime after 1870 he relocated his home to Virginia under a railroad contract, but returned to Bristol, Pennsylvania, in the same capacity. He belonged to the Order of Odd Fellows, and the Grand Army of the Republic (G.A.R.) Lieutenant Colonel Lee never married.[13] He passed away on July 28, 1897, due to the complications of a stroke, and is buried in Arlington National Cemetery, Arlington, Virginia.[14]

Joseph S. Jenkins, a resident of Hanover, York County, entered federal military service at age twenty-nine on August 11, 1861, and became the company commander of Company C. Wounded at the Battle of Antietam, he recovered to participate in the battles at Fredericksburg and Chancellorsville. On January 1, 1863, he was promoted to major and later mustered out of service as the nine-month term of service for the regiment had ended. On May 17, 1864, he reentered federal service, becoming the captain of Company G, 184th Regiment, Pennsylvania Volunteer Infantry.[15] Tragically, Captain Jenkins was killed in action while on picket duty during the Siege of Petersburg on November 6, 1864, leaving his wife Catherine and four young children. Catherine received a widow's pension of $20 plus an additional $8 for their children.[16] He is buried in the Mount Olivet Cemetery, Hanover, York County, Pennsylvania.[17]

---

12. "John Lee," Find-A-Grave, Memorial ID 49245993, viewed at https://www.findagrave.com/memorial/49245993/john-lee#add-to-vc; Bates, 207.
13. *The Sentinel*, Carlisle, Pennsylvania, Jul 29, 1897, Page 2.
14. "John Lee," Find-A-Grave, Memorial ID 49245993, viewed at https://www.findagrave.com/memorial/49245993/john-lee#add-to-vc
15. *Lewistown Gazette*, Lewistown, Pennsylvania, Wednesday, November 23, 1864, Page 1.
16. US Civil War "Widows Pensions", 1861-1910, Catherine B. Jenkins, widow's pension application no. 88023, Record Group 15, Roll no. 485, National Archives and Records Administration, Washington, DC.
17. "Joseph Samuel Jenkins," Find-A-Grave, Memorial ID 982274209, viewed at https://www.findagrave.com/memorial/98274209/joseph-samuel-jenkins.

H. Clay Marshall, in 1860 at age twenty-one, was working on his parents' family farm in West Pennsboro, Cumberland County.[18] Two years later he entered military service in Newville, Cumberland County, being mustered in on August 15, 1862. He joined Company E and was quickly promoted from second lieutenant to first lieutenant, and later became the regiment's adjutant.[19] On January 7, 1863, he was discharged by a Surgeon's Certificate.[20] By 1870 he was married and had one son, and entered into the manufacturing business living in Cromwell, Huntingdon County.[21] He later moved his family to Upper Providence, Delaware County, where he became a US customs official.[22] By 1910, he and his wife of forty-four years had moved to Philadelphia.[23] H. Clay Marshall passed away on March 9, 1927, at the age of eighty-nine, in Media.[24] He was laid to rest in the Media Cemetery, Delaware County, Pennsylvania.[25]

John S. Low, born in Carlisle, Cumberland County, first enlisted on April 23, 1861, for a period of three months as a sergeant of Company C. On August 6, 1862, he again mustered into federal service as a private of Company G, and was quickly promoted to first lieutenant of the company. He soon became the regiment's adjutant and was later promoted to captain of Company G. After the war he returned to his home in Carlisle and became engaged in the mercantile business, becoming a proprietor of a grocery store and a senior partner in the coach making firm of

CAPTAIN JOHN S. LOW
(Cumberland County Historical Society, Carlisle, Pennsylvania)

---

18. 1860 US Census, Hanover, York County, Pennsylvania, Record Group 29; Series Number: 653; Roll: M653_1200; Page: 187; National Archives and Records Administration, Washington, DC.
19. Bates, 207.
20. Bates, 207.
21. 1870 US Census, Cromwell, Huntingdon, Pennsylvania; Roll: M593_1349, Page 571B; National Archives and Records Administration, Washington, DC.
22. 1900 US Census, Upper Providence, Delaware, Pennsylvania; Roll: 1406: Page 7; Enumeration District: 0193, National Archives and Records Administration, Washington, DC.
23. 1910 US Census, Philadelphia, Ward 8, Philadelphia, Pennsylvania; Roll T624_1387; Page 5a; Enumeration District: 0123, National Archives and Records Administration, Washington, DC.
24. *The Philadelphia Inquirer*, Philadelphia, March 10, 1927, Page 32.
25. "Henry Clay Marshall," Find-A-Grave, Memorial ID 158205323, viewed at https://www.findagrave.com/memorial/158205323/henry-clay-marshall.

Low & Lau. In 1880 he entered into the ice and bottling business.²⁶ Captain Low was married, and had five children. He passed away on April 7, 1891, at the age of fifty-four, due to Bright's disease and heart issues. He is buried in the Ashland Cemetery, Carlisle, Cumberland County, Pennsylvania.²⁷

John Hays of Cumberland County graduated from Dickinson College in 1857, later reading the law in the offices of Frederick Watts, and was admitted to the Cumberland County Bar in 1859. Entering federal military service at the age of twenty-five, on August 14, 1862, he became first lieutenant of Company A and later, on February 18, 1863, was promoted to the regiment's adjutant.²⁸ Upon recuperating from wounds that he received during the Battle of Chancellorsville, he mustered out with the regiment.²⁹ John then resumed his law practice in Carlisle with R. N. Henderson. From 1874 to 1893 he was the president of Carlisle

ADJUTANT JOHN HAYS, POST-WAR IMAGE
(U.S. Army Military History Institute)

Deposit Bank, and in 1899 he assumed the managership of the Carlisle Frog and Switch Company through 1918.³⁰ Until 1901 he was the editor and publisher of the *Carlisle Herald*.³¹ In 1865 he married Jan Vann Ness Smead. Together they had five children. John passed away on November 30, 1921, at the age of eighty-four, of natural causes.³² He is buried in the Ashland Cemetery, Carlisle, Cumberland County, Pennsylvania.³³

---

26. *The Carlisle Evening Herald*, Carlisle, Pennsylvania, April 8, 1891.
27. "John Spahr Low," Find-A-Grave, Memorial ID 43729909, viewed at https://www.findagrave.com/memorial/43729909/john-spahr-low.
28. "John M. Hays," Find-A-Grave, Memorial ID 4372448, viewed at https://www.findagrave.com/memorial/43732448/john-m-hays; Bates, 207.
29. Bates, 207.
30. *Harrisburg Telegraph*, Harrisburg, Pennsylvania, November 30, 1921, Page 11.
31. Raphael S. Hays II, *John Hays, Civil War Soldier, Lawyer, Businessman*, self-published for the 250th Anniversary of Cumberland County, 2000, 59. Raphael S. Hays, II (John Hay's great-grandson) interviewed by author, at Hays' office, (President Frog and Switch Company, Carlisle, Pennsylvania, October 27, 2006.
32. *Harrisburg Telegraph*, Harrisburg, Pennsylvania, November 30, 1921, Page 11.
33. "John M. Hays," Find-A-Grave, Memorial ID 4372448, viewed at https://www.findagrave.com/memorial/43732448/john-m-hays.

John R. Turner of Cumberland County was an older member of the regiment, enlisted at the age of forty-seven, mustering in on August 14, 1862. He was appointed the regiment's quartermaster, from his prior rank of first lieutenant, and survived the war uninjured, mustering out with the regiment.[34] By trade John was a carpenter, and is said to have assisted in the construction of the Adams County, Pennsylvania, Courthouse, and also designed the Clarion County Courthouse.[35] In 1833 he married Catherine Halbert, and together they had three children.[36] John passed away on September 28, 1888, at the age of seventy-three and is buried in the Old Graveyard, Carlisle, Cumberland County, Pennsylvania.[37] Numerous letters he had written are used in this book.

John S. Ramsey, a Philadelphia native and doctor, enlisted December 4, 1861, as assistant surgeon of the 55th Regiment, Pennsylvania Volunteer Infantry. Not quite a year later, on October 15, 1862, he was transferred to the newly formed 130th Regiment, Pennsylvania Volunteer Infantry, at the age of twenty-two, as surgeon, and was mustered out on May 21, 1863, with the regiment.[38] Married, with one daughter, Dr. Ramsey returned to Philadelphia to resume his medical practice. He passed away on January 30, 1894, at the age

SURGEON JOHN S. RAMSEY
(Courtesy of Jeff Donaldson)

---

34. Bates, 207.
35. 1860 US Census, Carlisle, Cumberland County, Pennsylvania, Record Group Number 29; Series Number: M653; Roll: M653_1101; Page 123; National Archives and Records Administration, Washington, DC.
36. 1860 U. S. Census, Carlisle, Cumberland County, Pennsylvania, Record Group Number 29; Series Number: M653; Roll: M653_1101; Page 123; National Archives and Records Administration, Washington, DC.
37. "John Rudisill Turner," Find-A-Grave, Memorial ID: 114968059, viewed at https://www.findagrave.com/memorial/114968059/john-rudisill-turner.
38. "Dr. John Sylvester Ramsey," Find-A-Grave, Memorial ID: 135949003, viewed at https://www.findagrave.com/memorial/135949003/john-sylvester-ramsey; Bates, 207.

Afterword

of fifty-four, and is buried in the Woodlands Cemetery, Philadelphia, Pennsylvania.[39]

Fred L. Haupt, born in Sunbury, studied medicine under Dr. R. H. Awl, and joined the regiment, at the age of twenty-six, as assistant surgeon on August 10, 1862.[40] During the Battle of Antietam, he was the only available surgeon for the regiment and overworked himself to the point of exhaustion.[41] Dr. Haupt resigned from military service on February, 20, 1863.[42] He returned to Sunbury and continued his practice for the next thirty years. Married, with four children, Dr. Haupt passed away on March 16, 1894, at the age of fifty-seven.[43] He is buried in the Pomfret Manor Cemetery, Sunbury, Northumberland County, Pennsylvania.[44]

John H. Longenecker, born in Lancaster County, graduated from the Jefferson Medical College, Philadelphia, in 1846.[45] On September 15, 1862, at age thirty-nine, he joined the ranks of the regiment as assistant surgeon, and remained until the regiment mustered out.[46] After the war John served as a civilian contract surgeon at the Annapolis Naval Hospital in Annapolis, Maryland, until May 3, 1865. He later practiced medicine in Brooklyn, New York, and Hudson, Massachusetts, finally settling in Islip, Suffolk, New York, where he passed away on August 19, 1902, at the age of seventy-nine. Dr.

ASSISTANT SURGEON
JOHN H. LONGENECKER,
POST-WAR IMAGE
(Find-A-Grave)

---

39. "Dr. John Sylvester Ramsey," Find-A-Grave, Memorial ID: 135949003, viewed at https://www.findagrave.com/memorial/135949003/john-sylvester-ramsey; Bates, 207.
40. "Dr. Fred L. Haupt," Find-A-Grave, Memorial ID: 150435446, viewed at https://www.findagrave.com/memorial/150435446/fred-l-haupt; Bates, 207.
41. *The Daily Item*, Sunbury, Pennsylvania, March 16, 1894, Page 1.
42. Bates, 207.
43. *The Daily Item*, Sunbury, Pennsylvania, March 16, 1894, Page 1.
44. "Dr. Fred L. Haupt," Find-A-Grave, Memorial ID: 150435446, viewed at https://www.findagrave.com/memorial/150435446/fred-l-haupt.
45. *Brooklyn Eagle, Brooklyn*, New York, August 20, 1902, Page 6.
46. "Dr. Fred L. Haupt," Find-A-Grave, Memorial ID: 150435446, viewed at https://www.findagrave.com/memorial/150435446/fred-l-haupt; Bates, 207.

Longenecker was married and had seven children. He is buried in the Lancaster Cemetery, Lancaster, Lancaster County, Pennsylvania.[47]

Peter Winter, born in Jenkins Township, Luzerne County, first learned the blacksmithing trade from his father, but desiring to achieve more in life, attended the Wyoming Seminary.[48] After graduation he taught school for three years, but then turned to surveying for the next seven years, followed by studying medicine under Dr. French of Hyde Park. In 1861 he entered the medical department of the University of the City of New York, graduating two years later.[49] Not long afterwards, he was appointed as assistant surgeon, joining the regiment at age thirty-two, on March 4, 1863, serving until the regiment mustered out.[50] He settled in Chenango Forks, Bloom County, NY, where he practiced medicine for one year. In 1865, Dr. Winter returned to Pennsylvania, settling in Dunmore, Lackawanna County, where he remained his entire life, establishing a medical practice.[51] Dr. Winter was married and had nine children. He is buried in the Dunmore Cemetery, Lackawanna County, Pennsylvania.[52]

ASSISTANT SURGEON
PETER WINTER
(POST-WAR IMAGE)
(National Archives and Records Administration)

Reverend George W. Chalfant, born in Mechanicsburg, Cumberland County, graduated from Jefferson College, Canonsburg, and later attended the Western Theological Seminary. His first pastorate was at the Mechanicsburg Presbyterian Church in April 1861.[53] On October 1, 1862, age twenty-six, he was appointed chaplain of the regiment until

---

47. "Dr. John Henry Longenecker," Find-A-Grave, Memorial ID: 32869859, viewed at https://www.findagrave.com/memorial/32869859/john_henry-longenecker#source.
48. "Dr. Peter Winters," Find-A-Grave, Memorial ID: 92806472, viewed at https://www.findagrave.com/memorial/92806472/peter-winters.
49. *The Scranton Tribune*, Scranton, Lackawanna County, Pennsylvania, Page 8.
50. Bates, 207.
51. *The Scranton Tribune*, Scranton, Lackawanna County, Pennsylvania, Page 8.
52. "Dr. Peter Winters," Find-A-Grave, Memorial ID: 92806472, viewed at https://www.findagrave.com/memorial/92806472/peter-winters.
53. *The Daily Notes*, Canonsburg, Pennsylvania, February 4, 1914, Page 6.

Afterword 175

he requested a discharge on January 7, 1863.[54] In his letter requesting a discharge, Chaplain Chalfant expressed his desire due to "recent events" to return home and care for his home pastorage and family.[55] He also mentioned a possible "fearful epidemic of smallpox."[56] He was discharged on January 7, 1863.[57] In 1864, he served on the United States Christian Commission in the Army of the Potomac. In 1881 Reverend Chalfant and his family moved to Pittsburgh, and he became the pastor of the Park Avenue Presbyterian Church until his retirement. He organized ten churches in Pittsburgh and was a member of numerous boards, fraternal organizations, and the McPherson Post Grand Army of the Republic (G.A.R.) Reverend Chalfant was married, with six children.[58] Three of his children became Presbyterian ministers, two became attorneys, and his daughter married a Presbyterian minister. Reverend Chalfant passed away at age seventy-seven on February 2, 1914, and is buried in the Homewood Cemetery, Pittsburgh, Pennsylvania.[59]

Reverend George M. Slaysman, age forty, from Lewistown, Mifflin County, succeeded Reverend George W. Chalfant as the regiment's chaplain on February 13, 1863, and served in this capacity until the regiment was mustered out.[60] Reverend Slaysman was the founder of the First Baptist Church of York, and returned to the pulpit, serving in several other Baptist churches in Pennsylvania and New York. He was later called to return to York and pastor his former church until 1892 when his health began to fail. Reverend Slaysman was elected the permanent chaplain of the 130th Regiment, serving at all of the regiment's reunions until his death on January 25, 1904, at age eighty-one.[61] He is buried in the Old Baptist Cemetery, Shirlysburg, Huntingdon County, Pennsylvania. Reverend Slaysman was married but had no children.[62]

---

54. Bates, 207.
55. Compiled Service Record, George W. Chalfant, 130th Regiment, P.V., Record Group, 94, National Archives and Records Administration, Washington, DC.
56. Compiled Service Record, George W. Chalfant, 130th Regiment, P.V., Record Group, 94, National Archives and Records Administration, Washington, DC.
57. Bates, 207.
58. *The Daily Notes*, Canonsburg, Pennsylvania, February 4, 1914, Page 6.
59. "Rev. George Wilson Chalfant," Find-A-Grave, Memorial ID: 90814203, viewed at https://www.findagrave.com/memorial/90814203/george-wilson-chalfant.
60. Bates, 207.
61. *The Gazette, York*, Pennsylvania, Jan. 25, 1904, Page 1.
62. "Rev. George Major Slaysman," Find-A-Grave, Memorial ID: 75469642, viewed at https://www.findagrave.com/memorial/75469642/george-major-slaysman.

William G. Bosler, most likely from Cheltenham, Montgomery County, mustered into service on August 11, 1862, was quickly promoted from corporal of Company C to the regiment's sergeant major on August 17, 1862. On January 1, 1863 he was again promoted, to second lieutenant, Company C. He was wounded during the Battle of Fredericksburg but recovered and was mustered out with the regiment.[63] William returned to his home in Cheltenham, taking over the family's milling business, the Cheltenham Flour Mills, on October 21, 1863. William, unmarried, passed away on January 1, 1872, at the age of thirty-one.[64] His gravesite is unknown.

William H. Eisenhart from York County entered military service at age twenty-four on August 9, 1862, as a sergeant of Company K, 130th Regiment. However, on January 1, 1863, he was promoted to replace William G. Bosler.[65] He survived the war, mustering out with the regiment on May 21, 1863.[66] Although there is no record of him receiving medical training, his obituary referred to him as "Dr. William H. Eisenhart." There, it appears that he died of a sudden heart attack. Although married, William had no children. He is buried in the Prospect Hill Cemetery, York, Pennsylvania.[67]

William T. Cutler entered his military service at the age of twenty-three, on August 11, 1861, as a first sergeant of Company A, but was soon promoted to quartermaster sergeant of the regiment, serving in this position until the regiment's mustering out.[68] It appears that he later served for a period of eighteen months as a private in the Signal Corps.[69] By 1870 he was married and had one young child, and was residing in Altoona with an occupation as a tinner.[70] William continued in this trade through

---

63. Bates, 211.
64. The Reporter, Lansdale, Pennsylvania, Apr 15, 1897, Page 3.
65. Bates, 202, 207.
66. Bates, 207, 222.
67. "Dr. William H. Eisenhart," Find-A-Grave, Memorial ID: 44888073, viewed at https://www.findagrave.com/memorial/44888073/william-henry-eisenhart.
68. Bates, 207.
69. Special Schedules of the Eleventh Census (1890) Enumerating Union Veterans and Widows of Union Veterans of the Civil War; (National Archives Microfilm Publication M123, 118 rolls); Records of the Department of Veterans Affairs, Record Group 15; National Archives in Washington, DC.
70. 1870 US Census, Altoona Ward 2, Blair Pennsylvania, Roll: M593_1309; Page 81A; National Archives and Records Administration, Washington, DC.

Afterword

1888, passing away on April 28, 1892, at age fifty-three. He is buried in the Fairview Cemetery, Altoona, Blair County, Pennsylvania.[71]

Joseph H. Halbert, born in Carlisle, Cumberland County, mustered into service on August 8, 1862, at age twenty-eight. He was later promoted from sergeant in Company G to the regiment's commissary sergeant, on January 1, 1863. He served in that capacity until the regiment's mustering out.[72] Joseph returned to his home in Carlisle and continued his trade as a plasterer.[73] He was married, with five children, and passed away on August 16, 1890, at the age of fifty-six. He is buried in the Old Graveyard, Carlisle, Cumberland County, Pennsylvania.[74]

John Geddes Barr from Newville, Cumberland County, at the age of thirty-two enlisted in what became Company E, mustering into service on August 12, 1862, at the rank of sergeant. On December 1, 1862, he was promoted as the regiment's hospital steward. On May 21, 1863, he mustered out with the regiment.[75] The local Newville newspaper reported that Dr. J. Geddes Barr had opened a medical office on April 14, 1859.[76] In the 1860 Newville, Pennsylvania US Census his occupation is cited as a physician.[77] There is no evidence that he had received any formal medical training which would account for his position as the regiment's hospital steward. On October 31, 1865, a York newspaper reported "Dr. J. Geddes Barr, of Newville, Cumberland County, Pa., fell dead at the breakfast table last Saturday."

HOSPITAL STEWARD JOHN GEDDES BARR, POST-WAR IMAGE
(Newville Historical Society)

---

71. "William Taylor Cutler," Find-A-Grave, Memorial ID: 90245136, viewed at https://www.findagrave.com/memorial/90245136/william-taylor-cutler#add-to-vc.
72. Bates, 207, 218.
73. 1870 US Census, Carlisle West Ward, Cumberland County, Pennsylvania; Roll: M593_1332: Page 326B; National Archives and Records Administration. Washington, DC.
74. "Joseph C. Halbert," Find-A-Grave, Memorial ID: 98690488, viewed at https://www.findagrave.com/memorial/98690488/joseph-c-halbert.
75. Bates, 207, 214.
76. *The Star and Enterprise*, Newville, Pennsylvania, November 8, 1860, Page 4.
77. 1860 US Census, Newville, Cumberland County, Pennsylvania; Record Group Number 29; Series Number M653; Roll: M653_1102; Page 564; National Archives and Records Administration, Washington, DC. (Name shown as Jno. G. Barr, The Borough of Newville, page 10.)

He was not married and had no children. John passed away on October 21, 1865, at the age of thirty-five, and is buried in the Big Spring Presbyterian Church Cemetery, Newville, Cumberland County, Pennsylvania.[78]

William M. Porter, of Carlisle, Cumberland County, the oldest of all of the 130th's company commanders, entered the service at age fifty-three on August 14, 1863, and became the commander of Company A. He survived the war uninjured and mustered out with the regiment.[79] Prior to the war, he was the editor of the *Carlisle Herald*, and was married, with five children. During his lifetime he served Carlisle in several notable positions as prothonotary, postmaster, and treasurer; and at the time of his death, he was a clerk in the Office of the Secretary of the Commonwealth.[80] He passed away on July 27, 1873, at the age of sixty-four, and is buried in the Old Graveyard, Carlisle, Cumberland County, Pennsylvania.[81]

Hamilton Glessner of York entered the service at age forty-one, on August 13, 1863, to become the commander of Company B. He survived the war.[82] Upon the mustering out of the 130th, Regiment Captain Glessner joined the 200th Regiment, Pennsylvania Volunteer Infantry, to become the company commander of Company K.[83] Upon his return to civilian life Hamilton entered the painting trade. In 1873 he and his family moved to Baltimore, Maryland.[84] Hamilton was married, with six children, and passed away on December 3, 1903, at age eighty-three. He is buried in an unmarked grave in the Loudon Park Cemetery, Baltimore, Maryland.[85]

---

78. "Dr. John Geddes Barr," Find-A-Grave, Memorial ID: 71483351, viewed at https://www.findagrave.com/memorial/71483351/john-geddes-barr.
79. Bates, 207.
80. *The News-Chronicle*, Shippensburg, Pennsylvania, Aug. 2, 1873, Page 3.
81. "Capt. William Montgomery Porter," Find-A-Grave, Memorial ID: 260438872, viewed at https://www.findagrave.com/memorial/26043872/william-montgomery-porter.
82. Bates, 209.
83. Special Schedules of the Eleventh Census (1890) Enumerating Union Veterans and Widows of Union Veterans of the Civil War; (National Archives Microfilm Publication M123, 118 Rolls); Records of the Department of Veteran Affairs, Record Group 15: National Archives, Washington, DC.
84. *The York Dispatch*, York, Pennsylvania, December 7, 1903, Page 8.
85. "Hamilton Andrew 'Ham' Glessner," Find-A-Grave, Memorial ID: 130638311 viewed at https://www.findagrave.com/memorial/130638311/hamilton-andrew-glessner.

Thomas B. Griffith enlisted at the age of twenty-four in Hanover, York County, entered federal service on August 11, 1862, and was appointed as first lieutenant of Company C.[86] On January 1, 1863, upon the promotion of the company's commander, Captain Joseph S. Jenkins, to the regimental staff, Thomas was promoted to captain of Company C.[87] He survived the war, mustering out with the regiment.[88] By 1865, Thomas had married, and would have five children.[89] In 1871, and for the next thirty-six years, Thomas and family resided in Montoursville, Lycoming County, where he was a druggist and practiced dentistry.[90] On August 27, 1907, at the age of sixty-nine, Thomas succumbed to a stroke and is buried in the Montoursville Cemetery, Montoursville, Lycoming County, Pennsylvania.[91]

James Kelso, at the age of forty-four, entered federal service on August 10, 1862, in what was known as the Shippensburg Guards, which would become Company D.[92] James was appointed the captain of Company D and survived the war uninjured. Prior to military service he was a farmer and returned to this occupation upon his discharge on May 21, 1863.[93] Captain Kelso was married, with six children. On January 13, 1879, at the age of sixty, he passed away, and is buried in the Old Jefferson Cemetery, Jefferson County, Pennsylvania.[94]

CAPTAIN JAMES KELSO, COMPANY D
(*The Chronicle*, Shippensburg, Pennsylvania)

---

86. Bates, 211.
87. Bates, 211.
88. Bates, 211.
89. "Thomas Benton Griffith," Find-A-Grave, Memorial ID:73024551, viewed at https://www.findagrave.com/memorial/73024551/thomas-benton-griffith
90. *The Baltimore Sun*, Baltimore, Maryland, Sep 3, 1907, Page 7; 1870 US Census, Stewarts, York, Pennsylvania; Roll: M593_1468; Page 500B; National Archives and Records Administration, Washington, DC.
91. "Thomas Benton Griffith," Find-A-Grave, Memorial ID:73024551, viewed at https://www.findagrave.com/memorial/73024551/thomas-benton-griffith
92. Bates, 212.
93. 1860 US Census, Clover, Jefferson, Pennsylvania, Record Group 29; Series Number: M653; Roll: M653_1118; Page 93; National Archives and Records Administration, Washington, DC.
94. "CPT James Kelso," Find-A-Grave, Memorial ID: 119724226, viewed at https://www.findagrave.com/memorial/119724226/james-kelso.

Joshua W. Sharp, at the age of thirty-one, and William Laughlin, both of Newville, Cumberland County, Pennsylvania, in the late summer of 1862 recruited a company of men which became Company E, with Joshua appointed as first lieutenant.[95] Both men mustered into federal service on August 15, 1863. Upon the death of Company E's Commander, Captain William Laughlin, during the Battle of Fredericksburg, First Lieutenant Sharp became the commander of the company, and would survive the war uninjured. He mustered out of service with the remainder of the regiment.[96] The following month he raised another company; however, he soon experienced a physical collapse and was mustered out of service. Later, he was given a commission as a first lieutenant in the Veteran Reserve Corps (V.R.C.) and assigned to the Provost Marshall in Washington for the remainder of the war.[97] At the end of the war, he received an appointment from President Andrew Johnson in the Regular Army as brevet major of volunteers and remained several years. Joshua long maintained a desire to travel abroad. In 1879, despite his fragile health, he traveled to Europe, later crossing the Mediterranean Sea to visit Egypt and Palestine.[98] At the advice of a doctor, seeing his health declining, Joshua traveled to Jaffa, where he died on April 7, 1881, at the age of forty-nine.[99] He is buried in the Jaffa Old Cemetery, Tel Aviv, Tel Aviv District, Israel. Captain Sharp never married and has no descendants.[100]

John S. Lyne from Carlisle, Cumberland County, became the second commander of Company G, being promoted to its captain on August 17, 1862, replacing John Lee who was promoted to major.[101] John Lyne was age twenty-seven when he entered federal service, on August 13, 1862.[102] Prior to military service, his trade was a tinner.[103] He would be discharged

---

95. "Capt. Joshua William Sharp," *Find-A-Grave*, Memorial ID: 53511819, viewed at https://www.findagrave.com/memorial/53511819/joshua-williams-sharp.

96. Bates, 214.

97. *The Valley Sentinel*, Carlisle, Pennsylvania, Friday, May 6, 1881, Page 5.

98. National Archives and Records Administration (NARA); Washington DC; NARA Series: Passport Applications, 1795-1905; Roll #: 288; Volume #: Roll 288-01 Apr 1879–16 May 1879.

99. *The Valley Sentinel*, Carlisle, Pennsylvania, Friday, May 6, 1881, Page 5.

100. "Capt. Joshua William Sharp," Find-A-Grave, Memorial ID: 53511819, viewed at https://www.findagrave.com/memorial/53511819/joshua-williams-sharp; "Joshua William Sharp," Find-A-Grave. Memorial ID: 86620019, viewed at https://www.findagrave.com/memorial/86620019/joshua-williams-sharp.

101. Bates, 217.

102. "John S. Lyne," Find-A-Grave, Memorial ID: 20047673, viewed at https://www.findagrave.com/memorial/20047673/john-s-lyne.

103. 1860 U. S. Census; Carlisle, Cumberland County, Pennsylvania; Group Number 29, Series Number M653; Roll: M653_1101; Page 118; National Archives and Records Administration, Washington, DC.

on February 5, 1863, on a Surgeon's Certificate, and was replaced by John S. Low.[104] John returned home to Carlisle, to his wife and three daughters, resuming his occupation as a tinner.[105] By 1880, John and his family had relocated to Altoona, Blair County, where he was a coppersmith, later moving to Colorado Springs, Colorado.[106] He passed away on August 20, 1918, at the age of eighty-four.[107] Official records indicate that John additionally served in Companies A and B, 2nd Pennsylvania Provincial Calvary; Company B, 17th Pennsylvania Cavalry; and Company C, 9th Regiment, Pennsylvania Volunteer Infantry.[108] He is buried in the Fairview Cemetery, Colorado Springs, El Paso County, Colorado.[109]

John C. Hoffaker of Middlesex Township, Cumberland County, entered federal service on September 2, 1862, at age thirty-six and became the commander of Company H.[110] In February of 1863, John Hoffaker was discharged due to a medical disability recorded as syphilis. Upon discharge he returned to his trade as a miller in West Pennsboro.[111] It appears that the long-term effects of syphilis caused his mental illness, evidenced by his false claims, of previous military service, and that someone else was receiving his military pension. An application for his military pension was submitted in March 1875, although no pension was ever issued. Captain Hoffaker was married, and had two children, and passed away on November 16, 1893, at the age of sixty-seven, in the Carlisle, Pennsylvania, Almshouse. He is buried in the Ashland Cemetery, Carlisle, Cumberland County, Pennsylvania.[112]

---

104. Bates, 217.
105. 1870 U. S. Census, Carlisle East Ward, Cumberland, Pennsylvania, Record Group Number 29; Series Number M653; Roll: M593_1332; Page 253A, National Archives and Records Administration, Washington, DC.
106. 1870 US Census, Carlisle East Ward, Cumberland, Pennsylvania, Record Group Number 29; Series Number M653; Roll: M593_1332; Page 253A, National Archives and Records Administration, Washington, DC.
107. 1910 Census, Colorado Springs, Ward 7, El Paso Colorado; Roll: T624_119; Page 2a, Enumeration District: 0054, National Archives and Records Administration, Washington, DC.
108. U. S. Civil War Pensions, 1861-1910, John S. Lyne, Invalid application no. 1201986, Publication T289, Record Group 15, Roll number 485, National Archives and Records Administration, Washington, DC.
109. "John S. Lyne," Find-A-Grave, Memorial ID: 20047673, viewed at https://www.findagrave.com/memorial/20047673/john-s-lyne.
110. Bates, 219.
111. 1870 Census, West Pennsboro, Cumberland County, Pennsylvania; Roll: M593_1333; Page 554B; National Archives and Records Administration, Washington, DC.
112. "John C. Hoffaker," Find-A-Grave, Memorial ID: 184368499, viewed at https://www.findagrave.com/memorial/184368499/john-c-hoffaker.

George C. Marshall had lived at home, helping his parents run their family farm, which was located in East Marlborough Township, Chester County.[113] Responding to the call for troops by President Lincoln, George, then twenty-two, enlisted for military service on April 19, 1861, and became sergeant, Company G, 2nd Regiment, Pennsylvania Volunteers.[114] This regiment was a ninety-day regiment and he was discharged on July 21, 1861[115] George, now age twenty-two, once again enlisted on August 18, 1862, and was appointed first lieutenant of Company H.[116] On March 1, 1863, he was promoted to the rank of captain and succeeded the previous commander, Captain John C. Hoffaker, who was discharged on a Surgeons Certificate. George survived the war and mustered out with the regiment.[117] Sometime after 1870 he married, and had three children, operating his own farm in Chester County.[118] Later in life he left farming to become a life insurance agent.[119] A widower, now retired, he passed away due to nephritis on April 28, 1921, and is buried in the Longwood Cemetery, Kennett Square, Chester County, Pennsylvania.[120]

Lewis Small was committed to the Union cause by first enlisting in the 16th Regiment, Pennsylvania Volunteers, for three months service as a corporal in Company A.[121] After his expiration of service, at thirty-three, he recruited and organized what would become Company I, where he served as the captain, entering federal service on August 9, 1862.[122] Not long after the 130th Regiment's expiration of its nine-months service,

---

113. 1860 Census; East Marlborough, Chester, Pennsylvania; Record Group Number: 19: Series Number: M653; Roll M653_1091, Page 213; National Archives and Records Administration, Washington, DC.
114. "George C. Marshall," Find-A-Grave, Memorial ID: 103009147, viewed at https://www.findagrave.com/memorial/103009147/george-c-marshall; Bates, 217.
115. National Archives at Washington DC; Washington DC, USA; Applications for Headstones For U. S. Military Veterans, 1925-1941; NAID: 596118; Record Group Number: 92; Record Group Title: Records of the Office of the Quartermaster General.
116. "George C. Marshall," Find-A-Grave, Memorial ID: 103009147, viewed at https://www.findagrave.com/memorial/103009147/george-c-marshall.
117. Bates, 219.
118. 1880 Census; Kennett, Chester, Pennsylvania; Record Group 29; Roll 1114; Page 263b; Enumeration District: 054; National Archives and Records Administration, Washington, DC.
119. 1900; Census, Kennett, Chester Ward 2, Delaware, Pennsylvania; Roll 1404; Page 213; Enumeration District: 0144; National Archives and Records Administration, Washington, DC.
120. "George C. Marshall," Find-A-Grave, Memorial ID: 103009147, viewed at https://www.findagrave.com/memorial/103009147/george-c-marshall.
121. Lewis Small," Find-A-Grave, Memorial ID: 58734150, viewed at https://www.findagrave.com/memorial/58734150/lewis-small.
122. "Lewis Small," Find-A-Grave, Memorial ID: 58734150, viewed at https://www.findagrave.com/memorial/58734150/lewis-small; Bates, 220.

Afterword 183

Lewis organized Company E, 207th Regiment, Pennsylvania Volunteers, where he served as captain until the end of the war. After the war's end he served as lieutenant of Company A, 8th Regiment, Pennsylvania National Guard, for five years. Lewis belonged to several York fraternal organizations, which included the General Sedgwick Post, No. 37, Grand Army of the Republic (G.A.R.) Captain Small was married with two sons.[123] He passed away on October 1, 1890, the age of sixty-one and is buried in the Prospect Hill Cemetery, York Pennsylvania.[124]

David Z. Seipe, from York County, at age twenty-five entered federal service on August 9, 1862, and was soon appointed as first lieutenant of Company K.[125] Within less than two weeks he was promoted to the captain of Company K, succeeding Levi Maish, who was promoted to the regiment's lieutenant colonel. Captain Seipe was fortunate to survive a wound that he received at the Battle of Antietam, and mustered out with the regiment on May 21, 1863.[126] Shortly thereafter he joined the first Battalion Pennsylvania Infantry, serving as captain of Company B for a period of six months.[127] David served a third time, joining the ranks of the 18th Regiment, Pennsylvania Volunteer Infantry, beginning on January 27,1864 as a major, until the war's end, mustering out on August 8, 1865.[128] He returned to York and entered the real estate business. He was a member of the General John Sedgwick Grand Army of the Republic (G.A.R.) Post 37 in York.[129] David, a bachelor, passed away on May 9, 1911, at age seventy-four, and is buried in the Greenmount Cemetery, York, Pennsylvania.[130]

---

123. *York Democratic Press*, York, Pennsylvania, Friday, October 10, 1890, Page 3
124. "Lewis Small," Find-A-Grave, Memorial ID: 58734150, viewed at https://www.findagrave.com/memorial/58734150/lewis-small.
125. "Maj. David Z. Seipe," Find-A-Grave, Memorial ID: 36897123, viewed at https://www.findagrave.com/memorial/36897123/david-z-seipe.
126. Bates, 222.
127. Pennsylvania (State), Civil War Muster Rolls and Related Records, 1861–1866. Records of the Department of Military and Veteran's Affairs. Record Group 19, Series 19.11. Pennsylvania Historical and Museum Commission, Harrisburg, Pennsylvania.
128. Pennsylvania Historical and Museum Commission; Harrisburg, Pennsylvania; Pennsylvania Veteran Burial Cards, 1929-1990; Series Number: Series 1.
129. *The York Daily*, York, Pennsylvania, Saturday, May 13, 1911, Page 3.
130. Pennsylvania Historical and Museum Commission: Harrisburg, PA, USA; Pennsylvania (State). Death Certificates, 1906–1968; Certificate Number Range 048401-051940; "Maj David Z. Seipe," Find-A-Grave, Memorial ID: 36897123, viewed at https://www.findagrave.com/memorial/36897123/david-z-seipe.

John Hemminger, born in Waynesboro, Franklin County, entered federal service at a stated age of eighteen, on August 12, 1862, joining Company E as a private. Fortunately, he remained uninjured during his tour of service and mustered out with the regiment on May 21,1863. John's military service continued with another two enlistments. On July 22, 1863, John enlisted a second time, serving at the rank of private in Company F, First Pennsylvania Battalion. During this enlistment he was assigned to guard the platform at Gettysburg when President Lincoln delivered his immortal "Gettysburg Address." He was discharged with his company on January 9, 1864. For his third enlistment, he joined Company G, 202nd Regiment, Pennsylvania Volunteer Infantry, as a corporal serving from August 31,1864 until August 3, 1865.[131] His military career ended after he participated in the Grand Review in Washington. As a young man John was taught the skills of a wagonmaker by his father, and returned to this trade, continuing through the 1880s.[132] Later his occupations were those of a bookkeeper, surveyor, and he retired as an accountant at a Building and Loan Association.[133] In addition to his invaluable Civil War Diary, John wrote the work, *Cumberland County Pennsylvania In the Civil War*, published in 1926.[134] He was actively involved with the Coldwell Post of The Grand Army of the Republic, (G.A.R.) and participated in many of

PRIVATE JOHN D. HEMMINGER, POST-WAR IMAGE
(U.S. Army Military History Institute)

---

131. Bates, 215.
132. 1860 U. S. Census, Mifflin, Cumberland, Pennsylvania; Roll M563, Page 345, The National Archives and Records Administration, Washington DC; 1870 U. S. Census, Frankford, Cumberland, Pennsylvania: Roll: M593_1332; Page 74B, The National Archives and Records Administration, Washington DC; 1880 U. S. Census, Frankford, Cumberland, Pennsylvania: Roll; 1400; Page 5; Enumeration District: 004, The National Archives and Records Administration, Washington DC.
133. 1900 U. S. Census, Carlisle Ward 3, Cumberland, Pennsylvania: Roll 1122; Page 305d; Enumeration District: 080. Page 74B, The National Archives and Records Administration, Washington DC; 1910 U. S. Census, Carlisle Ward 3, Cumberland, Pennsylvania: Roll T624_1335; Page 1b; Enumeration District: 5, The National Archives and Records Administration, Washington DC; 1920 U. S. Census, Carlisle Ward 3, Cumberland, Pennsylvania: Roll T625_1556; Page 8b; Enumeration District:5, The National Archives and Records Administration, Washington DC.
134. J.D. Hemminger, Cumberland County Pennsylvania In the Civil War, 1926, Carlisle, Pennsylvania.

the 130th's reunions serving in various positions.[135] John passed away at age eighty-three, coincidentally on the anniversary of the Battle of Antietam. He is buried in the Old Graveyard, Carlisle, Cumberland County, Pennsylvania. John was married twice and had three children.[136] Many of his diary entries are used in this book.

Edward W. Spangler was born on February 23, 1846 in Paradise Township, York County. As a young boy he worked on his widowed mother's farm. Desiring to enhance his education, at the age of thirteen he enrolled in the York Academy. After one year he became a clerk in a York dry goods store. In August 1862 at the age of sixteen, responding to President Lincoln's call for volunteers, Edward enlisted in Company K as a private.[137] Fortunately, after experiencing three major battles uninjured, he mustered out with the regiment on May 21, 1863.[138]

PRIVATE EDWARD SPANGLER, POST-WAR IMAGE (Find-A-Grave)

Upon his return home to York Edward was appointed deputy United States Marshall of York County. However, only a few weeks into service his leg was broken from a kick from a horse. Unable to serve in this position, he resigned. He later returned to his studies at the York Academy. Edward continued his studies in the law at the University of Pennsylvania and was admitted to the York bar in 1867. He soon was the head of the law firm of Spangler, Ross & Brenneman. In 1881 he became the president of the York Republican Club. By 1882 he, along with two partners, purchased the "York Daily Publishing House". In January of 1886 he organized and became the president of the Spangler Manufacturing Company.[139] Edward passed away on April 22, 1907 at

---

135. *The News-Chronicle*, Shippensburg, Pennsylvania, September 21, 1928, Page 19; *The Sentinel*, Carlisle, Pennsylvania, September 18, 1825, Page 2.
136. "John Daniel Hemminger," Find-A-Grave, Memorial ID: 26052320, viewed at https://www.findagrave.com/memorial/26052320/john-daniel-hemminger.
137. "Edward W. Spangler", Find a Grave, Memorial ID 13356374, viewed at https://www.findagrave.com/memorial/13356374/edward-webster-spangler.
138. Bates, 223.
139. *The Gazette*, York, Pennsylvania, Apr. 23, 1907, Page 1.

age 61. He is buried in the Prospect Hill Cemetery, York, Pennsylvania. Edward married Mary Francis Miller in 1873 and together they had two children.[140] A number of references for this book was taken from his work, *My Little War Experience,* printed by the York Daily Publishing Company, York, Pennsylvania in 1904.

Lewis Masonheimer, born in Waynesboro, Franklin County, entered federal service at the age of twenty-one in Company A. On September 17, 1862, Lewis was promoted from private to the rank of corporal, and survived the war, mustering out with the regiment.[141] On May 5, 1863, he married Eliza Wetzel, evidently being granted a furlough.[142] Prior to military service, as a young man Lewis learned the confectionary business, and opened and operated a store on West High Street in York. Later he entered into the livery and grocery businesses. Lewis was also a deputy prothonotary (clerk of courts) for almost nine years. He later held the position of teller at the Merchants Bank in York and was active in the Grand Army of the Republic (G.A.R.) along with several other fraternal organizations.[143] Lewis was married and had three children. He passed away on December 7, 1918, at the age of seventy-eight, and is buried in the Old Graveyard, Carlisle, Cumberland County, Pennsylvania.[144] Lewis would maintain a daily diary often referred to in this book.

John B. Landis, born in York County, entered federal service on August 9, 1862, at the age of twenty-two, and was appointed corporal in Company G.[145] Wounded during the Battle of Fredericksburg, Corporal Landis survived, and was discharged on February 12, 1863, as a result of his wounds. After recuperating, on September 6, 1864, John joined the 209th Regiment, Pennsylvania Volunteer Infantry, to become the

---

140. "Edward W. Spangler", Find a Grave, Memorial ID 13356374, viewed at https://www.findagrave.com/memorial/13356374/edward-webster-spangler.

141. Bates, 208.

142. "Lewis Masonheimer," Find-A-Grave, Memorial ID: 78293419, viewed at https://www.findagrave.com/memorial/78293419/lewis-masonheimer/photo.

143. *Carlisle Evening Herald*, Carlisle, Pennsylvania, December 9, 1918, Page 1.

144. "Lewis Masonheimer," Find-A-Grave, Memorial ID: 78293419, viewed at https://www.findagrave.com/memorial/78293419/lewis-masonheimer/photo.

145. Bates, 217; 1850 US Census, Spring Garden, York, Pennsylvania; Record Group: 29; Series M432; Roll 840, Page 175b, The National Archives and Records Administration, Washington DC.

captain of Company A, serving until the end of the war.¹⁴⁶ Upon his discharge John returned to Carlisle, Cumberland County, with his occupation as a revenue officer.¹⁴⁷ By 1880, John had become an attorney practicing in Carlisle.¹⁴⁸ He married Barbara Hessin Merkle and together they had five children, with the youngest dying at childbirth.¹⁴⁹ John passed away on October 31, 1905, at the age of sixty-four, and is buried in the Saint Johns Cemetery, Mechanicsburg, Cumberland County, Pennsylvania.¹⁵⁰ A number of his personal memoirs are used in this book.

PRIVATE JOHN B. LANDIS, POST-WAR IMAGE
(Cumberland County Historical Society, Carlisle, Pennsylvania)

Samuel H. Brehm, of Newville, Cumberland County, entered federal service at age twenty on August 12, 1862, in Company E, as a private, and survived the war uninjured.¹⁵¹ Prior to his enlistment Samuel graduated from Dickerson College. After his discharge Samuel graduated from the Jefferson Medical College in 1866, becoming a physician practicing medicine in Newville. About 1888, Samuel and his family moved to Hutchinson County, Kansas where he was said to be "one of the most successful and highstanding physicians in central Kansas."¹⁵² He belonged to the Masons, Woodmen, Mystic Circle Lodge, and the Grand Army of the Republic (G.A.R.).¹⁵³ Dr. Brehm passed away in 1894 at the age of fifty-four, and is buried in the

---

146. Samuel P. Bates, *History of the Pennsylvania Volunteers, Volume V* (Harrisburg: B. Singerly, State Publisher. 1870 Reprint, Wilmington NC.: Broadfoot Publishing Company, 1994), Page 743.

147. 1870 US Census, Carlisle County, Pennsylvania; Record Group: 29; Publication T9, 1,454 rolls, Roll: M593-1332: Page 267A, The National Archives and Records Administration, Washington DC.

148. 1880 US Census, Carlisle County, Pennsylvania; Record Group: 29; Publication T9, 1,454 rolls, Roll: 1122; Page 247b; Enumeration District:077, The National Archives and Records Administration, Washington DC.

149. "John B. Landis," Find-A-Grave, Memorial ID: 104411866, viewed at https://www.findagrave.com/memorial/104411866/john-b-landis.

150. *Carlisle Evening Herald*, Carlisle, Pennsylvania, November 3, 1905, Page 5; "John B. Landis," Find-A-Grave, Memorial ID: 104411866, viewed at https://www.findagrave.com/memorial/104411866/john-b-landis.

151. "Dr Samuel Henry Brehm," Find-A-Grave, Memorial ID: 39563479, viewed at https://www.findagrave.com/memorial/39563479/samuel-henry-brehm; Bates, 214.

152. *The Earth*, Brookville, Kansas, August 24, 1894, Page 2.

153. *The Hutchinson News-Herald*, Hutchinson, Kansas, August 20, 1894, Page 3.

Hutchinson Eastside Cemetery, Hutchinson, Kansas.[154] Samuel was married with four children.[155] Many of his diary entries are used in this book.

John S. Weiser from Pine Grove Furnace, Cumberland County, entered federal service on August 15, 1862, at the age of twenty-six, as a private in Company G. He survived the war uninjured and mustered out with the regiment on May 21, 1863.[156] On July 17, 1863 John joined Company B, 6th Pennsylvania Cavalry, as a second lieutenant, and later transferred to Company K, 185th Regiment, 22nd Pennsylvania Cavalry, to serve until the war's end.[157] By 1870, John was residing in Penn, Cumberland County, with the occupation of a carpenter.[158] However, in 1883 John and his wife moved to Ida Grove, Ida County, Iowa, where he purchased a 400-acre farm and became involved in the grocery business, and became a senior member of the firm Weiser and Van Wagoner.[159] On March 6, 1903, at the age of sixty-six, John died by accident from eating contaminated canned sausage.[160] He is buried in the Ida Grove Cemetery, Ida Grove, Ida County, Iowa. John was married twice although there is no record of any children.[161] A number of John Weiser's letters are used in this book.

---

154. "Dr Samuel Henry Brehm," Find-A-Grave, Memorial ID: 39563479, viewed at https://www.findagrave.com/memorial/39563479/samuel-henry-brehm.

155. *The Hutchinson News-Herald*, Hutchinson, Kansas, August 20, 1894, Page 3.

156. Bates, 219; "1LT John Solomon Weiser," Find-A-Grave, Memorial ID: 45731440, viewed at https://www.findagrave.com/memorial/45731440/john-solomon-weiser#source.

157. Samuel P. Bates, *History of the Pennsylvania Volunteers, Volume V* (Harrisburg: B. Singerly, State Publisher. 1870 Reprint, Wilmington NC.: Broadfoot Publishing Company, 1994), Page 175.

158. 1870 US Census, Penn Cumberland, Pennsylvania; Publication T132, 13 rolls, Roll: M593_1333; Page 356b; The National Archives and Records Administration, Washington DC.

159. https://www.findagrave.com/memorial/45731440/john-solomon-weiser#source.

160. *Evening Times-Republican*, Marshalltown, Iowa, March 7, 1903, Page 1; *Muscantine News-Tribune*, Muscantine, Iowa, March 10, 1903, Page 2.

161. "1LT John Solomon Weiser", Find-A-Grave, Memorial ID: 45731440, viewed at https://www.findagrave.com/memorial/45731440/john-solomon-weiser#source.

"We should therefore never fail to revere the memories of the great deeds of those who shed their blood for their country, nor forget the value of the great heritage which comes to us and succeeding generations through so much sacrifice and death."

—Edward W. Spangler, Private, Company K.

APPENDIX A

Additional Photographs

CORPORAL WALTER M. ALLISON, COMPANY A, POST-WAR IMAGE IN G.A.R. UNIFORM
(U.S. Army Military History Institute)

PRIVATE LEANDER C. CORMAN, COMPANY A
(U.S. Army Military History Institute)

Appendix A: Additional Photographs

PRIVATE WASHINGTON L. STOEY, COMPANY A, POST-WAR IMAGE
(Newville Historical Society)

PRIVATE JOHN H. ZEIGLER, COMPANY A, POST-WAR IMAGE
(Cumberland County Historical Society, Carlisle, Pennsylvania)

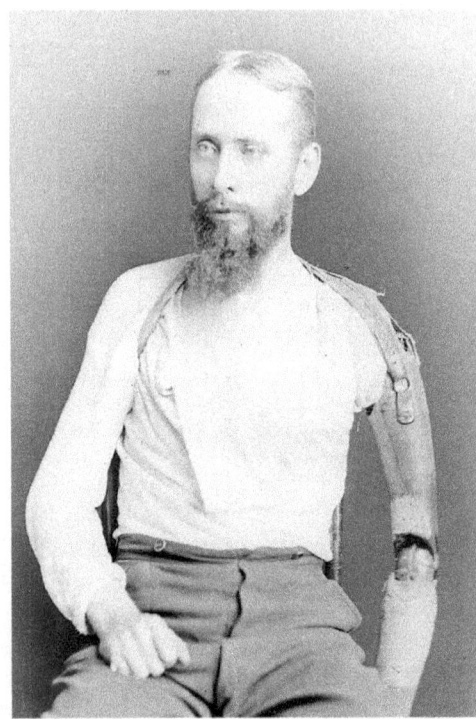

PRIVATE THOMAS NUMBERS, COMPANY C, POST-WAR IMAGE. DISABLED SOLDIERS SENT IMAGES OF THEIR WOUNDS TO THE PENSION BUREAU IN ORDER TO RECEIVE A DISABILITY PENSION.
(National Archives and Records Administration)

FIRST LIEUTENANT SAMUEL PATCHELL, COMPANY D
(*The Chronicle*, Shippensburg, Pennsylvania)

Appendix A: Additional Photographs

SECOND LIEUTENANT
DANIEL A. HARRIS,
COMPANY D
(*The Chronicle*, Shippensburg,
Pennsylvania)

SERGEANT JOHN HAYS,
COMPANY D,
POST-WAR IMAGE
(Newville Historical Society)

THIRD CORPORAL
GEORGE J. MCLEAN,
COMPANY D
(*The Chronicle*, Shippensburg,
Pennsylvania)

PRIVATE ALEXANDER
STEWART, COMPANY D
(*The Chronicle*, Shippensburg,
Pennsylvania)

Appendix A: Additional Photographs

CORPORAL FRANK BEST,
COMPANY E
(Cumberland County Historical
Society, Carlisle, Pennsylvania)

PRIVATE GEORGE W. WOLF,
COMPANY D,
POST-WAR IMAGE
(U.S. Army Military History
Institute)

SECOND LIEUTENANT
JOSEPH E. EGE, COMPANY E
(Courtesy of Susan M. Boardman)

PRIVATE WILLIAM
FINKENBINDER ON LEFT
AND EITHER SERGEANT
ALEXANDER KENNEDY,
SERGEANT CYRUS
KENNEDY OR PRIVATE
JOHN KENNEDY ON
RIGHT, COMPANY E
(Cumberland County
Historical Society,
Carlisle, Pennsylvania)

Appendix A: Additional Photographs

PRIVATE JACOB M. FLYER, COMPANY E, POST-WAR IMAGE
WITH DAUGHTERS MARY ON LEFT AND SUSAN ON RIGHT
(Cumberland County Historical Society, Carlisle, Pennsylvania)

MUSICIAN AUGUSTS G. KYLE, COMPANY E
(Cumberland County Historical Society, Carlisle, Pennsylvania)

Appendix A: Additional Photographs

PRIVATE ABRAHAM H. MCCOY, COMPANY E, POST-WAR IMAGE WITH WIFE
(Cumberland County Historical Society, Carlisle, Pennsylvania)

PRIVATE JOHN M. FARNER, COMPANY F, POST-WAR IMAGE WITH HIS WIFE FLORENCE (DAVIDSON)
(Cumberland County Historical Society, Carlisle, Pennsylvania)

PRIVATE SAMUEL A. MILLER,
COMPANY F, POST-WAR IMAGE
(Cumberland County Historical Society,
Carlisle, Pennsylvania)

PRIVATE SAMUEL OILER,
COMPANY G
(U.S. Army Military History Institute)

Appendix A: Additional Photographs

PRIVATE EDWIN D. QUIGLEY,
COMPANY G, POST-WAR IMAGE
(Cumberland County Historical Society,
Carlisle, Pennsylvania)

CORPORAL ISSAC BOWMAN,
COMPANY H, POST-WAR IMAGE
(U.S. Army Military History Institute)

PRIVATE WILLIAM H. MILLER, COMPANY K, POST-WAR IMAGE WITH HIS WIFE
(Cumberland County Historical Society, Carlisle, Pennsylvania)

UNIDENTIFIED CORPORAL, COMPANY H
(Flickr)

APPENDIX B

Commanders and Staff, August 1862

FIELD AND STAFF OFFICERS
Henry I. Zinn, Colonel, Commander
Levi Maish, Lieutenant Colonel
John Lee, Major
H. Clay Marshall, Adjutant
John R. Turner, Quartermaster
Surgeon, Vacant
Assistant Surgeon, Frederick L. Haupt (August 19, 1862)
Chaplain, Vacant

REGIMENTAL NONCOMMISSIONED OFFICERS
William G. Bosler, Sergeant Major
William F. Cutler, Quartermaster Sergeant
Joseph C. Halbert, Commissary Sergeant
John G. Barr, Hospital Steward

COMPANY A
(Cumberland County)

William M. Porter, Captain
John R. Turner, First Lieutenant
John Hays, First Lieutenant
John O. Halbert, Second Lieutenant
George Thayer, First Lieutenant
Alphonso B. Beisel, First Sergeant

COMPANY B
(York County)

Hamilton A. Glessner, Captain
William H. Tomes, First Lieutenant
Henry Reisinger, Second Lieutenant
George K. Shenberger, First Sergeant

COMPANY C
(York and Montgomery Counties)

Joseph S. Jenkins, Captain
Benjamin F. Myers, First Lieutenant
William G. Bosler, Second Lieutenant
Clinton Keister, First Sergeant

COMPANY D
(Cumberland County, Shippensburg—The Shippensburg Guards)

James Kelso, Captain
Samuel Patchell, First Lieutenant
Daniel A. Harris, Second Lieutenant
Jacob Steinman, First Sergeant

COMPANY E
(Cumberland County, Newville)

William Laughlin, Captain
Joshua W. Sharpe, First Lieutenant
Henry Clay Marshall, Second Lieutenant
Joseph A. Ege, First Sergeant

COMPANY F
(Cumberland County, Mechanicsburg)

Henry I. Zinn, Captain
(Promoted to Colonel and 130th's Commander, August 17, 1862)
John B. Zinn, Captain

(Promoted from First Lieutenant to Captain, August 17, 1862)
William A. Givler, Second Lieutenant
Levi M Haverstick, First Sergeant
(Promoted to First Lieutenant, August 17, 1862)

COMPANY G
(Cumberland County)

John Lee, Captain
(Promoted to Major, August 17, 1862)
John S. Lyne, First Lieutenant
(Promoted to Captain, August 17, 1862)
Thomas D. Caldwell, First Sergeant
(Promoted to Second Lieutenant, August 17, 1862)
Henry Keller, Sergeant
(Promoted to First Sergeant, August 17, 1862)

COMPANY H
(Cumberland, Dauphin, and Chester Counties)

John C. Hoffaker, Captain
George C. Marshall, First Lieutenant
John K. McGann, Second Lieutenant
First Sergeant—Not filled

COMPANY I
(York County)

Lewis Small, Captain
David Wilson Grove, First Lieutenant
Franklin G. Tolbert, Second Lieutenant
Jeremiah Oliver, First Sergeant

COMPANY K
(York County)

Levi Maish, Captain
(Promoted to Lieutenant Colonel, August 17, 1862)

David Z. Seipe, First Lieutenant
(Promoted to Captain, August 17, 1862)
James Lece, Second Lieutenant
(Promoted to First Lieutenant, August 17, 1862)
John J. Frick, First Sergeant
(Promoted to Second Lieutenant, August 17, 1862)
Jas. P. McGuigan, Sergeant
(Promoted to First Sergeant, August 17, 1862)

APPENDIX C

Special Order #122

Special Order #122
Headquarters 3rd Division 2nd Corps
Army of the Potomac, May 12, 1863
Special Order No. 122. Extract

III. The 130th and 132nd Pennsylvania Regiments of nine months will be relieved from duty with this Division, the first at retreat to-day and the latter at retreat on the 15th inst.

Transportation will be in readiness at Falmouth Station at 7 A.M., tomorrow for the 130th and for the 132nd on the 15th unless otherwise directed. A staff officer from these headquarters will proceed to Acquia Landing where by roll call he will ascertain that no unauthorized persons leave with the regiments. The General commanding the Division takes pleasure in promulgating in orders their gallantry, soldier like bearing, and efficiency, during their entire term of service.

Within the nine months for which they were enrolled they have participated in the battles of Antietam, Fredericksburg, and the series of engagements near Chancellorsville; each has lost in that short period the Colonel who first brought it into the field, the brave Zinn who led the 130th in Fredericksburg, and the gallant Oakford, of the 132nd, who fell at Antietam.

Soldiers you return to your native State which has received luster from your achievements, and by your devotion to your Country's cause. This Army and the Division to which you are attached, although they lose you, will always retain and cherish the credit which your military bearing on all occasions has so reflected on them.

Your Division Commander cherishes the belief, after a sojurn [sic] at your homes with the friends who are all anxiety to behold those of you who have passed unscathed through the midst of so many dangers, will again rally round that flag which you have so nobly defended. By command of

MAJOR GEN. FRENCH
Commanding Division
(Signed) John M. Norvell
Chief of Staff and A. A. G.
Headquarters, 2nd Brigade, May 12, 1863
Official, J. Parks Portler
Captain and A. A. A. G.[162]

---

162. *The York Gazette*, May 19, 1863.

APPENDIX D
130th Regiment Pennsylvania Volunteer Infantry
Regiment Strength and Casualty Statistics

	Assigned	Killed	Wounded	Died of Wounds	Died of Disease	Died Unknown	Deserted	Discharged Disability	Captured	Missing
Command/Staff	10	1	2	0	0	0	0	1	0	0
Company A	94	1	17	3	0	0	3	24	1	0
Company B	100	7	11	0	0	1	8	20	1	0
Company C	100	5	7	5	2	2	7	14	1	1
Company D	101	5	5	1	1	1	6	21	0	0
Company E	91	4	12	2	3	1	2	14	0	0
Company F	100	4	23	3	0	3	5	8	0	1
Company G	96	0	4	1	2	0	6	12	0	0
Company H	90	2	1	0	2	1	6	13	0	0
Company I	95	6	17	3	3	3	4	10	1	0
Company K	92	5	9	2	3	2	1	10	0	0
TOTALS	**969**	**40**	**108**	**20**	**16**	**14**	**14**	**147**	**4**	**2**

Sources: Samuel P Bates, History of the Pennsylvania Volunteers, 1861-5, 5 vols. (Harrisburg: B. Singerly, State Publisher, 1870). VOL VII. (Reprint, Wilmington, NC: Broadfoot Publishing Co., 1994); Roll of the Regiment, 130th Regiment Pennsylvania Volunteer Infantry, Roll #517, Record Group 19, Pennsylvania State Archives, Harrisburg, Pennsylvania. Microfilm.

APPENDIX E

Regimental Roster

FIELD AND STAFF

Name	Age	Joined at	Date Joined	Remarks
Colonels				
Henry I. Zinn	28	Harrisburg	July 23, 1862	Promoted from Capt., Co. F, August 17, 1862. Killed at Fredericksburg on December 13, 1862.
Levi Maish	25	York	August 4, 1862	Promoted from Capt. Co. K to Lt. Col. on August 17, 1863. Promoted to Col. vice Zinn on February 3, 1863. Wounded at Antietem on September 17, 1862 and Chancellorsville on May 3, 1863. Mustered out with regiment on May 21, 1863
Lieutenant Colonel				
John Lee	35	Harrisburg	July 25, 1862	Promoted from Capt., Co. G., to Maj., August 17, 1862. Promoted to Lt. Col. on Dec 14, 1862. Mustered out with regiment on May 21, 1862.
Majors				
Joseph S. Jenkins	31	Hanover	July 28, 1862	Promoted from Capt., Co. C, January 1, 1863. Mustered out with Regiment on May 21, 1863.
Adjutants				
Henry Clay Marshall	24	Newville	August 6, 1862	Promoted from 2LT, Co. E, August 17, 1862. Discharged on Surgeon's Certificate January 7, 1863.
John S. Low	26	Carlisle	July 26, 1862	Promoted from 2LT, Co. G, August 9, 1862. Promoted to Cpt. Co. G on January 18, 1863 vice Lyne.
John Hays	25	Carlisle	August 5, 1862	Promoted from 1LT, Co. A, February 18, 1863. Wounded at Chancellorsville on May 3, 1863. Mustered out with regiment on May 21, 1863.

Appendix E: Regimental Roster

Name	Age	Joined at	Date Joined	Remarks
Quartermaster				
John R. Turner	46	Carlisle	August 5, 1862	Promoted from 1LT, Co. A on August 17, 1862 to Regitment's Quartermaster Officer. Mustered out with regiment on May 21, 1863.
Surgeon				
John S. Ramsey	23	Washington	October 15, 1862	Promoted from Assistant Surgeon, 55th Regiment P.V. on October 15, 1862. Mustered out with regitment on May 21, 1863.
Assistant Surgeons				
Frederick L. Haupt	Ukn	Harrisburg	August 19, 1862	Discharged by Special Order 84 due to disability on February 20, 1863.
John H. Longenecker	42	Harrisburg	Sept. 12, 1862	Mustered out with regiment on May 21, 1863.
Peter Winter	33	Harrisburg	March 4, 1863	Mustered out with regiment on May 21, 1863.
Chaplains				
George W. Chalfant	Ukn	Harrisburg	October 7, 1862	Dismissed January 7, 1863 by Major General Sumner. Discharge changed to Honorable by S. O. 185, War Department on April 25, 1863.
George M. Slaysman	41	Harrisburg	February 11, 1863	Mustered out with regiment on May 21, 1863.
Sergeant Majors				
William G. Bosler	22	Cheltenham	August 6, 1862	Wounded at Fredericksburg on December 13, 1862. Promoted from Corporal, Co. C on August 17, 1862. Promoted to 2LT, Co. C on January 1, 1863. Mustered out with regiment on May 21, 1863.
William H. Eisenhart	24	York	August 4, 1862	Promoted from Sergeant, Co. K on January 1, 1863. Mustered out with regiment on May 21, 1863.
Quartermaster Officer				
John R. Turner	46	Harrisburg	July 30, 1862	Promoted from Company A on August 17, 1862.
Quartermaster Sergeant				
William F. Cutler	23	Carlisle	August 5, 1862	Promoted from 1st Sergeant, Co. A on August 17, 1862. Mustered out with regiment on May 21, 1863.
Commisary Sergeant				
Joseph C. Halbert	28	Carlisle	July 25, 1863	Promoted from Sergeant, Co. A on January 1, 1863. Mustered out with regiment on May 21, 1863.

Name	Age	Joined at	Date Joined	Remarks
Hospital Steward				
John G. Barr	32	Newville	August 6, 1862	Promoted from Sergeant, Co. E on December 1, 1862. Mustered out with regiment on May 21, 1863.

COMPANY A - Recruited in Carlisle

Name	Age	Joined at	Date Joined	Remarks
Captain				
William M. Porter	30	Harrisburg	July 30, 1862	Mustered out with Company on May 21, 1863.
First Lieutenants				
John R. Turner	46	Harrisburg	July 30, 1862	Promoted to Regimental Quartermaster Officer on August 17, 1862.
John Hays	25	Harrisburg	July 30, 1862	Promoted from 2LT on August 17, 1862; to Adjutant on February 18, 1863.
George Thayer	42	Carlisle	August 5, 1862	Promoted from Sergeant to 1st Sergeant on August 17, 1862; to 1LT on February 18, 1863. Mustered out with Company on May 21, 1863.
Second Lieutenant				
John O. Halbert	24	Carlisle	August 5, 1862	Promoted from Sergeant on December 28, 1862. Mustered out with Company on May 21, 1863.
First Sergeants				
Alphonso B. Beisel	26	Carlisle	August 5, 1862	Promoted to Corporal to Sergeant on August 17, 1862; to 1st Sergeant on March 1, 1863. Mustered out with Company on May 21, 1863.
William F. Cutler	23	Carlisle	August 5, 1862	Promoted to Regimental Quartermaster Sergeant on August 18, 1862.
Sergeants				
James Underwood	38	Carlisle	August 5, 1862	Mustered out with Company on May 21, 1863.
William Vance	37	Carlisle	August 5, 1862	Promoted from Corporal on August 17, 1862. Mustered out with Company on May 21, 1863.
Abram L. Line	21	Carlisle	August 5, 1862	Promoted from Corporal on March 1, 1863. Mustered out with Company on May 21, 1863.

Appendix E: Regimental Roster 213

Name	Age	Joined at	Date Joined	Remarks
Samuel Wetzel	24	Carlisle	August 5, 1862	Promoted to Corporal on September 17, 1862; to Sergeant on March 1, 1863. Mustered out with Company on May 21, 1863.
Charles A. Smith	30	Carlisle	August 5, 1862	Promoted to Corporal on September 17, 1862. Wounded at Antietam, Maryland on September 17, 1862. Discharged on Surgeon's Certificate on February 16, 1863.
Corporals				
Lewis Masonheimer	21	Carlisle	August 5, 1862	Promoted to Corporal on September 17, 1862. Mustered out with Company on May 21, 1863.
William W. Neely	22	Carlisle	August 5, 1862	Promoted to Corporal on September 17, 1862. Mustered out with Company on May 21, 1863.
Charles D. Hall	30	Carlisle	August 5, 1862	Promoted to Corporal on September 17, 1862. Mustered out with Company on May 21, 1863.
Patrick Madden	27	Carlisle	August 5, 1862	Promoted to Corporal on September 17, 1862. Mustered out with Company on May 21, 1863.
Charles A. Aughinsbaugh	21	Carlisle	August 5, 1862	Promoted to Corporal on January 1, 1863. Mustered out with Company on May 21, 1863.
Walter M. Allison	20	Carlisle	August 5, 1862	Promoted to Corporal on January 1, 1863. Mustered out with Company on May 21, 1863.
Courtney H. Early	16	Carlisle	August 5, 1862	Promoted to Corporal on January 1, 1863. Mustered out with Company on May 21, 1863.
Robert J. McPherson	20	Carlisle	August 5, 1862	Promoted to Corporal on January 1, 1863. Mustered out with Company on May 21, 1863.
Musicians				
Henry Hipple	20	Carlisle	August 5, 1862	Mustered out with Company on May 21, 1863.
David Laughlin	34	Carlisle	August 5, 1862	Mustered out with Company on May 21, 1863.
Privates				
Askin, Robert Y.	23	Carlisle	August 5, 1862	Mustered out with Company on May 21, 1863.
Baker, William	22	Carlisle	August 5, 1862	Mustered out with Company on May 21, 1863.
Boas, Davis K.	18	Carlisle	August 5, 1862	Mustered out with Company on May 21, 1863.

Name	Age	Joined at	Date Joined	Remarks
Blain, Zachariah F.	18	Carlisle	August 5, 1862	Mustered out with Company on May 21, 1863.
Bouholtzer, Peter C.	27	Carlisle	August 5, 1862	Mustered out with Company on May 21, 1863.
Bowers, George W.	19	Carlisle	August 5, 1862	Mustered out with Company on May 21, 1863.
Brownewell, A. P.	18	Carlisle	August 5, 1862	Died on September 18 of wounds received at Antietam, Maryland on September 17, 1862.
Cocklin, Samuel F.	18	Carlisle	August 5, 1862	Mustered out with Company on May 21, 1863.
Comfort, Henry D.	21	Carlisle	August 5, 1862	Mustered out with Company on May 21, 1863.
Cornman, William O.	21	Carlisle	August 5, 1862	Wounded at Fredericksburg, Virginia on December 13, 1862. Mustered out with Company on May 21, 1863.
Cornman, William H.	23	Carlisle	August 5, 1862	Discharged on Surgeon's Certificate on December 4, 1862.
Cornman, Leander C.	24	Carlisle	August 5, 1862	Discharged on February 10, 1863 for wounds received at Antietam, Maryland on September 17, 1862.
Crabby, Henry A.	21	Carlisle	August 5, 1862	Deserted on September 19, 1862. Sent to the rear sick and never returned for duty.
Dubesey, Joseph	39	Carlisle	August 5, 1862	Deserted on September 28, 1862.
Eckels, Davidson H	20	Carlisle	August 5, 1862	Mustered out with Company on May 21, 1863.
Eitelbush, Peter F.	20	Carlisle	August 5, 1862	Wounded at Antietam, Maryland on September 17, 1862. Absent, in hospital, at muster out.
Evans, George	18	Carlisle	August 5, 1862	Mustered out with Company on May 21, 1863.
Evans, Johnson	20	Carlisle	August 5, 1862	Mustered out with Company on May 21, 1863.
Fiester, William	21	Carlisle	August 5, 1862	Wounded at Fredericksburg, Virginia on December 13, 1862. Mustered out with Company on May 21, 1863.
Fought, William E.	20	Carlisle	August 5, 1862	Discharged on Surgeon's Certificate on December 4, 1862.
Fagan, Alexander H.	30	Carlisle	August 5, 1862	Discharged on Surgeon's Certificate on December 5, 1862.
Faust, Ambrose J.	33	Carlisle	August 5, 1862	Discharged on Surgeon's Certificate on December 26, 1862.

Appendix E: Regimental Roster

Name	Age	Joined at	Date Joined	Remarks
Feuicle, William	21	Carlisle	August 5, 1862	Wounded at Antietam, Maryland on September 17, 1862. Discharged on Surgeon's Certificate on Fenruary 9, 1863.
Forber, Phillip	31	Carlisle	August 5, 1862	Killed at Fredericksburg, Virginia on December 13, 1862.
Green, George W.	19	Carlisle	August 5, 1862	Mustered out with Company on May 21, 1863.
Gould, Edward B.	20	Carlisle	August 5, 1862	Discharged on Surgeon's Certificate on December 5, 1862.
Gutshall, Francis A.	18	Carlisle	August 5, 1862	Discharged on Surgeon's Certificate on February 17, 1863.
Glass, Peter K.	43	Carlisle	August 5, 1862	Discharged on Surgeon's Certificate on March 27, 1863.
Greason, William H.	21	Carlisle	August 5, 1862	Died on September 18 of wounds received in action at Antietam, Maryland on September 17, 1862.
Heagy, William H.	19	Carlisle	August 5, 1862	Wounded at Fredericksburg, Virginia on December 13, 1862. Mustered out with Company on May 21, 1863.
Hunerich, William A.	22	Carlisle	August 5, 1862	Wounded at Antietam, Maryland on September 17, 1862. Absent, in hospital, at muster out.
Huyett, Daniel K.	18	Carlisle	August 5, 1862	Wounded at Antietam, Maryland on September 17, 1862. Discharged on Surgeon's Certificate on Fenruary 1, 1863.
Hackett, James	45	Carlisle	August 5, 1862	Discharged on Surgeon's Certificate on March 31, 1863.
Irvine, Samuel J.	22	Carlisle	August 5, 1862	Sent to hospital sick on September 23, 1862. Detailed from Camp Curtin as Clerk by Captain Lane on October 17, 1862. Absent, in hospital. War Department advised he was discharged with Company on May 21, 1863.
Jones, James	21	Carlisle	August 5, 1862	Mustered out with Company on May 21, 1863.
Kerr, James A.	23	Carlisle	August 5, 1862	Mustered out with Company on May 21, 1863.
Kerr, Andrew	21	Carlisle	August 5, 1862	Prisoner from November 18, 1862 to January 1, 1863. Mustered out with Company on May 21, 1863.
Kutz, Emanuel C.	21	Carlisle	August 5, 1862	Wounded at Antietam, Maryland on September 17, 1862. Absent, in hospital, at muster out.

Name	Age	Joined at	Date Joined	Remarks
Keeney, Daniel B	24	Carlisle	August 5, 1862	September 17, 1862. Discharged on Surgeon's Certificate on February 4, 1863.
Leas, Ephraim C	18	Carlisle	August 11, 1862	Mustered out with Company on May 21, 1863.
Loudon, Duffield	29	Carlisle	August 5, 1862	Mustered out with Company on May 21, 1863.
Lynch, John D.	18	Carlisle	August 5, 1862	Mustered out with Company on May 21, 1863.
Lynch, William P.	23	Carlisle	August 5, 1862	Deserted, wounded at Antietam on September 17, 1862. Sent to Hospital and never returned. Discharged on Surgeon's Certificate on February 14, 1863.
Lyne, George W.	Unk	Unk	August 5, 1862	Wounded at Antietam, Maryland on September 17, 1862. Absent, at muster out.
Matlack, Joseph R.	35	Carlisle	August 5, 1862	Mustered out with Company on May 21, 1863.
Marsh, William H.	25	Carlisle	August 5, 1862	Mustered out with Company on May 21, 1863.
Mell, George W.	24	Carlisle	August 5, 1862	Mustered out with Company on May 21, 1863.
Mitchell, Edward A.	19	Carlisle	August 5, 1862	Mustered out with Company on May 21, 1863.
Morrison, Winfried S.	18	Carlisle	August 5, 1862	Mustered out with Company on May 21, 1863.
Moore, Joseph P.	18	Carlisle	August 5, 1862	Mustered out with Company on May 21, 1863.
Moore, Thomas W.	24	Carlisle	August 5, 1862	Discharged on Surgeon's Certificate on October 23, 1863.
Meartin, James	28	Carlisle	August 5, 1862	Discharged on February 15, 1863.
McQuate, Peter	21	Carlisle	August 5, 1862	Mustered out with Company on May 21, 1863.
McKibbin, William L.	20	Carlisle	August 5, 1862	Mustered out with Company on May 21, 1863.
Powley, Samuel A.	37	Carlisle	August 5, 1862	Mustered out with Company on May 21, 1863.
Pannebacker, Samuel B.	28	Carlisle	August 5, 1862	Discharged on Surgeon's Certificate on December 29, 1862.
Powley, William B.	25	Carlisle	August 5, 1862	Deserted from Bolivan Heights on September 27, 1862.
Rickanbaugh, Henry	24	Carlisle	August 5, 1862	Mustered out with Company on May 21, 1863.

Appendix E: Regimental Roster 217

Name	Age	Joined at	Date Joined	Remarks
Richey, William	48	Carlisle	August 5, 1862	Discharged on Surgeon's Certificate on April 8, 1863.
Smith, John B.	22	Carlisle	August 5, 1862	Mustered out with Company on May 21, 1863.
Smith, William H.	22	Carlisle	August 5, 1862	Mustered out with Company on May 21, 1863.
Sperow, William	19	Carlisle	August 5, 1862	Mustered out with Company on May 21, 1863.
Steiner, William D.	28	Carlisle	August 5, 1862	Wounded at Antietam, Maryland on September 17, 1862. Absent, in hospital, at muster out.
Stoey, Washington L.	20	Carlisle	August 5, 1862	Wounded at Antietam, Maryland on September 17, 1862 and at Chancellorsville, Virginia on May 1, 1863. Absent, in hospital, at muster out.
Smith, George S.	28	Carlisle	August 5, 1862	Discharged on Surgeon's Certificate on November 13, 1862.
Smith, Theodore U.	25	Carlisle	August 5, 1862	Discharged on Surgeon's Certificate on December 24, 1862.
Stoey, John R.	33	Carlisle	August 5, 1862	Discharged on Surgeon's Certificate on December 24, 1862.
Spangler, Benjamin K.	35	Carlisle	August 5, 1862	Discharged on Surgeon's Certificate on December 6, 1862.
Smith, James A.	19	Carlisle	August 5, 1862	Discharged on Surgeon's Certificate on December 10, 1862.
Stout, Charles	21	Carlisle	August 5, 1862	September 20, 1862 sent to hospital, never returned. Absent at muster out.
Washmoud, Andrew	18	Carlisle	August 5, 1862	Mustered out with Company on May 21, 1863.
Wetzel. Andrew	17	Carlisle	August 5, 1862	Mustered out with Company on May 21, 1863.
Weaver, Joseph	21	Carlisle	August 5, 1862	Died on September 18 of wounds received at Antietam, Maryland on September 17, 1862.
Zeigler, John H.	20	Carlisle	August 5, 1862	Discharged on Surgeon's Certificate on March 23, 1863.

COMPANY B - Recruited in York

Name	Age	Joined at	Date Joined	Remarks
Captain				
Hamilton A. Glessner	42	Harrisburg	July 29, 1862	Mustered out with Company on May 21, 1863.

Name	Age	Joined at	Date Joined	Remarks
First Lieutenant				
William H. Tomes	24	Harrisburg	July 29, 1862	Wounded at Antietam, Maryland on September 17, 1862. Mustered out with Company on May 21, 1863.
Second Lieutenant				
Henry Reisinger	26	Harrisburg	August 9, 1862	Wounded at Antietam, Maryland on September 17, 1862. Mustered out with Company on May 21, 1863.
First Sergeant				
George K. Shenberger	21	York	August 10, 1862	Promoted from Private on January 1, 1863. Wounded at Chancellorsville, Virginia on May 3, 1863. Mustered out with Company on May 21, 1863.
Sergeants				
Henry R. Weaver	21	York	July 21, 1862	Mustered out with Company on May 21, 1863.
Henry Oaks	29	York	August 6, 1862	Mustered out with Company on May 21, 1863.
Augustus Flury	23	York	August 6, 1862	Promoted from Corporal on January 1, 1863. Mustered out with Company on May 21, 1863.
Charles Harkins	22	York	August 7, 1862	Promoted from Private on January 1, 1863. Mustered out with Company on May 21, 1863.
Charles Shetter	22	York	August 6, 1862	Killed at Antietam, Maryland on September 17, 1862. Buried in Prospect Hill Cemetery in York, Pennsylvania
Charles Austin	29	York	July 25, 1862	Wounded at Antietam, Maryland on September 17, 1862. Discharged on Surgeon's Certificate on February 11, 1863.
Corporals				
Levi H. Rankin	26	York	August 6, 1862	Mustered out with Company on May 21, 1863.
Jonathan Shenberger	22	York	August 6, 1862	Mustered out with Company on May 21, 1863.
John Sharp	25	York	August 8, 1862	Mustered out with Company on May 21, 1863.
Lyman Humes	22	York	August 7, 1862	Promoted to Corporal on January 1, 1863. Mustered out with Company on May 21, 1863.
Martin Bheuler	21	York	August 7, 1862	Promoted to Corporal on January 1, 1863. Mustered out with Company on May 21, 1863.

Appendix E: Regimental Roster

Name	Age	Joined at	Date Joined	Remarks
John H. Keller	23	York	August 6, 1862	Discharged on Surgeon's Certificate due to disability on November 13, 1863.
Henry Kidd	20	York	August 7, 1862	Discharged on Surgeon's Certificate on January 10, 1863.
Musicians				
Charles Watson	24	York	July 29, 1862	Mustered out with Company on May 21, 1863.
Frederick Snyder	17	York	July 25, 1862	Discharged on Surgeon's Certificate due to disability on January 10, 1863.
Privates				
Altland, George	19	York	August 7, 1862	Mustered out with Company on May 21, 1863.
Berlin, Geroge A.	24	York	July 23, 1862	Mustered out with Company on May 21, 1863.
Bisker, John H.	21	York	August 7, 1862	Mustered out with Company on May 21, 1863.
Bitner, Jacob	22	York	August 9, 1862	Mustered out with Company on May 21, 1863.
Butt, William P.	23	York	August 4, 1862	Wounded at Antietam, Maryland on September 17, 1862. Discharged on Surgeon's Certificate on December 22, 1862.
Berger, Samuel	18	York	August 8, 1862	Wounded at Antietam, Maryland on September 17, 1862. Discharged on Surgeon's Certificate on November 22, 1862.
Blum, Mathias	31	York	August 8, 1862	Discharged on Surgeon's Certificate on February 26, 1863.
Coble, Jacob	23	York	July 23, 1862	Mustered out with Company on May 21, 1863.
Coble, Jesse	24	York	July 31, 1862	Mustered out with Company on May 21, 1863.
Danner, Van Buren	25	York	July 7, 1862	Discharged on Surgeon's Certificate on February 27, 1863.
Flury, William A.	23	York	July 6, 1862	Mustered out with Company on May 21, 1863.
Fitzkee, Adam	21	York	July 6, 1862	Mustered out with Company on May 21, 1863.
Freet, Oliver	21	York	August 10, 1862	Mustered out with Company on May 21, 1863.
Fitzkee, Adam G.	21	York	August 7, 1862	Discharged on Surgeon's Certificate on November 8, 1862.

Name	Age	Joined at	Date Joined	Remarks
Flinn, George	24	York	July 28, 1862	Wounded at Antietam, Maryland on September 17, 1862. Discharged on Surgeon's Certificate on November 29, 1862.
Flury, Joshua	25	York	August 8, 1862	Deserted on October 31, 1862.
Franklin, George K.	24	York	July 31, 1862	In confinement at Georgetown, DC on October 31, 1862. Deserted on September 17, 1862.
Gohn, Franklin R.	23	York	July 6, 1862	Wounded at Chancellorsville, Virginia on May 3, 1863. Mustered out with Company on May 21, 1863.
Grim, George	21	York	July 6, 1862	Mustered out with Company on May 21, 1863.
Grace, Alonzo	22	York	July 6, 1862	Mustered out with Company on May 21, 1863.
Grouver, Josiah	25	York	July 7, 1862	Mustered out with Company on May 21, 1863.
Gardner, John Y.	23	York	July 7, 1862	Mustered out with Company on May 21, 1863.
Hibner, Henry	23	York	July 22, 1862	Mustered out with Company on May 21, 1863.
Hammer, Henry A.	21	York	August 8, 1862	Mustered out with Company on May 21, 1863.
Hyde, William A.	24	York	August 9, 1862	Mustered out with Company on May 21, 1863.
Heppenstall, Emanuel	22	York	August 9, 1862	Mustered out with Company on May 21, 1863.
Herr, Barton	32	York	August 9, 1862	Mustered out with Company on May 21, 1863.
Hosler, Daniel	23	York	July 7, 1862	Killed at Antietam, Maryland on September 17, 1862.
Harkey, John	25	York	July 19, 1862	Discharged on Surgeon's Certificate due to disability on February 6, 1862.
Hoover, Samuel	21	York	August 8, 1862	Discharged on Surgeon's Certificate due to disability on March 18, 1862.
Hoops, Hiram	32	York	August 6, 1862	Deserted on October 8, 1862.
Hopson, Joseph	22	York	August 5, 1862	Deserted on September 18, 1862.
Hostler, Daniel	24	York	August 7, 1862	Killed at Antietam, Maryland on September 17, 1862.
Jacobs, Barton	22	York	August 9, 1862	Mustered out with Company on May 21, 1863.

Appendix E: Regimental Roster 221

Name	Age	Joined at	Date Joined	Remarks
Jack, Andrew B.	21	York	August 7, 1862	Mustered out with Company on May 21, 1863.
Kendig, Henry	32	York	July 22, 1862	Mustered out with Company on May 21, 1863.
Krall, George B.	21	York	August 8, 1862	Mustered out with Company on May 21, 1863.
Krall, Joseph	27	York	August 9, 1862	Mustered out with Company on May 21, 1863.
Kahr, Jacob	27	York	August 7, 1862	Mustered out with Company on May 21, 1863.
Keinard, John	22	York	August 7, 1862	Wounded at Antietam, Maryland in September 17, 1862. Mustered out with Company on May 21, 1863.
Loncks, Samuel	25	York	August 7, 1862	Wounded at Fredricksburg, Virginia on December 13, 1862. Mustered out with Company on May 21, 1863.
Lowkart, Abraham C.	21	York	August 6, 1862	Mustered out with Company on May 21, 1863.
Lentz, Peter R.	22	York	August 6, 1862	Mustered out with Company on May 21, 1863.
Leibhert, Henry	22	York	August 7, 1862	Mustered out with Company on May 21, 1863.
Lentz, Andrew	44	York	July 21, 1862	Killed at Antietam, Maryland on September 17, 1862.
Leber, Jacob G.	24	York	August 10, 1862	Discharged on Surgeon's Certificate on November 15, 1862.
Leinhart, Samuel	25	York	August 7, 1862	Wounded at Antietam, Maryland on September 17, 1862. Discharged on Surgeon's Certificate on February 11, 1863.
Miller, Leander F.	28	York	August 8, 1862	Mustered out with Company on May 21, 1863.
Moore, Alfred	22	York	July 28, 1862	Deserted on August 18, 1862. Apprehended August 4, 1864. Court martialed on December 30, 1864 and sentenced to serve nine months without pay.
Moul, Daniel	21	York	August 9, 1862	Died at Falmouth, Virginia on December 17, 1862.
Neff, Aaron	21	York	August 7, 1862	Mustered out with Company on May 21, 1863.
Ness, Noah	21	York	August 7, 1862	Discharged on Surgeon's Certificate on January 10, 1863.
Otstop, Henry	28	York	July 28, 1862	Mustered out with Company on May 21, 1863.

Name	Age	Joined at	Date Joined	Remarks
Owens, William	42	York	August 6, 1862	Discharged on Surgeon's Certificate on February 5, 1863.
Phillips, Witman A.	21	York	August 8, 1862	Absent, in arrest, at muster out.
Pluffer, Christian	25	York	July 25, 1862	Absent, sick at hospital, at muster out.
Petry, John	22	York	August 7, 1862	Deserted on October 3, 1862.
Petry, William	21	York	August 7, 1862	Deserted on October 3, 1862. Returned on April 20, 1863. Mustered out with Company on May 21, 1863.
Ropp, Edward C.	21	York	August 7, 1862	Mustered out with Company on May 21, 1863.
Synder, John	21	York	July 22, 1862	Mustered out with Company on May 21, 1863.
St. Clair, Charles	21	York	August 7, 1862	Mustered out with Company on May 21, 1863.
Stavner, Henry	24	York	August 7, 1862	Mustered out with Company on May 21, 1863.
Steward, Michael	18	York	August 8, 1862	Captured at U.S Ford. Virginia. Mustered out with Company on May 21, 1863.
Sheetz, William	23	York	July 23, 1862	Mustered out with Company on May 21, 1863.
Smith, Henry C.	21	York	July 25, 1862	Mustered out with Company on May 21, 1863.
Shutter, Jacob	21	York	August 8, 1862	Killed at Antietam, Maryland on September 17, 1862.
Sutton, Washington	20	York	August 8, 1862	Discharged on Surgeon's Certificate on August 28, 1862.
Strike, Eli	22	York	August 6, 1862	Discharged on Surgeon's Certificate on February 10, 1863.
Soulia, John	44	York	August 8, 1862	Discharged on Surgeon's Certificate on February 10, 1863.
Sleegar, Frederick	21	York	August 8, 1862	Discharged on Surgeon's Certificate on February 5, 1863.
Spyker, Franklin	24	York	August 6, 1862	Deserted on September 1, 1862.
Troup, Cornelius	21	York	July 28, 1862	Mustered out with Company on May 21, 1863.
Troup, David	21	York	July 21, 1862	Deserted on November 23, 1862. Returned on April 20, 1863. Mustered out with Company on May 21, 1863. Change of desertion removed on March 10, 1890.

Appendix E: Regimental Roster 223

Name	Age	Joined at	Date Joined	Remarks
Toben, Thomas	30	York	July 25, 1862	Killed at Antietam, Maryland on September 17, 1862.
Tray, John	21	York	July 25, 1862	Killed at Antietam, Maryland on September 17, 1862.
Upp, John K.	22	York	August 7, 1862	Mustered out with Company on May 21, 1863.
Wertz, Phillip	26	York	August 6, 1862	Mustered out with Company on May 21, 1863.
Whitcomb, Joseph	18	York	August 7, 1862	Mustered out with Company on May 21, 1863.
Wilson, Thomas	19	York	August 10, 1862	Mustered out with Company on May 21, 1863.
Wilson, Thomas J.	23	York	August 10, 1862	Mustered out with Company on May 21, 1863. Charged with desertion, dropped on March. 10, 1890.
Woodmansee, Howard	29	York	August 8, 1862	Mustered out with Company on May 21, 1863.
Zeigler, Henry	19	York	August 6, 1862	Killed at Antietam, Maryland on September 17, 1862.

COMPANY C - Recruited in York

Name	Age	Joined at	Date Joined	Remarks
Captains				
Joesph S. Jenkins	30	Hanover	July 19, 1862	Wounded at Antietam, Maryland on September 17, 1862. Promoted to Major on December 13, 1862. Killed at Petersburg.
Thomas B. Griffin	25	Hanover	July 19, 1862	Promoted from First Lieutenant on January 1, 1863. Mustered out with Company on May 21, 1863.
Fisrt Lieutenant				
Benjamen. R. Myers	30	Cheltenham	August 6, 1862	Promoted to Second Lieutenant on January 1, 1863. Mustered out with Company on May 21, 1863.
Second Lieutenant				
William G. Bosler	22	Cheltenham	August 6, 1862	Promoted from Sergeant Major on January 1, 1862. Mustered out with Company on May 21, 1863.
First Sergeant				
Clinton Keister	22	Hanover	August 6, 1862	Mustered out with Company on May 21, 1863.

Name	Age	Joined at	Date Joined	Remarks
Sergeants				
John S. Forrest	27	Hanover	August 3, 1862	Mustered out with Company on May 21, 1863.
Charles Fiscus	37	Hanover	August 3, 1862	Mustered out with Company on May 21, 1863.
Adam Reiling	28	Hanover	July 31, 1862	Mustered out with Company on May 21, 1863.
Joseph W. Klinefelter	23	Hanover	August 6, 1862	Mustered out with Company on May 21, 1863.
Corporals				
Alfred D. Kohler	18	Hanover	August 9, 1862	Mustered out with Company on May 21, 1863.
Benjamin F. Dean	25	Cheltenham	August 6, 1862	Mustered out with Company on May 21, 1863.
Henry John Koutz	21	Hanover	August 6, 1862	Wounded at Antietam, Maryland, on September 17, 1862. Died of disease at Lincoln General Hospital, Washington, DC, May 8, 1863.
Levi Rinely	21	Hanover	August 7, 1862	Mustered out with Company on May 21, 1863.
Franklin J. McClair	21	Hanover	July 31, 1862	Promoted to Corporal on January 1, 1863. Mustered out with Company on May 21, 1863.
William H. Griffith	18	Hanover	August 6, 1862	Promoted to Corporal on March 1, 1863. Mustered out with Company on May 21, 1863.
Henry Wagner	18	Hanover	August 6, 1862	Promoted to Corporal on March 1, 1863. Mustered out with Company on May 21, 1863.
Wesley Taylor	42	Hanover	August 9, 1862	Discharged by Special Order on May 9, 1863.
William Metzgar	33	Hanover	August 6, 1862	Discharged by Special Order on January 20, 1863.
Christian H. Shuster	40	Hanover	August 6, 1862	Died on September 27, 1862 of wounds received on September 17, 1862.
Wagoneer				
Leapson, John A.	80	Cheltenham	August 6, 1862	Killed at Antietem, Maryland on September 14, 1862.
Musicians				
David A. Miller	19	Hanover	August 6, 1862	Mustered out with Company on May 21, 1863.
George W. Stahl	21	Hanover	August 7, 1862	Mustered out with Company on May 21, 1863.

Appendix E: Regimental Roster

Name	Age	Joined at	Date Joined	Remarks
Privates				
Aubel, George	26	Hanover	August 6, 1862	Mustered out with Company on May 21, 1863.
Ayres, Franklin	22	Cheltenham	August 6, 1862	Left sick at Harper's Ferry. Absent, sick, at muster out.
Austine, Jacob	19	Hanover	August 6, 1862	Mustered out with Company on May 21, 1863.
Brubaker, Lyman	21	Hanover	August 6, 1862	Wounded and missing in action at Fredricksburg, Virginia on December 13, 1862.
Bell, George E.	19	Hanover	August 6, 1862	Mustered out with Company on May 21, 1863.
Brubaker, Milton K.	21	Hanover	August 6, 1862	Mustered out with Company on May 21, 1863.
Boll, Samuel	21	Hanover	August 9, 1862	Mustered out with Company on May 21, 1863.
Berger, Henry C.	18	Hanover	August 8, 1862	Mustered out with Company on May 21, 1863.
Childs, John L.	23	Cheltenham	August 6, 1862	Sick in hospital at West Philadelphia. Desertion charge dropped.
Childs, Alfred	21	Cheltenham	August 6, 1862	Mustered out with Company on May 21, 1863.
Conway, Charles H.	19	Hanover	August 6, 1862	Mustered out with Company on May 21, 1863.
Caskey, William B.	21	Cheltenham	August 6, 1862	Mustered out with Company on May 21, 1863.
Coble, Henry	21	Hanover	August 7, 1862	Discharged by Special Order on February 11, 1863.
Day, Josiah D.	44	Cheltenham	August 6, 1862	Mustered out with Company on May 21, 1863.
Day, Henry C.	18	Cheltenham	August 6, 1862	Mustered out with Company on May 21, 1863.
Dinwiddie, John J.	30	Hanover	August 6, 1862	Mustered out with Company on May 21, 1863.
Edie, John R.	23	Hanover	August 6, 1862	Captured. Absent at Camp Parole, Annapolis, Maryland at muster out.
Eaton, Thomas	26	Hanover	August 6, 1862	Killed at Antietam, Maryland on September 17, 1862.
Folk, George	32	Hanover	July 29, 1862	Mustered out with Company on May 21, 1863.
Fortenbach, Martin	21	Hanover	August 7, 1862	Mustered out with Company on May 21, 1863.
Friscan, Michael	20	Hanover	July 21, 1862	Absent. Sick at muster out. Sent to Division Hopsital on March 30, 1863.

Name	Age	Joined at	Date Joined	Remarks
Gable, James H.	19	Hanover	August 10, 1862	Mustered out with Company on May 21, 1863.
Gibbs, Joseph S.	18	Hanover	August 6, 1862	Mustered out with Company on May 21, 1863.
Gibbs, William A.	19	Hanover	August 6, 1862	Discharged by Special Order on January 24, 1863.
Grey, John	19	Hanover	July 30, 1862	Deserted from Camp Curtin on August 20, 1862.
Haley, Thomas	21	Hanover	August 6, 1862	Mustered out with Company on May 21, 1863.
Hamm, Henry	21	Hanover	August 9, 1862	Mustered out with Company on May 21, 1863.
Heiss, George W.	21	Hanover	August 9, 1862	Mustered out with Company on May 21, 1863.
Hamilton, John	23	Cheltenham	August 6, 1862	Died near Falmouth, Virginia on December 28, 1862.
Henry, Thomas	25	Hanover	July 30, 1862	Deserted from Camp Curtin on August 20, 1862.
Iliff, William	40	Cheltenham	August 6, 1862	Mustered out with Company on May 21, 1863.
Jennings, Henry	21	Hanover	August 7, 1862	Mustered out with Company on May 21, 1863.
Jontz, Joseph	18	Hanover	August 6, 1862	Discharged by Special Order on March 19, 1863.
Kane, John	21	Cheltenham	August 6, 1862	Mustered out with Company on May 21, 1863.
Keister, Calvin	19	Hanover	August 6, 1862	Mustered out with Company on May 21, 1863.
Kohler, Henry	21	Hanover	August 9, 1862	Mustered out with Company on May 21, 1863.
Leapson, James M.	23	Cheltenham	August 6, 1862	Mustered out with Company on May 21, 1863.
Lefevre, Jacob	20	Hanover	August 6, 1862	Mustered out with Company on May 21, 1863.
Leschy, Lewis C.	18	Hanover	August 1, 1862	Discharged by Special Order on January 14, 1863.
Miller, Charles H.	27	Harrisburg	August 9, 1863	Mustered out with Company on May 21, 1863.
Myers, William R.	20	Cheltenham	August 6, 1862	Mustered out with Company on May 21, 1863.
Miller, Louis	19	Cheltenham	July 30, 1862	Mustered out with Company on May 21, 1863.
Myers, Adam	22	Cheltenham	August 6, 1862	Died of wounds received at Antietam, Maryland on September 17, 1862.

Appendix E: Regimental Roster

Name	Age	Joined at	Date Joined	Remarks
Mitzell, Andrew	27	Hanover	August 7, 1862	Died of disease at Belle Plain, Virginia on December 3, 1862.
Miller, Bloomfield	24	Cheltenham	August 6, 1862	Died on December 2 of wounds received at Antietam, Maryland on September 17, 1862.
Miller, Isaiah	24	Hanover	August 7, 1863	Killed at Antietam, Maryland on September 17, 1862.
Miller, Harman R.	18	Hanover	August 6, 1863	Killed at Antietam, Maryland on September 17, 1862.
Morris, William	24	Hanover	July 30, 1862	Deserted on September 12, 1862 while on march through Maryland.
Numbers, Thomas	18	Hanover	August 11, 1862	Discharged on March 30, 1863 for wounds with loss of arm received at Antietam, Maryland on September 17, 1862.
Phaff, Lewis	44	Hanover	August 7, 1862	Discharged on Surgeon's Certificate on March 9, 1863.
Rutter, Issac	28	Hanover	July 29, 1862	Mustered out with Company on May 21, 1863.
Rapp, John	28	Hanover	August 6, 1862	Discharged by Special Order, March 14, 1863.
Ruhl, Noah	19	Hanover	August 6, 1863	Died near Falmouth, Virginia on March 3, 1862.
Seitz, William N.	19	Hanover	August 6, 1862	Mustered out with Company on May 21, 1863.
Shenberger, Michael	25	Hanover	August 6, 1862	Mustered out with Company on May 21, 1863.
Seifert, William H.	23	Hanover	August 1, 1862	Mustered out with Company on May 21, 1863.
Sweitzer, Emanuel	22	Hanover	August 4, 1862	Mustered out with Company on May 21, 1863.
Sadler, John C.	23	Hanover	August 6, 1862	Mustered out with Company on May 21, 1863.
Stegner, Peter	22	Hanover	August 7, 1862	Mustered out with Company on May 21, 1863.
Smith, William J.	23	Hanover	August 7, 1862	Mustered out with Company on May 21, 1863.
Stanley, William	44	Hanover	August 7, 1862	Discharged by Special Order on March 5, 1863.
Smith, Daniel L.	18	Hanover	August 6, 1862	Discharged on Surgeon's Certificate on February 16, 1863.
Smith, John E.	25	Hanover	August 7, 1862	Discharged on Surgeon's Certificate on March 27, 1863.

Name	Age	Joined at	Date Joined	Remarks
Smith, William	40	Hanover	August 7, 1862	Discharged on Surgeon's Certificate on October 20, 1863.
Smith, Henry	29	Hanover	July 29, 1862	Deserted from Camp Curtin on August 19, 1862.
Tomilinson, Harvey	25	Cheltenham	August 6, 1862	Mustered out with Company on May 21, 1863.
Trim, William	19	Hanover	July 29, 1862	Mustered out with Company on May 21, 1863.
Tomilinson, Benjamin	19	Cheltenham	August 6, 1862	Killed at Antietam, Maryland on September 17, 1862.
Toll, James	39	Hanover	July 29, 1862	Deserted from Camp Curtin on August 19, 1862.
Towson, Robert	18	Hanover	August 6, 1862	Deserted on September 16, 1862 while on march through Maryland.
Vanartsdalen, Harvey	25	Hanover	August 6, 1862	Died on September 20, 1862 of wounds received at Antietam, Maryland on September 17, 1862.
Watts, Lewis	35	Hanover	July 29, 1862	Mustered out with Company on May 21, 1863.
Wiley, Edward	21	Cheltenham	August 6, 1862	Mustered out with Company on May 21, 1863.
Wite, Albin K.	22	Hanover	August 6, 1862	Mustered out with Company on May 21, 1863.
Wentz, George E.	18	Hanover	August 6, 1862	Mustered out with Company on May 21, 1863.
Wagner, George	22	Harrisburg	August 8, 1862	Discharged by Special Order on May 1, 1863.
Waltemyer, Adam H.	24	Hanover	August 7, 1862	Died on January 20, 1863 of smallpox while on furlough from hospital.
Welsh, Michael	20	Hanover	July 31, 1862	Deserted from Camp Curtin, Pennsylvania on August 19, 1862.
Zeigler, William N.	18	Hanover	August 6, 1862	Mustered out with Company on May 21, 1863.

COMPANY D - Recruited in Shippensburg

Name	Age	Joined at	Date Joined	Remarks
Captain				
James Kelso	43	Shippensburg	August 4, 1862	Mustered out with Company on May 21, 1863.
First Lieutenant				
Samuel Patchell	24	Shippensburg	August 4, 1862	Mustered out with Company on May 21, 1863.

Appendix E: Regimental Roster

Name	Age	Joined at	Date Joined	Remarks
Second Lieutenant				
Daniel A. Harris	27	Shippensburg	August 4, 1862	Mustered out with Company on May 21, 1863.
First Sergeants				
Jacob Steinman	33	Shippensburg	August 4, 1862	Promoted from Sergeant on January 1, 1863. Mustered out with Company on May 21, 1863.
Issac Willis	28	Shippensburg	August 4, 1862	Discharged on Surgeon's Certificate on December 29, 1862.
Sergeants				
John A. Kenower	33	Shippensburg	August 4, 1862	Mustered out with Company on May 21, 1863.
John Hayes	21	Shippensburg	August 4, 1862	Promoted from Private on January 1, 1863. Mustered out with Company on May 21, 1863.
William H. H. Rebuck	20	Shippensburg	August 4, 1862	Promoted from Corporal on January 1, 1863. Mustered out wih Company on May 21, 1863.
John Witmer	25	Shippensburg	August 4, 1862	Promoted from Corporal on January 1, 1863. Mustered out wih Company on May 21, 1863.
Geroge Brenizer	26	Shippensburg	August 4, 1862	Died at Shippensburg, Pennsylvania on October 20, 1862.
Samuel Harris	18	Shippensburg	August 4, 1862	Mustered out with Company on May 21, 1863.
William H. McClure	19	Shippensburg	August 4, 1862	Promoted to Corporal on January 1, 1863. Mustered out with Company on May 21, 1863.
Robert Duke	21	Shippensburg	August 4, 1862	Mustered out with Company on May 21, 1863.
John C. Hays	21	Shippensburg	August 4, 1862	Promoted to Corporal on January 1, 1863. Mustered out with Company on May 21, 1863.
Esrem Landis	22	Shippensburg	August 4, 1862	Promoted to Corporal on January 1, 1863. Mustered out with Company on May 21, 1863.
John S. Stahly	32	Shippensburg	August 4, 1862	Promoted to Corporal on January 1, 1863. Mustered out with Company on May 21, 1863.
William H. Mathews	22	Shippensburg	August 4, 1862	Promoted to Corporal on January 1, 1863. Absent on detached service as clerk in Quartermaster Department at muster out.
James H. Taylor	19	Shippensburg	August 4, 1862	Promoted to Corporal on January 1, 1863. Mustered out with Company on May 21, 1863.

Name	Age	Joined at	Date Joined	Remarks
Samuel C. Boher	25	Shippensburg	August 4, 1862	Discharged on Surgeon's Certificate on February 28, 1863.
Samuel Croft	25	Shippensburg	August 4, 1862	Discharged on Surgeon's Certificate on February 13, 1863.
George McLean	21	Shippensburg	August 4, 1862	Died on December 23 of wounds received at Fredricksburg, Virginia on December 13, 1862.
Musicians				
William W. Synder	38	Shippensburg	August 4, 1862	Mustered out with Company on May 21, 1863.
Samuel Dubbs	22	Shippensburg	August 4, 1862	Mustered out with Company on May 21, 1863.
Wagoneer				
Michael O. Hubley	20	Shippensburg	August 4, 1862	Mustered out with Company on May 21, 1863.
Privates				
Arrison, John	18	Shippensburg	August 4, 1862	Mustered out with Company on May 21, 1863.
Anderson, William J.	22	Shippensburg	August 4, 1862	Mustered out with Company on May 21, 1863.
Brown, George W.	19	Shippensburg	August 4, 1862	Mustered out with Company on May 21, 1863.
Baker, Thomas	25	Shippensburg	August 4, 1862	Mustered out with Company on May 21, 1863.
Burdsall, Stephen	28	Shippensburg	August 4, 1862	Discharged at Philadelphia on Surgeon's Certificate on December 31, 1863.
Boher, David W.	23	Shippensburg	August 4, 1862	Discharged on Surgeon's Certificate on February 11, 1863.
Burns, George	44	Shippensburg	August 4, 1862	Discharged on Surgeon's Certificate on March 20, 1863.
Bowermaster, Sam	23	Shippensburg	August 4, 1862	Deserted from Antietam, Maryland on September 18, 1862.
Coover, Jeremiah	33	Shippensburg	August 4, 1862	Mustered out with Company on May 21, 1863.
Coover, Jacob	19	Shippensburg	August 4, 1862	Mustered out with Company on May 21, 1863.
Clough, Eli	38	Shippensburg	August 4, 1862	Discharged at Philadelphia on Surgeon's Certificate on January 10, 1863.
Carbaugh, Marion	21	Shippensburg	August 4, 1862	Died at Georgetown, DC of disease on November 19, 1862. Buried in Military Asylum Cemetery.
Carabaugh, Solomon	21	Shippensburg	August 4, 1862	Deserted from Antietam, Maryland on September 18, 1862.

Appendix E: Regimental Roster

Name	Age	Joined at	Date Joined	Remarks
Donelly, Thaddeus	24	Shippensburg	August 4, 1862	Mustered out with Company on May 21, 1863.
Dubbs, William H.	25	Shippensburg	August 4, 1862	Discharged at Germanton, Pennsylvania on Surgeon's Certificate on March 25, 1863.
Deihl, Elijah M.	19	Shippensburg	August 4, 1862	Killed at Antietam, Maryland on September 17, 1862.
Eckenrode, Joseph	38	Shippensburg	August 4, 1862	Wounded at Antietam, Maryland on September 17, 1862. Mustered out with Company on May 21, 1863.
Eshman, Lewis	30	Shippensburg	August 4, 1862	Mustered out with Company on May 21, 1863.
Elm, Jacob R.	21	Shippensburg	August 4, 1862	Mustered out with Company on May 21, 1863.
Eckenrode, William	32	Shippensburg	August 4, 1862	Discharged at Philadelphia, Pennsylvania on Surgeon's Certificate on February 19, 1863.
Foglesenger, George W.	28	Shippensburg	August 4, 1862	Mustered out with Company on May 21, 1863.
Fagam, George	21	Shippensburg	August 4, 1862	Mustered out with Company on May 21, 1863.
Forney, Henry	18	Shippensburg	August 4, 1862	Mustered out with Company on May 21, 1863.
Fornwalt, William	28	Shippensburg	August 4, 1862	Mustered out with Company on May 21, 1863.
Frantz, David	23	Shippensburg	August 4, 1862	Mustered out with Company on May 21, 1863.
Fry, Thomas	24	Shippensburg	August 4, 1862	Mustered out with Company on May 21, 1863.
Grabill, William B.	18	Shippensburg	August 4, 1862	Wounded at Antietam, Maryland on September 17, 1862. Mustered out with Company on May 21, 1863.
Gussman, John E.	19	Shippensburg	August 4, 1862	Mustered out with Company on May 21, 1863.
Gussman, George K.	21	Shippensburg	August 4, 1862	Discharged at Washington, DC on Surgeon's Certificate on June 4, 1863.
Gross, John	41	Shippensburg	August 4, 1862	Discharged at Germanton, Pennsylvania on Surgeon's Certificate on April 1, 1863.
Hoch, Peter	20	Shippensburg	August 4, 1862	Mustered out with Company on May 21, 1863.
Howard, Samuel	21	Shippensburg	August 4, 1862	Mustered out with Company on May 21, 1863.
Hatton, William M.	21	Shippensburg	August 4, 1862	Mustered out with Company on May 21, 1863.

Name	Age	Joined at	Date Joined	Remarks
Hannon, William M.	21	Shippensburg	August 4, 1862	Mustered out with Company on May 21, 1863.
Harr, Jacob	28	Shippensburg	August 4, 1862	Mustered out with Company on May 21, 1863.
Hartline, William R.	30	Shippensburg	August 4, 1862	Mustered out with Company on May 21, 1863.
Heller, Adam R.	18	Shippensburg	August 4, 1862	Mustered out with Company on May 21, 1863.
Inghram. Josiah	17	Shippensburg	August 4, 1862	Discharged at Falmouth, Virginia on Surgeon's Certificate on February 16, 1863.
Jones, William	21	Shippensburg	August 4, 1862	Mustered out with Company on May 21, 1863.
Johnston, John E.	21	Shippensburg	August 4, 1862	Discharged by Special Order pm December 15, 1862.
Lenher, Nicholas	23	Shippensburg	August 4, 1862	Killed at Antietam, Maryland on September 17, 1862.
Maredith, William M.	36	Shippensburg	August 4, 1862	Wounded at Antietam, Maryland on September 17, 1862. Mustered out with Company on May 21, 1863.
Martin, James A.	23	Shippensburg	August 4, 1862	Mustered out with Company on May 21, 1863.
Mackey, James L.	18	Shippensburg	August 4, 1862	Mustered out with Company on May 21, 1863.
Martin, Samuel B.	23	Shippensburg	August 4, 1862	Discharged at Portsmouth, Rhode Island on Surgeon's Certificate on May, 1863.
Miller, Harry	29	Shippensburg	August 4, 1862	Killed at Antietam, Maryland on September 17, 1862.
Mathews, Joseph A.	18	Shippensburg	August 4, 1862	Killed at Antietam, Maryland on September 17, 1862.
Martin, William J.	21	Shippensburg	August 4, 1862	Deserted from Antietam, Maryland on September 18, 1862.
McClay, John A.	18	Shippensburg	August 4, 1862	Discharged at Philadelphia, Pennsylvania on Surgeon's Certificate on January 7, 1863.
McGaghey, Jerome	19	Shippensburg	August 4, 1862	Deserted from Antietam, Maryland on September 18, 1862.
Null, John R.	21	Shippensburg	August 4, 1862	Mustered out with Company on May 21, 1863.
Nicholas, Henry	19	Shippensburg	August 4, 1862	Mustered out with Company on May 21, 1863.
Numer, David W.	31	Shippensburg	August 4, 1862	Mustered out with Company on May 21, 1863.

Appendix E: Regimental Roster

Name	Age	Joined at	Date Joined	Remarks
Prague, Alfred	19	Shippensburg	August 4, 1862	Mustered out with Company on May 21, 1863.
Piper, Samuel D. H.	24	Shippensburg	August 4, 1862	Mustered out with Company on May 21, 1863.
Rebuck, Jacob H.	22	Shippensburg	August 4, 1862	Mustered out with Company on May 21, 1863.
Reside, George	23	Shippensburg	August 4, 1862	Discharged at Philadelphia, Pennsylvania on Surgeon's Certificate on February 16, 1863.
Rankin, Joseph P.	18	Shippensburg	August 4, 1862	Discharged at Philadelphia, Pennsylvania on Surgeon's Certificate on January 6, 1863.
Reesman, David M.	29	Shippensburg	August 4, 1862	Discharged at Washington, DC on Surgeon's Certificate on February 10, 1863.
Rhen, David	28	Shippensburg	August 4, 1862	Discharged on Surgeon's Certificate on February 13, 1863.
Rhen, Jermiah	26	Shippensburg	August 4, 1862	Deserted from Bolivar Heights on September 25, 1862.
Rhen, Jacob	32	Shippensburg	August 4, 1862	Deserted from Bolivar Heights on September 25, 1862.
Sims, Jacob H.	21	Shippensburg	August 4, 1862	Mustered out with Company on May 21, 1863.
Stevens, William	21	Shippensburg	August 4, 1862	Mustered out with Company on May 21, 1863.
Shapley, Joseph	19	Shippensburg	August 4, 1862	Mustered out with Company on May 21, 1863.
Stewart, Alexander	18	Shippensburg	August 4, 1862	Absent, on detached service in Harrisburg, Virginia at muster out.
Spangler, Joseph	28	Shippensburg	August 4, 1862	Mustered out with Company on May 21, 1863.
Shuster, James R.	19	Shippensburg	August 4, 1862	Discharged on March 17, 1863 for wounds received at Fredericksburg, Virginia on December 13, 1862.
Smith, Nicholas	28	Shippensburg	August 4, 1862	Discharged at Washington, DC on Surgeon's Certificate on March 1, 1863.
Smith, Alexander	32	Shippensburg	August 4, 1862	Killed at Antietam, Maryland on September 17, 1862.
Tritt, William H.	20	Shippensburg	August 4, 1862	Mustered out with Company on May 21, 1863.
Tucky, John	18	Shippensburg	August 4, 1862	Dropped from the rolls due to not having consent of parents, date unknown.
Winters, David	21	Shippensburg	August 4, 1862	Mustered out with Company on May 21, 1863.

Name	Age	Joined at	Date Joined	Remarks
Witherow, Washington P.	21	Shippensburg	August 4, 1862	Mustered out with Company on May 21, 1863.
White, Henry	Unk	Shippensburg	August 4, 1862	Absent, on detached service at muster out.
Wolf, George W.	19	Shippensburg	August 4, 1862	Mustered out with Company on May 21, 1863.
Wolf, John A.	21	Shippensburg	August 4, 1862	Mustered out with Company on May 21, 1863.

COMPANY E - Recruited in Newville

Name	Age	Joined at	Date Joined	Remarks
Captains				
William Laughlin	42	Newville	August 6, 1862	Killed at Fredericksburg, Virginia on December 13, 1862. Buried in Big Spring Cemetery, Newville, Pennsylvania.
Joshua W. Sharp	31	Newville	August 6, 1862	Promoted to First Lieutenant on December 13, 1862. Mustered out with Company on May 21, 1863.
First Lieutenants				
John P. Wagner	22	Newville	August 12, 1862	Promoted from First Sergeant to Second Lieutenant on August 17, 1862. To First Lieutenant on December 13, 1862. Mustered out with Company on May 21, 1863.
Henry Clay Marshall	24	Newville	August 6, 1862	Promoted to Regimental Adjutant on August 17, 1862.
Second Lieutenant				
Joseph A. Ege	21	Newville	August 6, 1862	Promoted to First Sergeant on August 17, 1862. To Second Lieutenant on December 13, 1862. Mustered out with Company on May 21, 1863.
First Sergeant				
William Vanard	29	Newville	August 6, 1862	Promoted from Sergeant to First Sergeant on December 13, 1862. Mustered out with Company on May 21, 1863.
Sergeants				
Harrison Trego	22	Newville	August 6, 1862	Mustered out with Compay on May 21, 1863.
Edward W. Eby	21	Newville	August 6, 1862	Promoted to Corporal on December 13, 1862. Mustered out with Company on May 21, 1863.

Appendix E: Regimental Roster

Name	Age	Joined at	Date Joined	Remarks
Alexander Henry	22	Newville	August 6, 1862	Promoted from Private on December 13, 1862. Mustered out with Company on May 21, 1863.
Zebulon Mull	29	Newville	August 6, 1862	Promoted from Corporal on August 17, 1862. Mustered out with Company on May 21, 1863.
John G. Barr	32	Newville	August 6, 1862	Promoted from Corporal on August 17, 1863. Promoted to Regimental Hospital Steward on December 1, 1862.
Corporals				
George Wagner	18	Newville	August 6, 1862	Mustered out with Company on May 21, 1863.
William Hefflefinger	19	Newville	August 6, 1862	Mustered out with Company on May 21, 1863.
Alexander Kennedy	24	Newville	August 6, 1862	Wounded at Antietam, Maryland on September 17, 1862. Mustered out with Company on May 21, 1863.
Cyrus Kennedy	24	Newville	August 6, 1862	Wounded at Antietam, Maryland on September 17, 1862. Mustered out with Company on May 21, 1863.
Charles F. Hykes	28	Newville	August 6, 1862	Promoted to Corporal on August 17, 1862. Mustered out with Cmpany on May 21, 1863.
John B. Woodrow	19	Newville	August 6, 1862	Promoted to Corporal on August 17, 1862. Mustered out with Company on May 21, 1863.
Jacob W. Sharar	19	Newville	August 6, 1862	Promoted to Corporal on December 13, 1862. Mustered out with Cmpany on May 21, 1863.
George Carothers	19	Newville	August 6, 1862	Promoted to Corporal on December, 1862. Mustered out with Cmpany on May 21, 1863.
Frank Best	20	Newville	August 6, 1862	Discharged at Washington, DC by Special Order on January 22, 1863.
Phillip C. Smith	25	Newville	August 6, 1862	Transferred to Company F, 117th Pennsylvania, date unkown.
John H. Stickler	22	Newville	August 6, 1862	Died on October 4, 1862 of wounds received at Antietam, Maryland on September 17, 1862.
Wagoneer				
Kendig, Emanuel	Unk	Newville	August 12, 1862	Mustered out with Company on May 21, 1863.
Musicians				
Augustus G. Kyle	28	Newville	August 6, 1862	Mustered out with Company on May 21, 1863.

Name	Age	Joined at	Date Joined	Remarks
William Johnson	16	Newville	August 6, 1862	Deserted near Sharpsburg on September 19, 1862.
Privates				
Allen, Jesse K.	21	Newville	August 6, 1862	Mustered out with Company on May 21, 1863.
Allison, Reuben H.	21	Newville	August 6, 1862	Mustered out with Company on May 21, 1863.
Best, Richard	18	Newville	August 6, 1862	Mustered out with Company on May 21, 1863.
Bixier, Samuel	18	Newville	August 6, 1862	Mustered out with Company on May 21, 1863.
Brehm, Samuel	21	Newville	August 6, 1862	Mustered out with Company on May 21, 1863.
Bargstresser, Henry	21	Newville	August 6, 1862	Mustered out with Company on May 21, 1863.
Boyles, Theodore	21	Newville	August 6, 1862	Discharged at Harrisburg, Virgnia by Special Order on February 11, 1863.
Bargstesser, William	23	Newville	August 6, 1862	Discharged at Harrisburg, Virginia by Special Order on February 11, 1863.
Charlton, John L.	19	Newville	August 6, 1862	Mustered out with Company on May 21, 1863.
Crider, David W.	20	Newville	August 6, 1862	Mustered out with Company on May 21, 1863.
Crull, John W.	22	Newville	August 6, 1862	Died at Armory Square Hospital of disease at Washinton, DC on January 9, 1863. Buried in Military Asylum Cemetery.
Conery, Joseph	19	Newville	August 6, 1862	Died at 3rd Division, Second Corps Hospital on March 20, 1863.
Diven, Andrew F.	24	Newville	August 6, 1862	Mustered out with Company on May 21, 1863.
Dillman, George W.	27	Newville	August 6, 1862	Mustered out with Company on May 21, 1863.
Davidson, Robert M.	19	Newville	August 6, 1862	Mustered out with Company on May 21, 1863.
Donnelly, Geroge	19	Newville	August 6, 1862	Discharged on Surgeon's Certificate on February 16, 1863.
Ewing, George A.	28	Newville	August 6, 1862	Mustered out with Company on May 21, 1863.
Evilhock, Thomas	28	Newville	August 6, 1862	Mustered out with Company on May 21, 1863.
Finkenbinder, William	26	Newville	August 6, 1862	Wounded at Antietam, Maryland on September 17, 1862. Mustered out with Company on May 21, 1863.

Appendix E: Regimental Roster

Name	Age	Joined at	Date Joined	Remarks
Fyler, Jacob M.	22	Newville	August 6, 1862	Mustered out with Company on May 21, 1863.
Gillespie, Thomas G.	19	Newville	August 6, 1862	Wounded at Antietam, Maryland on September 17, 1862. Mustered out with Company on May 21, 1863.
Green, William	19	Newville	August 6, 1862	Mustered out with Company on May 21, 1863.
Hawk, James B.	21	Newville	August 6, 1862	Mustered out with Company on May 21, 1863.
Hamilton, William	18	Newville	August 6, 1862	Mustered out with Company on May 21, 1863.
Henry, Benjamin	22	Newville	August 6, 1862	Mustered out with Company on May 21, 1863.
Henry, Abraham	22	Newville	August 6, 1862	Mustered out with Company on May 21, 1863.
Hart, David	22	Newville	August 6, 1862	Mustered out with Company on May 21, 1863.
Hoetter, Josiah	18	Newville	August 6, 1862	Mustered out with Company on May 21, 1863.
Hemminger, John D.	18	Newville	August 6, 1862	Mustered out with Company on May 21, 1863.
Ickes, Charles	45	Newville	August 6, 1862	Mustered out with Company on May 21, 1863.
Jones, William	26	Newville	August 6, 1862	Absent at muster out.
King, Peter	38	Newville	August 6, 1862	Mustered out with Company on May 21, 1863.
Knettle, John	18	Newville	August 6, 1862	Mustered out with Company on May 21, 1863.
Kennedy, John	18	Newville	August 6, 1862	Discharged on March 17, 1863 for wounds received at Antietam, Maryland on September 17, 1862.
Kendig, Michael	20	Newville	August 6, 1862	Died of disease on May 14, 1863.
Landis, George	18	Newville	August 6, 1862	Mustered out with Company on May 21, 1863.
Lewis, James	18	Newville	August 6, 1862	Mustered out with Company on May 21, 1863.
Leidigh, Jacob M.	18	Newville	August 6, 1862	Wounded at Antietam, Maryland on September 17, 1862. Discharged on Surgeon's Certificate on February 11, 1863.
Lester, Henry C.	18	Newville	August 6, 1862	Discharged on Surgeon's Certificate on February 16, 1863.

Name	Age	Joined at	Date Joined	Remarks
Limpkilder, Frederick	33	Newville	August 6, 1862	Discharged on April 15, 1863 for wounds received at Antietam, Maryland on September 17, 1862.
Lockery, William	21	Newville	August 6, 1862	Died on November, 1862 of wounds received at Antietam, Maryland on September 17, 1862.
Miller, Jacob W.	23	Newville	August 6, 1862	Mustered out with Company on May 21, 1863.
Myers, Henry T.	26	Newville	August 6, 1862	Mustered out with Company on May 21, 1863.
Martin, John R.	24	Newville	August 6, 1862	Mustered out with Company on May 21, 1863.
Mateer, William	18	Newville	August 6, 1862	Wounded at Antietam, Maryland on September 17, 1862. Mustered out with Company on May 21, 1863.
Moul, Lewis	18	Newville	August 6, 1862	Mustered out with Company on May 21, 1863.
Miller, James	29	Newville	August 6, 1862	Discharged on March 10, 1863 for wounds received at Fredricksburg, Virginia on December 13, 1862.
Miller, David L.	28	Newville	August 6, 1862	Killed at Antietam, Maryland on September 17, 1862.
McLaughlin, Robert	30	Newville	August 6, 1862	Mustered out with Company on May 21, 1863.
McCune, Theodore	18	Newville	August 6, 1862	Discharged at Baltimore, Maryland on Surgeon's Certificate on February 16, 1863.
McCoy, Abraham H.	24	Newville	August 6, 1862	Discharged at Harrisburg on Surgeon's Certificate on March 6, 1863.
McCune, Samuel N.	21	Newville	August 6, 1862	Discharged at Harrisburg on Surgeon's Certificate on March 1, 1863.
McKeehan, Thaddaeu	23	Newville	August 6, 1862	Killed at Antietam, Maryland on September 17, 1862.
McCune, William A.	21	Newville	August 6, 1862	Killed at Antietam, Maryland on September 17, 1862.
Null, Daniel	18	Newville	August 6, 1862	Mustered out with Company on May 21, 1863.
Peck, Henry	19	Newville	August 6, 1862	Mustered out with Company on May 21, 1863.
Rife, Samuel	22	Newville	August 6, 1862	Mustered out with Company on May 21, 1863.
Ritner, William	18	Newville	August 6, 1862	Mustered out with Company on May 21, 1863.
Reddick, Samuel	24	Newville	August 6, 1862	Mustered out with Company on May 21, 1863.

Appendix E: Regimental Roster

Name	Age	Joined at	Date Joined	Remarks
Stoner, John H.	19	Newville	August 6, 1862	Mustered out with Company on May 21, 1863.
Vanasdlin, John	22	Newville	August 6, 1862	Deserted near Sharpsburg, Virginia on September 17, 1862.
Wheeler, Henry	20	Newville	August 6, 1862	Mustered out with Company on May 21, 1863.
Weakly, Josiah	23	Newville	August 6, 1862	Mustered out with Company on May 21, 1863.
Whislor, Simon M.	20	Newville	August 6, 1862	Mustered out with Company on May 21, 1863.
Ward, John	34	Newville	August 6, 1862	Wounded at Antietam, Maryland on on September 17, 1862. Discharged on February 11, 1863.
Warner, Wilson	14	Newville	August 6, 1862	Discharged near Falmouth, Virginia by Special Order on February 22, 1863.
Woods, William	21	Newville	August 6, 1862	Died of disease in November, 1862.

COMPANY F - Recruited in Mechanicsburg

Name	Age	Joined at	Date Joined	Remarks
Captains				
Henry I. Zinn	27	Mechanicsburg	July 23, 1862	Promoted to Colonel on August 17, 1862.
John B. Zinn	37	Mechanicsburg	July 23, 1862	Promoted from First Lieutenant to Captain on August 9, 1862. Resigned on March 19, 1863.
Levi Haverstick	21	Mechanicsburg	August 9, 1862	Promoted from First Sergeant to First Lieutenant on August 17, 1862. To Captain on March 19, 1863. Wounded at Antietam, Maryland on September 17, 1862 and at Fredericksburg, Virginia on December 13, 1862. Mustered out with Company on May 21, 1863.
First Lieutenant				
Michael W. French	23	Mechanicsburg	August 6, 1862	Promoted from Sergeant to Second Lieutenant on September 17, 1862. To First Lieutenant on March 19, 1863. Mustered out with Company on May 21, 1863.
Second Lieutenant				
William A. Givler	25	Mechanicsburg	July 23, 1862	Killed at Antietam, Maryland on September 17, 1862.

Name	Age	Joined at	Date Joined	Remarks
Thomas Tyndal	28	Harrisburg	August 9, 1862	Promoted to First Sergeant on September 17, 1862. To Second Lieutenant on March 19, 1863. Mustered out with Company on May 21, 1863.
First Sergeants				
Archibald L. Mullin	21	Mechanicsburg	August 9, 1862	Promoted from Corporal to Sergeant on December 7, 1862. To First Sergeant on March 19, 1863. Mustered out with Company on May 21, 1863.
Benjamin F. Barshinger	24	Mechanicsburg	August 9, 1862	Died at Emory Hospital on December 7, 1862 at Washington, DC.
Sergeants				
William E. Zinn	19	Mechanicsburg	August 8, 1862	Promoted from Corporal to Sergeant on September 17, 1862. Mustered out with Company on May 21, 1863. Sent to hosptial October 24, 1862.
William H. Miller	35	Mechanicsburg	August 8, 1862	Promoted from Corporal to Sergeant on September 17, 1862. Mustered out with Company on May 21, 1863.
Jonn C. Fink	19	Mechanicsburg	August 8, 1862	Promoted from Corporal to Sergeant on March 19, 1863. Mustered out with Company on May 21, 1863.
George W. Moltz	29	Mechanicsburg	August 8, 1862	Promoted from Private on December 28, 1862. Mustered out with Company on May 21, 1863.
Corporals				
Samuel. D. Culberston	23	Mechanicsburg	August 9, 1862	Promoted to Corporal. Wounded at Fredericksburg, Virginia on December 13, 1862. Mustered out with Company on May 21, 1863.
Lewis G. Saddler	22	Mechanicsburg	August 8, 1862	Mustered out with Company on May 21, 1863.
James Hughes	35	Mechanicsburg	July 23, 1862	Promoted to Corporal on December 28, 1862. Mustered out with Company on May 21, 1863.
Issac W. Basehore	21	Mechanicsburg	August 7, 1862	Promoted to Corporal on December 28, 1863. Mustered out with Company on May 21, 1863.
John E. Mann	22	Harrisburg	August 9, 1862	Promoted to Corporal on December 28, 1862. Mustered out with Company on May 21, 1863.
Henry W. Miller	21	Harrisburg	August 8, 1862	Promoted to Corporal on December 28, 1862. Mustered out with Company on May 21, 1863.
John Livingston	37	Harrisburg	August 8, 1862	Promoted to Corporal on December 28, 1862. Mustered out with Company on May 21, 1863.

Appendix E: Regimental Roster

Name	Age	Joined at	Date Joined	Remarks
Henry S. Lambert	24	Harrisburg	August 5, 1862	Missing in action at Fredericksburg, Virginia on December 13, 1862.
John B. Landis	21	Harrisburg	August 8, 1862	Discharged at Alexandria, Virginia on February 12, 1863 for wounds received at Fredericksburg, Virginia on December 13, 1862.
William A. Morreett	26	Harrisburg	August 9, 1862	Discharged at Harrisburg, Virginia on Surgeon's Certificate on February 10, 1863.
Musicians				
Jacob Earnest	18	Harrisburg	August 9, 1862	Mustered out with Company on May 21, 1863.
George Fishel	27	Mechanicsburg	August 9, 1862	Mustered out with Company on May 21, 1863.
Wagoneer				
Fink, John	23	Mechanicsburg	August 8, 1862	Mustered out with Company on May 21, 1863.
Privates				
Ashenfelter, George N.	19	Mechanicsburg	August 4, 1862	Mustered out with Company on May 21, 1863.
Baird, John A.	18	Mechanicsburg	July 23, 1862	Wounded at Antietam, Maryland on September 17, 1862. Mustered out with Company on May 21, 1863.
Brougher, Augustus O.	25	Harrisburg	August 9, 1862	Mustered out with Company on May 21, 1863.
Baker, Joseph	18	Mechanicsburg	August 5, 1862	Wounded at Chancellorsville, Virginia on May 3, 1863. Mustered out with Company on May 21, 1863.
Baker, Mathias	18	Mechanicsburg	August 8, 1862	Mustered out with Company on May 21, 1863.
Brougher, Johnson	21	Mechanicsburg	August 8, 1862	Wounded at Fredericksburg, Virginia on December 13, 1862. Mustered out with Company on May 21, 1863.
Bates, Samuel W.	27	Harrisburg	August 9, 1862	Wounded at Fredericksburg, Virginia on December 13, 1862. Sent to Hospital on December 14, 1862. Mustered out with Company on May 21, 1863.
Boyer, John	21	Harrisburg	August 9, 1862	Mustered out with Company on May 21, 1863.
Brillhart, Martin B.	18	Mechanicsburg	August 2, 1862	Absent, sick at muster out. At Convalescent Center, Alexandria, Virginia.
Brown, Benjamin	20	Harrisburg	August 9, 1862	Absent, sick at muster out. At Odd Fellows Camp, Georgetown, Washington, DC.

Name	Age	Joined at	Date Joined	Remarks
Bender, Levi	19	Mechanicsburg	August 9, 1862	Died at Field Hospital on September 25, 1862 of wounds received at Antietam, Maryland on September 17, 1862.
Bobb, Keller	18	Mechanicsburg	August 8, 1862	Died at Judiciary Square Hospital in Washington, DC on January 21, 1863 of wounds received at Fredericksburg, Virginia on December 13, 1862.
Brougher, Ira D.	19	Mechanicsburg	August 8, 1862	Discharged from Harrisburg, Virginia on December 25, 1862 for wounds received at Antietam, Maryland on September 17, 1862.
Bechtel, Moses H.	27	Harrisburg	August 9, 1862	Deserted at Bolivar Heights on October 15, 1862.
Crist, John C.	21	Mechanicsburg	August 2, 1862	Mustered out with Company on May 21, 1863.
Crist, Joesph W.	19	Mechanicsburg	August 5, 1862	Wounded at Chancellorsville, Virginia on May 3, 1863. Mustered out with Company on May 21, 1863.
Chamberlain, John	22	Mechanicsburg	August 8, 1862	Mustered out with Company on May 21, 1863.
Crone, Charles	25	Mechanicsburg	August 8, 1862	Sent to Hospital in Washington, DC on September 13, 1862. Discharged on Surgeon's Certificate, date unknown.
Daugherty, George	23	Mechanicsburg	August 7, 1862	Mustered out with Company on May 21, 1863.
Daugherty, William	20	Harrisburg	August 9, 1862	Mustered out with Company on May 21, 1863.
Erford, Jacob	18	Harrisburg	August 9, 1862	Mustered out with Company on May 21, 1863.
Emig, George S.	23	Mechanicsburg	August 9, 1862	Mustered out with Company on May 21, 1863.
English, Thomas W.	42	Mechanicsburg	August 8, 1862	Killed at Antietam, Maryland on September 17, 1862.
Ebersole, William	28	Harrisburg	August 9, 1862	Discharged from Harrisburg, Virginia on November 13, 1862 for wounds received at Antietam, Maryland on September 17, 1862.
Fink, Abraham	18	Mechanicsburg	August 8, 1862	Mustered out with Company on May 21, 1863.
Forney, Joseph	19	Mechanicsburg	August 9, 1862	Mustered out with Company on May 21, 1863.
Fosnot, Joshua V.	22	Mechanicsburg	August 8, 1862	Mustered out with Company on May 21, 1863.

Appendix E: Regimental Roster 243

Name	Age	Joined at	Date Joined	Remarks
Forror, Geroge	36	Harrisburg	August 9, 1862	Wounded at Fredericksburg, Virginia on December 13, 1862. Sent to Hospital on December 14, 1862. Absent, in Hospital at muster out.
Farner, John M.	19	Mechanicsburg	August 8, 1862	Wounded at Fredericksburg, Virginia on December 13, 1862. Mustered out with Company on May 21, 1863.
Fetzer, John	21	Mechanicsburg	August 8, 1862	Killed at Fredericksburg, December 13, 1862. Head blown off by a shell.
Gebhart, Jacob	41	Mechanicsburg	August 7, 1862	Mustered out with Company on May 21, 1863.
Glantz, John	28	Mechanicsburg	August 8, 1862	Mustered out with Company on May 21, 1863.
Gentsinger, Joseph	19	Harrisburg	August 7, 1862	Mustered out with Company on May 21, 1863.
Gravlin, George	32	Harrisburg	August 7, 1862	Mustered out with Company on May 21, 1863.
Guistwite, Samuel	22	Mechanicsburg	August 6, 1862	Deserted at Antietam, Maryland on September 17, 1862.
Hoover, Elijah J.	18	Harrisburg	August 9, 1862	Mustered out with Company on May 21, 1863.
Hess, George	21	Harrisburg	August 9, 1862	Mustered out with Company on May 21, 1863.
Hyde, John	20	Mechanicsburg	August 7, 1862	Deserted on September 17, 1862. Returned on April 5, 1863. Absent, sick at muster out.
Hoon, Joseph	26	Harrisburg	August 9, 1862	Discharged due to disease at Harrisburg, Virginia on Surgeon's Certificate on November 13, 1862.
Heiges, Joseph	21	Mechanicsburg	August 9, 1862	Deserted at Bolivar Heights on September 30, 1862.
Jones, Josiah R.	28	Mechanicsburg	August 9, 1862	Mustered out with Company on May 21, 1863.
Knisley, Anthony T.	20	Mechanicsburg	August 6, 1862	Wounded at Fredericksburg, Virginia on December 13, 1862. Mustered out with Company on May 21, 1863.
Kraber, John C.	21	Harrisburg	August 9, 1862	Mustered out with Company on May 21, 1863.
Koons, Jacob	24	Harrisburg	August 9, 1862	Mustered out with Company on May 21, 1863.
Knisley, Peter T.	18	Mechanicsburg	August 6, 1862	Died near Falmouth, Virginia on February 16, 1863.
Leidig, John W.	19	Mechanicsburg	August 8, 1862	Sent to Hospital on December 28, 1862. Absent, in Hospital at muster out.

Name	Age	Joined at	Date Joined	Remarks
Landis, Daniel D.	27	Mechanicsburg	August 7, 1862	Discharged at Harrisburg on February 26, 1862 for wounds received at Antietam, Maryland on September 17, 1862.
Maxwell, John R.	18	Mechanicsburg	August 6, 1862	Mustered out with Company on May 21, 1863.
Morrett, Hiram W.	18	Mechanicsburg	August 6, 1862	Mustered out with Company on May 21, 1863.
Minich, William	21	Mechanicsburg	August 8, 1862	Mustered out with Company on May 21, 1863.
Miller, John D.	21	Mechanicsburg	August 9, 1862	Mustered out with Company on May 21, 1863.
Miller, Robert B.	18	Mechanicsburg	August 8, 1862	Mustered out with Company on May 21, 1863.
Miller, Samuel A.	21	Mechanicsburg	August 8, 1862	Wounded at Antietam, Maryland on September 17, 1862. Sent to Hospital on September 18, 1862. Absent, in Hospital at muster out.
May, Samuel K.	19	Mechanicsburg	August 6, 1862	Died on September 21, 1862 of wounds received at Antietem, Maryland on September 17, 1862.
McFadden, John	22	Mechanicsburg	August 7, 1862	Mustered out with Company on May 21, 1863.
Pretz, John	27	Mechanicsburg	August 8, 1862	Mustered out with Company on May 21, 1863.
Rinehart, George H.	19	Mechanicsburg	August 9, 1862	Mustered out with Company on May 21, 1863.
Saddler, Benjamin E.	20	Mechanicsburg	August 8, 1862	Mustered out with Company on May 21, 1863.
Stonesifer, Ishmael	19	Mechanicsburg	August 8, 1862	Mustered out with Company on May 21, 1863.
Steigleman, Isaiah	33	Mechanicsburg	August 2, 1862	Wounded at Fredericksburg, Virginia on December 13, 1862. Mustered out with Company on May 21, 1863.
Strine, John	21	Mechanicsburg	August 8, 1862	Mustered out with Company on May 21, 1863.
Shaffer, William H.	18	Mechanicsburg	July 26, 1862	Mustered out with Company on May 21, 1863.
Sites, David	23	Mechanicsburg	August 8, 1862	Mustered out with Company on May 21, 1863.
Smith, John W. M.	18	Mechanicsburg	August 8, 1862	Mustered out with Company on May 21, 1863.
Shaull, William H.	24	Harrisburg	August 9, 1862	Mustered out with Company on May 21, 1863.
Shumberger, Simon	21	Harrisburg	August 9, 1862	Mustered out with Company on May 21, 1863.

Appendix E: Regimental Roster

Name	Age	Joined at	Date Joined	Remarks
Stewart, John W.	30	Harrisburg	August 9, 1862	Wounded at Fredericksburg, Virginia on December 13, 1862. Mustered out with Company on May 21, 1863.
Snavely, John	21	Mechanicsburg	July 23, 1862	Discharged on November 15, 1862 for wounds received at Antietam, Maryland on September 17, 1862.
Stevenson, Emanuel	28	Mechanicsburg	August 6, 1862	Deserted at Camp Curtin on August 15, 1862.
Wertz, Joseph	21	Mechanicsburg	August 8, 1862	Mustered out with Company on May 21, 1863.
Wood, John A.	19	Mechanicsburg	August 6, 1862	Wounded at Antietam, Maryland on September 17, 1862. Mustered out with Company on May 21, 1863.
Weyles, William	18	Mechanicsburg	August 7, 1862	Mustered out with Company on May 21, 1863.
White, William B.	21	Mechanicsburg	August 8, 1862	Wounded at Fredericksburg, Virginia on December 13, 1862. Mustered out with Company on May 21, 1863.
Wolf, George	19	Mechanicsburg	August 7, 1862	Absent, on detached service at muster out.
White, George	21	Mechanicsburg	August 9, 1862	Died at Windmill Point, Virginia on February 4, 1863.
Zinn, Thomas R.	18	Mechanicsburg	August 8, 1862	Killed at Antietam, Maryland on September 17, 1862.

COMPANY G - Recruited in Carlisle

Name	Age	Joined at	Date Joined	Remarks
Captains				
John Lee	38	Carlisle	July 25, 1862	Promoted to Major on August 17, 1862. Promoted to Lieutenant Colonel on December 14, 1862 .
John S. Lyne	26	Carlisle	July 25, 1862	Promoted from First Lieutenant on August 17, 1862. Discharged on Surgeon's Certificate on February 5, 1863.
John S. Low	26	Carlisle	July 25, 1862	Promoted to Adjuant on February 5, 1863. Mustered out with Company on May 21, 1863.
First Lieutenant				
Thomas D. Caldwell	25	Carlisle	July 25, 1862	Promoted from First Sergeant to Second Lieutenant on August 17, 1862. To first Lieutenant on January 7, 1863. Mustered out with Company on May 21, 1863.

Name	Age	Joined at	Date Joined	Remarks
Second Lieutenant				
Martin Kuhn	25	Carlisle	July 25, 1862	Promoted from Corporal to Sergeant on September 25, 1862. To Second Lieutenant on January 7, 1863. Mustered out with Company on May 21, 1863.
First Sergaent				
Henry Keller	21	Carlisle	July 25, 1862	Promoted from Sergeant on August 17, 1862. Mustered out with Company on May 21, 1863.
Sergeants				
Frank Cart	21	Carlisle	July 25, 1862	Promoted from Private on January 1, 1863. Mustered out with Company on May 21, 1863.
Alfred C. Harder	23	Carlisle	July 25, 1862	Mustered out with Company on May 21, 1863.
Issac S. Walker	24	Carlisle	July 25, 1862	Promoted from Corporal on January 1, 1863. Mustered out with Company on May 21, 1863.
William S. Keeler	26	Carlisle	July 25, 1862	Promoted from Private on January 1, 1863. Mustered out with Company on May 21, 1863.
Joseph C. Halbert	28	Carlisle	July 25, 1862	Promoted to Regiment's Commissary Sergeant on January 1, 1863.
William Sanderson	26	Carlisle	July 25, 1862	Deserted from Boonesboro, Maryland on September 6, 1862.
Corporals				
Charls H. Spotswood	26	Carlisle	July 25, 1862	Mustered out with Company on May 21, 1863.
Alexander Law	22	Carlisle	July 25, 1862	Mustered out with Company on May 21, 1863.
Samuel C. Bailey	21	Carlisle	July 25, 1862	Promoted to Corporal on January 1, 1863. Mustered out with Company on May 21, 1863.
Alexander G. Lyne	20	Carlisle	July 25, 1862	Mustered out with Company on May 21, 1863.
William McAllister	26	Carlisle	July 25, 1862	Promoted to Corporal on January 1, 1863. Mustered out with Company on May 21, 1863.
John Neeter	19	Carlisle	July 25, 1862	Promoted to Corporal on February 1, 1863. Mustered out with Company on May 21, 1863.
Samuel Miles	21	Carlisle	July 25, 1862	Promoted to Corporal on February 1, 1863. Mustered out with Company on May 21, 1863.

Appendix E: Regimental Roster

Name	Age	Joined at	Date Joined	Remarks
David Baxter	24	Carlisle	July 25, 1862	Promoted to Corporal on February 1, 1863. Mustered out with Company on May 21, 1863.
Issac Parsons	19	Carlisle	July 25, 1862	Discharged due to disability on Surgeon's Certificate on March 7, 1863.
John W. Alexander	38	Carlisle	July 25, 1862	Deserted from Camp Marcy, Virginia on September 5, 1862.
Musicians				
John Riley	18	Carlisle	July 25, 1862	Mustered out with Company on May 21, 1863.
George Ruggles	18	Carlisle	July 25, 1862	Mustered out with Company on May 21, 1863.
Privates				
Alexander, James J.	18	Carlisle	July 25, 1862	Mustered out with Company on May 21, 1863.
Boner, Willam F.	18	Carlisle	July 25, 1862	Mustered out with Company on May 21, 1863.
Boner, David	35	Carlisle	July 25, 1862	Mustered out with Company on May 21, 1863.
Bear, Benjamin F.	18	Carlisle	July 25, 1862	Mustered out with Company on May 21, 1863.
Bodge, Charles H	41	Carlisle	July 25, 1862	Mustered out with Company on May 21, 1863.
Boughamer, John	21	Carlisle	July 25, 1862	Mustered out with Company on May 21, 1863.
Baily, David M.	22	Carlisle	July 25, 1862	Discharged due to disability on Surgeon's Certtificate on February 10, 1863.
Bartley, John	19	Carlisle	July 25, 1862	Died from disease at Potomac Creek, Virginia on May 6, 1863.
Crouse, Henry C	18	Carlisle	July 25, 1862	Mustered out with Company on May 21, 1863.
Cornman, Martin	18	Carlisle	July 25, 1862	Mustered out with Company on May 21, 1863.
Corbett, William A.	18	Carlisle	July 25, 1862	Mustered out with Company on May 21, 1863.
Carothers, George W.	24	Carlisle	July 25, 1862	Mustered out with Company on May 21, 1863.
Cornman, John P.	20	Carlisle	July 25, 1862	Mustered out with Company on May 21, 1863.
Carbaugh, Daniel A.	24	Carlisle	July 25, 1862	Mustered out with Company on May 21, 1863.
Dixon, Henry T.	18	Carlisle	July 25, 1862	Mustered out with Company on May 21, 1863.

Name	Age	Joined at	Date Joined	Remarks
Douglass, George	20	Carlisle	July 25, 1862	Mustered out with Company on May 21, 1863.
Duffey, William W.	30	Carlisle	July 25, 1862	Wounded at Fredericksburg, Virginia on December 13, 1862. Mustered out with Company on May 21, 1863.
Drewit, George	38	Carlisle	July 25, 1862	Discharged due to disability on Surgeon's Certtificate on January 12, 1863.
Goodyear, John A.	24	Carlisle	July 25, 1862	Mustered out with Company on May 21, 1863.
Gorgas, John	24	Carlisle	July 25, 1862	Mustered out with Company on May 21, 1863.
Heckendorn, George	19	Carlisle	July 25, 1862	Mustered out with Company on May 21, 1863.
Heller, Jacob	26	Carlisle	July 25, 1862	Mustered out with Company on May 21, 1863.
Hart, Isaiah H.	38	Carlisle	July 25, 1862	Mustered out with Company on May 21, 1863.
Hannan, Robert M.	18	Carlisle	July 25, 1862	Mustered out with Company on May 21, 1863.
Hannan, William P.	18	Carlisle	July 25, 1862	Mustered out with Company on May 21, 1863.
Hipple, Jacob	21	Carlisle	July 25, 1862	Discharged due to disability on Surgeon's Certificate on December 24, 1862.
Ingram, David	30	Carlisle	July 25, 1862	Mustered out with Company on May 21, 1863.
Jacobs, Abraham	18	Carlisle	July 25, 1862	Mustered out with Company on May 21, 1863.
Kelly, Henry J.	42	Carlisle	July 25, 1862	Discharged due to disability on Surgeon's Certificate on March 17, 1863.
Lytle, William	38	Carlisle	July 25, 1862	Mustered out with Company on May 21, 1863.
Miller, George H	38	Carlisle	July 25, 1862	Mustered out with Company on May 21, 1863.
Martin, Thomas	19	Carlisle	July 25, 1862	Mustered out with Company on May 21, 1863.
Mondy, George	23	Carlisle	July 25, 1862	Mustered out with Company on May 21, 1863.
Minich, John W	24	Carlisle	July 25, 1862	Mustered out with Company on May 21, 1863.
Matthews, Robert	18	Carlisle	July 25, 1862	Mustered out with Company on May 21, 1863.
Murttorff, Emanuel	35	Carlisle	July 25, 1862	Mustered out with Company on May 21, 1863.

Appendix E: Regimental Roster

Name	Age	Joined at	Date Joined	Remarks
Murttorff, William	22	Carlisle	July 25, 1862	Wounded at Antietam, Maryland on September 17, 1862. Mustered out with Company on May 21, 1863.
Miller, Eli F.	21	Carlisle	July 25, 1862	Mustered out with Company on May 21, 1863.
McDonald, Edward A.	29	Carlisle	July 25, 1862	Mustered out with Company on May 21, 1863.
McNaughton, Samuel	40	Carlisle	July 25, 1862	Died of wounds received at Antietam, Maryland on September 17, 1862.
Noggle, Benjamin	26	Carlisle	July 25, 1862	Mustered out with Company on May 21, 1863.
Neely, Joseph	33	Carlisle	July 25, 1862	Discharged due to disability on Surgeon's Certificate on October 16, 1862.
Nonemaker, William	35	Carlisle	July 25, 1862	Discharged due to disability on Surgeon's Certificate on April 10, 1862.
Oiler, Samuel	19	Carlisle	July 25, 1862	Discharged due to disability on Surgeon's Certificate on March 11, 1862.
Oiler, Andrew	18	Carlisle	July 25, 1862	Discharged due to disability on Surgeon's Certificate on March 14, 1862.
Pie, David	28	Carlisle	July 25, 1862	Mustered out with Company on May 21, 1863.
Quigley, Edwin D.	30	Carlisle	July 25, 1862	Mustered out with Company on May 21, 1863.
Rodgers, Alexander	23	Carlisle	July 25, 1862	Mustered out with Company on May 21, 1863.
Ruggles, William	19	Carlisle	July 25, 1862	Mustered out with Company on May 21, 1863.
Robinson, Armstrong	18	Carlisle	July 25, 1862	Mustered out with Company on May 21, 1863.
Ramsey, William S.	29	Carlisle	July 25, 1862	Mustered out with Company on May 21, 1863.
Schuchman, Frederick	18	Carlisle	July 25, 1862	Mustered out with Company on May 21, 1863.
Stroble, Frederick	22	Carlisle	July 25, 1862	Mustered out with Company on May 21, 1863.
Stoner, Samuel A.	19	Carlisle	July 25, 1862	Mustered out with Company on May 21, 1863.
Shoemaker, Michael	26	Carlisle	July 25, 1862	Mustered out with Company on May 21, 1863.
Sites, Charles W.	29	Carlisle	July 25, 1862	Mustered out with Company on May 21, 1863.

Name	Age	Joined at	Date Joined	Remarks
Swoveland, Henry	30	Carlisle	July 25, 1862	Mustered out with Company on May 21, 1863.
Slusser, George W.	21	Carlisle	July 25, 1862	Wounded at Antietem, Maryland on September 17, 1862. Mustered out with Company on May 21, 1863.
Sours, Napoleon	26	Carlisle	July 25, 1862	Discharged due to disability on Surgeon's Certificate on March 14, 1862.
Sites, Alfred	18	Carlisle	July 25, 1862	Discharged due to disability on Surgeon's Certificate on February 26, 1862.
Shriver, Benjamin	21	Carlisle	July 25, 1862	Deserted from Camp Simmons in Harrisburg on August 16, 1863.
Saddler, Samuel G.	21	Carlisle	July 25, 1862	Deserted from Battle of Antietem on August 24, 1862.
Woodley, William W.	24	Carlisle	July 25, 1862	Mustered out with Company on May 21, 1863.
Waggoner, Benjamen	19	Carlisle	July 25, 1862	Mustered out with Company on May 21, 1863.
Wharfe, James	40	Carlisle	July 25, 1862	Mustered out with Company on May 21, 1863.
Windomaker, John	20	Carlisle	July 25, 1862	Mustered out with Company on May 21, 1863.
Wert, Joseph	23	Carlisle	July 25, 1862	Mustered out with Company on May 21, 1863.
Weiser, John S	25	Carlisle	July 25, 1862	Mustered out with Company on May 21, 1863.
Witherow, James	18	Carlisle	July 25, 1862	Died from disease near Falmouth, Virginia on January 17, 1863.
Warren, Joseph B	34	Carlisle	July 25, 1862	Deserted from Camp Simmons in Harrisburg on August 16, 1863.
Windomaker, Jacob	34	Carlisle	July 25, 1862	Deserted from Camp Simmons in Harrisburg on August 16, 1863.
Yeingst, William	18	Carlisle	July 25, 1862	Mustered out with Company on May 21, 1863.
Zeigler, George	39	Carlisle	July 25, 1862	Mustered out with Company on May 21, 1863.

COMPANY H - Recruited in Part at New Cumberland

Name	Age	Joined at	Date Joined	Remarks
Captains				
John C. Hoffaker	36	Harrisburg	Unknown	Discharged due to disability on Surgeon's Certificate on February 17, 1863.

Appendix E: Regimental Roster

Name	Age	Joined at	Date Joined	Remarks
George C. Marshall	22	Harrisburg	July 24, 1862	Promoted from First Lieutenant on March 1, 1863. Mustered out with Company on May 21, 1863.
First Lieutenant				
John K. McGann	26	Harrisburg	July 24, 1862	Promoted from First Lieutenant on March 1, 1863. Mustered out with Company on May 21, 1863.
Second Lieutenant				
Charles A. Hood	22	New Cumberland	August 5, 1862	Promoted from Private to First Sergeant on November 15, 1862. To Second Lieutenant on April 25, 1863. Mustered out with Company on May 21, 1863.
First Sergeant				
Peter Ludwig	25	New Cumberland	July 31, 1862	Promoted from Private to Sergeant on August 17, 1862. To First Sergeant on February 17, 1863. Mustered out with Company on May 21, 1863.
Sergeants				
John H. Young	26	New Cumberland	August 9, 1862	Promoted from Private on December 25, 1862. Mustered out with Company on May 21, 1863.
Thomas Maloney	25	West Chester	August 26, 1862	Promoted from Private on December 25, 1862. Mustered out with Company on May 21, 1863.
Andrew M. Rubner	25	West Chester	July 26, 1862	Promoted from Private on December 25, 1862. Mustered out with Company on May 21, 1863.
John J. Hull	29	New Cumberland	August 9, 1862	Promoted from Private on December 25, 1862. Mustered out with Company on May 21, 1863.
Corporals				
Benjamin F. Hoyer	36	New Cumberland	August 9, 1862	Promoted to Corporal on August 17, 1862. Mustered out with Company on May 21, 1863.
Charles A. Stewart	21	New Cumberland	August 9, 1862	Promoted to Corporal on August 17, 1862. Mustered out with Company on May 21, 1863.
Richard Green	24	Mechanicsburg	July 26, 1862	Promoted to Corporal on August 17, 1862. Mustered out with Company on May 21, 1863.
Joseph Yinger	33	New Cumberland	August 9, 1862	Promoted to Corporal on August 17, 1862. Mustered out with Company on May 21, 1863.
John Wise Sr.	43	Camp Curtin	August 9, 1862	Promoted to Corporal on August 17, 1862. Mustered out with Company on May 21, 1863.

Name	Age	Joined at	Date Joined	Remarks
James Bridgehouse	19	West Chester	August 9, 1862	Promoted to Corporal on February 26, 1862. Mustered out with Company on May 21, 1863.
David B. Kauffman	21	New Cumberland	August 9, 1862	Promoted to Corporal on January 31, 1863. Absent, wounded at muster out.
Peter B. Lyter	24	Camp Simmons	August 9, 1862	Promoted to Corporal on January 31, 1863. Absent, wounded at muster out.
Isaac Bowman	24	Fishersville	August 9, 1862	Discharged from Washington, D. C. on Surgeon's Certificate on January 20, 1863.
Chauncey C. Wilder	28	New Cumberland	August 9, 1862	Discharged on Surgeon's Certificate on February 25, 1863.
Wagoneer				
Koch, Charles	Unk	Unk	August 12, 1862	Mustered out with Company on May 21, 1863.
Musicians				
John A. Miller	28	Halifax	August 9, 1862	Mustered out with Company on May 21, 1863.
Wesley King	16	Mechanicsburg	August 9, 1862	Deserted from Bolivar Heights on September 23, 1862.
Privates				
Anderson, John	18	Camp Curtin	August 9, 1862	Discharged due to disability on Surgeon's Certificate on March 5, 1863.
Billet, Jacob M.	17	New Cumberland	August 8, 1862	Mustered out with Company on May 21, 1863.
Bothoroyd, John	40	West Chester	August 7, 1862	Discharged due to disability on Surgeon's Certificate on December 17, 1863.
Bradley, John	19	West Chester	August 6, 1862	Deserted from Camp Marcy, Virginia on August 25, 1862.
Christy, Henry	25	West Chester	August 9, 1862	Mustered out with Company on May 21, 1863.
Cummings, Watson	32	New Cumberland	August 9, 1862	Mustered out with Company on May 21, 1863.
Coon, Christopher	19	West Chester	August 9, 1862	Mustered out with Company on May 21, 1863.
Cole, Humphrey	19	West Chester	August 12, 1862	Mustered out with Company on May 21, 1863.
Dougherty, James	22	West Chester	August 9, 1862	Mustered out with Company on May 21, 1863.
Doner, William	18	Harrisburg	August 30, 1862	Not on muster-out roll.
Eisenberger, Franklin	18	Camp Curtin	August 9, 1862	Mustered out with Company on May 21, 1863.

Appendix E: Regimental Roster

Name	Age	Joined at	Date Joined	Remarks
Evans, Jacob	21	Mechanicsburg	August 2, 1862	Mustered out with Company on May 21, 1863.
Fauber, Nathaniel	18	Fishersville	August 8, 1862	Mustered out with Company on May 21, 1863.
Fisher, Samuel S.	31	New Cumberland	August 8, 1862	Mustered out with Company on May 21, 1863.
Fetrow, Abel	18	New Cumberland	August 6, 1862	Discharged due to disability on Surgeon's Certificate on February 10, 1863.
Gabriel, Stager	26	Mechanicsburg	August 6, 1862	Sent to hospital on December 25, 1862. Absent, sick at muster out.
Guistwite, Daniel	19	New Cumberland	August 4, 1862	Mustered out with Company on May 21, 1863.
Harris, James	18	New Cumberland	August 8, 1862	Mustered out with Company on May 21, 1863.
Hopes, Rufus C.	20	West Chester	August 6, 1862	Deserted from Harrisburg, Pennsylvania on August 17, 1862.
Knouff, Joseph	18	Halifax	August 8 1862	Mustered out with Company on May 21, 1863.
Kriner, Charles	21	Halifax	August 9, 1862	Mustered out with Company on May 21, 1863.
Kirk, John	18	New Cumberland	August 9, 1862	Mustered out with Company on May 21, 1863.
Kopenhaver, Samuel	18	Fishersville	August 9, 1862	Mustered out with Company on May 21, 1863.
Kauffman, David S.	21	New Cumberland	August 12, 1862	Mustered out with Company on May 21, 1863.
Kennedy, George	36	Harrisburg	August 26, 1862	Not on muster-out roll.
Lentz, Jacob	20	Fishersville	August 8, 1862	Mustered out with Company on May 21, 1863.
Matson, Jesse C.	24	West Chester	August 8, 1862	Mustered out with Company on May 21, 1863.
Mateer, Albert W.	21	Camp Simmons	August 9, 1862	Mustered out with Company on May 21, 1863.
Moyer, Solomon	22	New Cumberland	August 19, 1862	Mustered out with Company on May 21, 1863.
Miller, John	26	Mechanicsburg	August 1, 1862	Deserted from Washington, DC on August 18, 1862.
Morgan, Charles A.	23	Mechanicsburg	July 29, 1862	Deserted from Harrisburg, Pennsylvania on August 17, 1862.
McLaughlin, Alexander	36	Mechanicsburg	August 8, 1862	Mustered out with Company on May 21, 1863.
McSloy, John	26	West Chester	August 7, 1862	Absent without leave at muster out.

Name	Age	Joined at	Date Joined	Remarks
McCalley, John	21	West Chester	August 9, 1862	Deserted from Camp Marcy, Virginia on August 25, 1862.
Nelson, Frank	25	New Cumberland	August 31, 1862	Mustered out with Company on May 21, 1863.
Nelson, David W.	40	New Cumberland	August 9, 1862	Mustered out with Company on May 21, 1863.
Naylor, Isaac M.	18	New Cumberland	August 8, 1862	Mustered out with Company on May 21, 1863.
Pray, William C.	21	New Cumberland	August 8, 1862	Mustered out with Company on May 21, 1863.
Powle, Daniel	18	Fishersville	August 8, 1862	Mustered out with Company on May 21, 1863.
Preston, William H.	27	West Chester	August 6, 1862	Discharged due to disability from Philadelphia, Pennsylvania on Surgeon's Certificate on March 27, 1863.
Pray, John S.	24	New Cumberland	August 9, 1862	Died due to disease near Falmouth, Virginia, date unknown.
Peskey, John	22	Harrisburg	August 30, 1862	Not on muster-out roll.
Roler, Ferdinand	20	New Cumberland	August 8, 1862	Mustered out with Company on May 21, 1863.
Rhoads, Cyrus	25	New Cumberland	August 6, 1862	Discharged due to disability on Surgeon's Certificate on March 7, 1863.
Reese, William H.	22	West Chester	August 8, 1862	Discharged due to disability on Surgeon's Certificate on January 14, 1863.
Rahn, Michael	43	New Cumberland	August 9, 1862	Died of disease at Bolivar Heights on December 6, 1862.
Rock, Michael	40	Harrisburg	August 29, 1862	Not on muster-out roll.
Snyder, Jacob	34	New Cumberland	August 6, 1862	Mustered out with Company on May 21, 1863.
Shanton, Alfred C	18	New Cumberland	August 5, 1862	Mustered out with Company on May 21, 1863.
Shoop, Samuel	21	Halifax	August 9, 1862	Mustered out with Company on May 21, 1863.
Stoner, Albert	19	New Cumberland	August 9, 1862	Mustered out with Company on May 21, 1863.
Strickley, Levi	19	West Chester	August 7, 1862	Sent to Hospital on September 23, 1862. Absent, sick at muster out.
Semily, Joseph H.	36	West Chester	August 6, 1862	Mustered out with Company on May 21, 1863.
Stringfellow, Joseph G.	22	West Chester	August 7, 1862	Discharged due to disability on Surgeon's Certificate on April 1, 1863.

Appendix E: Regimental Roster

Name	Age	Joined at	Date Joined	Remarks
Snavley, John B.	18	Mechanicsburg	August 4, 1862	Killed at Antietam, Maryland on September 17, 1862.
Sennett, John W.	18	Harrisburg	August 23, 1862	Not on muster-out roll.
Trout, Abraham	36	New Cumberland	August 8, 1862	Mustered out with Company on May 21, 1863.
Townsend, Anteriken	42	West Chester	August 8, 1862	Discharged due to disability on Surgeon's Certificate on February 13, 1863.
Trust, John	23	New Cumberland	August 9, 1862	Killed at Antietam, Maryland on September 17, 1862.
Uhler, Isaac	19	Fishersville	August 8, 1862	Discharged on Surgeon's Certificate on February 28, 1863.
Weitzel, Joseph M.	18	New Cumberland	July 31, 1862	Mustered out with Company on May 21, 1863.
Walker, William	26	Fishersville	August 8, 1862	Mustered out with Company on May 21, 1863.
Wert, Adam	21	West Chester	August 8, 1862	Mustered out with Company on May 21, 1863.
Waterson, Joseph	30	West Chester	August 9, 1862	Mustered out with Company on May 21, 1863.
Wise, John M.	24	Mechanicsburg	August 8, 1862	Mustered out with Company on May 21, 1863.
Watson, Gibbons	24	West Chester	August 6, 1862	Discharged due to disability on Surgeon's Certificate on March 6, 1863.
Wertzel, William R.	27	New Cumberland	August 9, 1862	Died at Washington, DC on March 13, 1863.
Wallet, Daniel	18	Harrisburg	August 29, 1862	Not on muster-out roll.

COMPANY I - Recruited in York

Name	Age	Joined at	Date Joined	Remarks
Captain				
Lewis Small	34	Harrisburg	August 7, 1862	Mustered out with Company on May 21, 1863.
First Lieutenant				
D. Wilson Grove	38	Harrisburg	August 7, 1862	Wounded at Fredericksburg, Virginia on December 13, 1862. Mustered out with Company on May 21, 1863.
Second Lieutenants				
Franklin G. Torbert	22	Harrisburg	August 7, 1862	Killed at Fredericksburg, Virginia on December 13, 1862.

Name	Age	Joined at	Date Joined	Remarks
Jeremiah Oliver	31	York	August 7, 1862	Promooted from First Sergeant on December 13, 1862. Mustered out with Company on May 21, 1863.
First Sergeant				
Osburn E. Stephens	44	York	August 7, 1862	Promoted from Sergeant on December 13, 1862. Mustered out with Company in May 21, 1863.
Sergeants				
John M. Torbit	30	York	August 7, 1862	Wounded at Fredericksburg, Virginia on December 13, 1862. Mustered out with Company in May 21, 1863.
Samuel C. Monroe	33	York	August 7, 1862	Promoted from Corporal on December 12, 1862. Mustered out with Company on May 21, 1863.
Samuel G. Ilginfritz	21	York	August 7, 1862	Promoted from Corporal on December 13, 1862. Wounded at Fredericksburg, Virginia on December 13, 1862. Mustered out with Company on May 21, 1863.
Nathan B. Wails	22	York	August 7, 1862	Promoted to Corporal on December 13, 1862. Mustered out with Company on May 21, 1863.
Christian B. Miller	25	York	August 7, 1862	Died on January 3, 1863 of wounds received at Fredericksburg, Virginia on December 13, 1862.
William W. Clark	26	York	August 7, 1862	Killed at Fredericksburg, Virginia on December 13, 1862.
Corporals				
James E. Anderson	24	York	August 7, 1862	Wounded at Fredericksburg, Virginia on December 13, 1862. Mustered out with Company in May 21, 1863.
Joseph B. Grove	21	York	August 7, 1862	Wounded at Fredericksburg, Virginia on December 13, 1862. Mustered out with Company in May 21, 1863.
James C. McCurdy	21	York	August 7, 1862	Mustered out with Company on May 21, 1863.
John A. Channell	21	York	August 7, 1862	Promoted to Corporal on December 13, 1862. Wounded at Chancellorsville on December 3, 1862. Mustered out with Company on May 21, 1863.
John Bell	21	York	August 7, 1862	Promoted to Corporal on December 13, 1862. Mustered out with Company on May 21, 1863.
Thomas A. Morgan	18	York	August 7, 1862	Promoted to Corporal on December 13, 1862. Mustered out with Company on May 21, 1863.

Appendix E: Regimental Roster

Name	Age	Joined at	Date Joined	Remarks
John H. Geesy	28	York	August 7, 1862	Promoted to Corporal on December 13, 1862. Mustered out with Company on May 21, 1863.
Samuel Warnbaugh	37	York	August 7, 1862	Promoted to Corporal on December 13, 1862. Mustered out with Company on May 21, 1863.
James E. Watson	37	York	August 7, 1862	Discharged due to disability on Surgeon's Certificate on March 14, 1863.
Samuel B. Montooth	27	York	August 7, 1862	Died of disease on March 8, 1863.
Wagoneer				
Gordon, James E.	Unk	Unk	August 9, 1862	Mustered out with Company on May 21, 1863.
Musicians				
David Kane	21	York	August 7, 1862	Discharged due to disability on Surgeon's Certificate on December 22, 1862.
Joseph W. Stokes	31	York	August 7, 1862	Discharged at Falmouth, Virginia on Surgeon's Certificate, date unknown.
Privates				
Blackburn, William	31	York	August 7, 1862	Mustered out with Company on May 21, 1863.
Burkholder, John F.	23	York	August 7, 1862	Mustered out with Company on May 21, 1863.
Brooks, Thomas H.	21	York	August 7, 1862	Mustered out with Company on May 21, 1863.
Barton, Thomas	21	York	August 7, 1862	Mustered out with Company on May 21, 1863.
Boyd, Wells N.	19	York	August 7, 1862	Mustered out with Company on May 21, 1863.
Burkins, Edward	22	York	August 7, 1862	Discharged at Philadelphia, Pennsylvania due to disability on Surgeon's Certificate on February 7, 1863.
Cripple, William H.	24	York	August 7, 1862	Mustered out with Company on May 21, 1863.
Channell, James C.	19	York	August 7, 1862	Mustered out with Company on May 21, 1863.
Collins, Thomas J.	23	York	August 7, 1862	Wounded at Fredericksburg, Virginia on December 13, 1862. Mustered out with Company on May 21, 1863.
Cooper, John R.	21	York	August 7, 1862	Mustered out with Company on May 21, 1863.
Downs, Charles T.	21	York	August 7, 1862	Killed at Fredericksburg, Virginia on December 13, 1862.

Name	Age	Joined at	Date Joined	Remarks
Edgar, Hugh	31	York	August 7, 1862	Mustered out with Company on May 21, 1863.
Evans, Joseph E.	18	York	August 7, 1862	Wounded at Antietam, Maryland on September 17, 1862. Mustered out with Company on May 21, 1863.
Edwards, Daniel	21	York	August 7, 1862	Mustered out with Company on May 21, 1863.
Eicholtz, Rolandes	20	York	August 7, 1862	Mustered out with Company on May 21, 1863.
Evans, John G.	21	York	August 7, 1862	Deserted from Antietam, Maryland on September 17, 1862.
Fantom, Robert	18	York	August 7, 1862	Mustered out with Company on May 21, 1863.
Frestan, Joseph E.	21	York	August 7, 1862	Mustered out with Company on May 21, 1863.
Fisher, Edward	18	York	August 7, 1862	Mustered out with Company on May 21, 1863.
Gibson, Henry	25	York	August 7, 1862	Mustered out with Company on May 21, 1863.
Geesy, Warrington	18	York	August 7, 1862	Mustered out with Company on May 21, 1863.
Gordon, Henry C.	20	York	August 7, 1862	Discharged from Philadelphia, Pennsylvania due to disability on Surgeon's Certificate on February 5, 1863.
Grim, William	21	York	August 7, 1862	Discharged from Philadelphia, Pennsylvania due to disability on Surgeon's Certificate on December 31, 1862.
Griffith, Robert W.	28	York	August 7, 1862	Deserted from Antietam, Maryland on September 17, 1862.
Hunter, Frederick	19	York	August 7, 1862	Captured at Chancellorsville, Virginia on May 2, 1863. Mustered out with Company on May 21, 1863.
Harvey, William A.	33	York	August 7, 1862	Mustered out with Company on May 21, 1863.
Hughes, John O.	22	York	August 7, 1862	Mustered out with Company on May 21, 1863.
Hart, William	23	York	August 7, 1862	Wounded at Chancellorsville, Virginia on May 3, 1863. Died on January 21, 1863. Buried in Military Asylum Cemetery in Washington, DC.
Hitchcock, Charles A.	18	York	August 7, 1862	Died in October, 1862 of wounds received at Antietam, Maryland on September 17, 1862. Buried in National Cemetery in Winchester, Virginia, lot 26.

Appendix E: Regimental Roster

Name	Age	Joined at	Date Joined	Remarks
Hart, Charles	21	York	August 9, 1862	Killed at Fredericksburg, Virginia on December 13, 1862.
Hertz, Charles	21	York	August 9, 1862	Deserted from Bolivar Heights, Maryland, date unknown.
Jones, Thomas T.	22	York	August 7, 1862	Mustered out with Company on May 21, 1863.
Jones, William D.	23	York	August 7, 1862	Died of disease at USA Hospital in Frederick City, Maryland on December 14, 1862. Burial record December 16, 1862. Buried in National Cemetery in Antietam, Maryland. Marker #4062, Section 26, Lot E, Grave 481.
Koplin, Samuel E.	22	York	August 7, 1862	Mustered out with Company on May 21, 1863.
Kilgore, Nelson S.	25	York	August 7, 1862	Wounded at Antietam, Maryland on September 17, 1862. Mustered out with Company on May 21, 1863.
Keene, Conrad	37	York	August 7, 1862	Mustered out with Company on May 21, 1863.
Krone, George	21	York	August 7, 1862	Discharged due to disability at Harrisburg on Surgeon's Certificate on February 13, 1863.
Knight, Thomas V.	44	York	August 7, 1862	Discharged due to disability from USA Hospital in Washington, DC on Surgeon's Certificate on January 12, 1863.
Lehr, Alexander	20	York	August 7, 1862	Mustered out with Company on May 21, 1863.
Meyer, Augustus	35	York	August 7, 1862	Wounded at Antietam, Maryland on September 17, 1862. Mustered out with Company on May 21, 1863.
Minnich, Alfred	31	York	August 7, 1862	Mustered out with Company on May 21, 1863.
Miller, George	21	York	August 7, 1862	Wounded at Antietam, Maryland on September 17, 1862. Mustered out with Company on May 21, 1863.
Mitchell, John	27	York	August 7, 1862	Died at Washington, DC on January 2, 1863.
McCollough, Jacob	26	York	August 7, 1862	Mustered out with Company on May 21, 1863.
McKinley, William J.	22	York	August 7, 1862	Wounded at Fredericksburg, Virginia on December 13, 1862. Mustered out with Company on May 21, 1863.
McCall, Matthew H.	26	York	August 7, 1862	Mustered out with Company on May 21, 1863.

Name	Age	Joined at	Date Joined	Remarks
McCaulay, George W.	21	York	August 7, 1862	Discharged due to disability from USA Hospital in Washington, DC on Surgeon's Certificate on April 6, 1863.
McCauley, William A.	19	York	August 7, 1862	Died of disease at York, in August, 1862.
Ness, Henry R.	21	York	August 7, 1862	Killed at Antietam, Maryland on September 17, 1862.
Olp, Eli	39	York	August 7, 1862	Died on February 25, 1863. Buried in Military Asylum Cemetery in Wasington, DC.
Peterson, Christian	21	York	August 7, 1862	Mustered out with Company on May 21, 1863.
Posey, Robert	21	York	August 7, 1862	Died on March 5, 1863.
Rowan, Samuel G.	24	York	August 7, 1862	Mustered out with Company on May 21, 1863.
Rhoades, Henry G.	19	York	August 7, 1862	Mustered out with Company on May 21, 1863.
Ruff, Ezekiel G.	21	York	August 7, 1862	Mustered out with Company on May 21, 1863.
Runt, William	21	York	August 7, 1862	Deserted from hospital at York, date unknown.
Smeigh, Samuel	21	York	August 7, 1862	Mustered out with Company on May 21, 1863.
Sherwood, Marion	24	York	August 7, 1862	Mustered out with Company on May 21, 1863.
Schriber, Michael	25	York	August 7, 1862	Mustered out with Company on May 21, 1863.
Schwerin, Christopher	33	York	August 7, 1862	Discharged from USA Georgetown Hospital at Washington, DC on Surgeon's Certificate on December 15, 1862.
Smith, Richard M.	18	York	August 7, 1862	Killed at Antietam, Maryland on September 17, 1862.
Wisman, Adam	18	York	August 7, 1862	Mustered out with Company on May 21, 1863.
Wise, Elijah H.	24	York	August 7, 1862	Wounded at Antietam, Maryland on September 17, 1862. Mustered out with Company on May 21, 1863.
Wails, William H.	21	York	August 7, 1862	Mustered out with Company on May 21, 1863.
Wisenall, Charles A.	18	York	August 7, 1862	Mustered out with Company on May 21, 1863.
Wiley, John T.	21	York	August 7, 1862	Mustered out with Company on May 21, 1863.

Appendix E: Regimental Roster

Name	Age	Joined at	Date Joined	Remarks
Wise, Jacob H.	21	York	August 7, 1862	Mustered out with Company on May 21, 1863.
Wilson, Henry M.	26	York	August 7, 1862	Wounded at Antietam, Maryland on September 17, 1862 and at Chancellorsville, Virginia on May 3, 1863. Mustered out with Company on May 21, 1863.
Wilson, William H.	18	York	August 7, 1862	Mustered out with Company on May 21, 1863.
Yost, Daniel T.	21	York	August 7, 1862	Absent, sick at muster out.
Zeigler, Peter W.	21	York	August 7, 1862	Mustered out with Company on May 21, 1863. Left at Hospital at Bolivar Heights, Maryland.

COMPANY K - Recruited in York

Name	Age	Joined at	Date Joined	Remarks
Captains				
Levi Maish	24	York	August 4, 1862	Promoted to Lieutenant Colonel, August 17, 1862. Promoted to Colonel February 3, 1863.
David Z. Seipe	22	Washington	Unknown	Promoted from First Lieutenant on August 17, 1862. Wounded at Antietam, Maryland on September 17, 1862. Mustered out with Company on May 21, 1863.
First Lieutenant				
James Lece	33	Harrisburg	August 17, 1862	Promoted from Second Lieutenant on August 17, 1862. Mustered out with Company on May 21, 1863.
Second Lieutenant				
John J. Frick	19	Harrisburg	August 17, 1862	Promoted from First Sergeant on August 17, 1862. Mustered out with Company on May 21, 1863.
First Sergeant				
James P. McGuigan	21	York	August 4, 1862	Promoted from Sergeant on August 17, 1862. Mustered out with Company on May 21, 1863.
Sergeants				
Samuel S. Ensminger	33	York	August 4, 1862	Mustered out with Company on May 21, 1863.
C. Jabez Epley	20	York	August 4, 1862	Promoted from Corporal on August 17, 1862. Mustered out with Company on May 21, 1863.

Name	Age	Joined at	Date Joined	Remarks
Benjamin F. Spangler	18	York	August 4, 1862	Promoted from Corporal on January 1, 1863. Mustered out with Company on May 21, 1863.
Lewis E. Smyser	20	York	August 4, 1862	Promoted from Corporal on April 1, 1863. Mustered out with Company on May 21, 1863.
William H. Eisenhart	24	York	August 4, 1862	Promoted to Regimental Sergeant Major on January 1, 1863.
Corporals				
Alexander C. Ward	34	York	August 4, 1862	Mustered out with Company on May 21, 1863.
George Dosch	23	York	August 4, 1862	Mustered out with Company on May 21, 1863.
Charles McCreary	23	York	August 4, 1862	Promoted to Corporal on August 17, 1863. Mustered out with Company on May 21, 1863.
Joseph T. Hendrickson	21	York	August 4, 1862	Promoted to Corporal on August 17, 1863. Mustered out with Company on May 21, 1863.
John H. Schultz	29	York	August 4, 1862	Promoted to Corporal on August 17, 1863. Absent, sick at muster out.
James McComas	29	York	August 4, 1862	Promoted to Corporal on August 17, 1863. Mustered out with Company on May 21, 1863.
Joseph A. Drexler	19	York	August 4, 1862	Discharged due to disability from York on Surgeon's Certificate on December 15, 1862.
Thomas Doran	21	York	August 4, 1862	Deserted from Bolivar Heights, Maryland on September 26, 1862.
Musicians				
John McHale	33	York	August 4, 1862	Mustered out with Company on May 21, 1863.
Vinton Welsh	16	York	August 4, 1862	Discharged due to disability at Washington, D. C. on Surgeon's Certificate on January 25, 1863.
Privates				
Bratton, George K.	38	York	August 4, 1862	Wounded at Chancellorsville, Virginia on May 3, 1863. Mustered out with Company on May 21, 1863.
Butt, John	42	York	August 4, 1862	Mustered out with Company on May 21, 1863.
Barnett, Stephen S.	20	York	August 4, 1862	Wounded at Antietam, Maryland on September 17, 1862. Absent in hospital at York at muster out.
Berkheimer, William	23	York	August 4, 1862	Mustered out with Company on May 21, 1863.

Appendix E: Regimental Roster

Name	Age	Joined at	Date Joined	Remarks
Beers, John	21	York	August 4, 1862	Discharged due to disability at Harrisburg, Pennsylvania on Surgeon's Certificate on October 29, 1862.
Bupp, John	25	York	August 4, 1862	Wounded at Antietam, Maryland on September 17, 1862. Discharged at York, Pennsylvania on March 3, 1863.
Brown, Adam	25	York	August 4, 1862	Killed at Antietam, Maryland on September 17, 1862. Buried in National Cemetery Section 26, Lot A, Grave I, Marker # 3599.
Cline, Lewis	26	York	August 4, 1862	Mustered out with Company on May 21, 1863.
Clemmens, William	24	York	August 4, 1862	Mustered out with Company on May 21, 1863.
Campbell, Samuel C.	32	York	August 4, 1862	Died at Washington, DC on March 2, 1863. Buried in Military Asylum Cemetery.
Diehl, Adam	25	York	August 4, 1862	Mustered out with Company on May 21, 1863.
Dugan, John T.	21	York	August 4, 1862	Discharged on Surgeon's Certificate on February 16, 1863.
Fickes, Harrison	21	York	August 4, 1862	Discharged on Surgeon's Certificate on February 16, 1863.
Fetrow, John R.	23	York	August 4, 1862	Mustered out with Company on May 21, 1863.
Folckemmer, Henry	25	York	August 4, 1862	Mustered out with Company on May 21, 1863.
Foster, Robert N.	25	York	August 4, 1862	Mustered out with Company on May 21, 1863.
Frey, Alexander	20	York	August 4, 1862	Killed at Antietam, Maryland on September 17, 1862.
Grove, Andrew	25	York	August 4, 1862	Mustered out with Company on May 21, 1863.
Garrety, Edward A.	18	York	August 4, 1862	Mustered out with Company on May 21, 1863.
Goff, Jacob	30	York	August 4, 1862	Discharged due to disability at Washington, DC on Surgeon's Certificate on March 2, 1863.
Good, Christian	18	York	August 4, 1862	Killed at Antietam, Maryland on September 18, 1862. Buried in National Cemetery, Section 26, Lot A, Grave 18, Marker #3598.
Horn, David R.	18	York	August 4, 1862	Absent, sick at muster out. Left at Division Hospital Acquia Creek, Virginia.
Horn, Charles	18	York	August 4, 1862	Mustered out with Company on May 21, 1863.

Name	Age	Joined at	Date Joined	Remarks
Horn, Henry 1st	19	York	August 4, 1862	Mustered out with Company on May 21, 1863.
Horn, Herny 2nd	19	York	August 4, 1862	Mustered out with Company on May 21, 1863.
Hammer, John D.	21	York	August 4, 1862	Mustered out with Company on May 21, 1863.
Hubley, George	19	York	August 4, 1862	Mustered out with Company on May 21, 1863.
Harris, William	42	York	August 4, 1862	Mustered out with Company on May 21, 1863.
Hedrick, Geroge A.	18	York	August 4, 1862	Mustered out with Company on May 21, 1863.
Hammond, Russell	25	York	August 4, 1862	Mustered out with Company on May 21, 1863.
Herman, John C.	26	York	August 4, 1862	Mustered out with Company on May 21, 1863.
Hoover, Phillip C.	23	York	August 4, 1862	Mustered out with Company on May 21, 1863.
Ilgenfritz, William F.	26	York	August 4, 1862	Mustered out with Company on May 21, 1863.
Jennings, Andrew	26	York	August 4, 1862	Mustered out with Company on May 21, 1863.
Jennings, Burger	30	York	August 4, 1862	Mustered out with Company on May 21, 1863.
Kister, Jacob	29	York	August 4, 1862	Mustered out with Company on May 21, 1863.
Kline, Marion	20	York	August 4, 1862	Mustered out with Company on May 21, 1863.
Krall, Christian	22	York	August 4, 1862	Died on January 4, 1863 of wounds received at Fredericksburg, Virginia on December 13, 1862
Levenight, Henry	28	York	August 4, 1862	Mustered out with Company on May 21, 1863.
Lauman, George	20	York	August 4, 1862	Discharged due to disability on March 3, 1863 at Washington, DC.
Miller, William H.	20	York	August 4, 1862	Mustered out with Company on May 21, 1863.
Millard, Jonathan J.	41	York	August 4, 1862	Mustered out with Company on May 21, 1863.
Miller, Jesse B.	18	York	August 4, 1862	Mustered out with Company on May 21, 1863.
Miller, Elias B.	20	York	August 4, 1862	Mustered out with Company on May 21, 1863.

Appendix E: Regimental Roster 265

Name	Age	Joined at	Date Joined	Remarks
Miller, Jacob	23	York	August 4, 1862	Transferred to the 18th US Infantry on December 12, 1862 at Harrisburg.
Myers, George	31	York	August 4, 1862	Discharged on March 3, 1863 at York, Pennsylvania. Wounded at Battle of Antietam on September 17, 1862.
Manifold, Joseph E.	26	York	August 4, 1862	Died of diease near Falmouth, Virginia on December 15, 1862.
Myers, Eli W.	21	York	August 4, 1862	Died December 18, 1862 of wounds received at Fredericksburg, Virginia on December 13, 1862. Buried in Prospect Hill Cemetery, York.
Palmer, Charles	32	York	August 4, 1862	Mustered out with Company on May 21, 1863.
Potts, Rankin C.	28	York	August 4, 1862	Mustered out with Company on May 21, 1863.
Palmer, William W.	22	York	August 4, 1862	Killed at Antietam, Maryland on September 18, 1862.
Repman, Henry D.	29	York	August 4, 1862	Wounded at Chancellorsville, Virginia on May 3, 1863. Absent in hospital at muster out.
Rutledge, William T.	18	York	August 4, 1862	Mustered out with Company on May 21, 1863.
Richard, Peter S.	22	York	August 4, 1862	Mustered out with Company on May 21, 1863.
Raffensberger, Edward T.	21	York	August 4, 1862	Mustered out with Company on May 21, 1863.
Raffensberger, Daniel T.	22	York	August 4, 1862	Died of diease near Falmouth, Virginia on February 11, 1863. Buried in Military Asylum Cemetery.
Reever, Jacob G.	22	York	August 4, 1862	Mustered out with Company on May 21, 1863.
Ruby, Walter B.	18	York	August 4, 1862	Discharged due to disability at York, Pennsylvania on December 31, 1862.
Seipe, Jacob	21	York	August 4, 1862	Mustered out with Company on May 21, 1863.
Seipe, Herman	24	York	August 4, 1862	Mustered out with Company on May 21, 1863.
Sutton, Abraham	25	York	August 4, 1862	Mustered out with Company on May 21, 1863.
Spangler, Edward W.	18	York	August 4, 1862	Mustered out with Company on May 21, 1863.
Shuler, Edward	18	York	August 4, 1862	Mustered out with Company on May 21, 1863.
Stallman, William H.	21	York	August 4, 1862	Mustered out with Company on May 21, 1863.

Name	Age	Joined at	Date Joined	Remarks
Steig, Augustus	21	York	August 4, 1862	Mustered out with Company on May 21, 1863.
Spangler, Benjamin	39	York	August 4, 1862	Wounded at Antietam, Maryland on September 17, 1862. Discharged at Reading, Pennsylvania on April 10, 1863.
Smith, Jacob	19	York	August 4, 1862	Killed at Antietam, Maryland on September 17, 1862.
Stroman, Thaddeus	18	York	August 4, 1862	Died near Hillsboro, Virginia on October 30, 1862. Buried in National Cemetery in Winchester, Virginia, lot 25.
Watson, John H.	19	York	August 4, 1862	Mustered out with Company on May 21, 1863.
Walters, John A.	21	York	August 4, 1862	Discharged at Alexandria, Virginia on February 16, 1863.
Young, George E.	19	York	August 4, 1862	Mustered out with Company on May 21, 1863.
Young, William H.	22	York	August 4, 1862	Mustered out with Company on May 21, 1863.
Young, Edward J.	18	York	August 4, 1862	Mustered out with Company on May 21, 1863.

SOURCES:

Bates, Samuel P., *History of the Pennsylvania Volunteers*, 1861-5, 5 vols. Harrisburg. B. Singerly, State Publisher. 1870. Reprint, Wilmington, NC: Broadfoot Publishing Co. 1994.

Roll of the Regiment, 130th Regiment Pennsylvania Volunteer Infantry, Roll #517, Record Group 19, Pennsylvania State Archives, Harrisburg, Pennsylvania. Microfilm.

American Democrat, August 20, 1862.

Carlisle Herald, August 29, 1862.

Shippensburg News, August 23, 1862.

Hemminger, J.D., *Cumberland County Pennsylvania In the Civil War*, Carlisle, Pennsylvania, 1926.

PA-Roots, 130th Pennsylvania Volunteers, Muster Rolls, November 10, 2003, http://www.pa-roots.com/pacw/130th/.

NOTE: When a discrepancy occurred, two primary source documents were considered validation. Samuel Bates' *History of the Pennsylvania Volunteers*, 1861–1865 contained a number of errors.

BIBLIOGRAPHY

PRIMARY SOURCES

Books:

Bates, David Homer. *Lincoln in the Telegraph Office*. New York: Century Co., 1907. Reprint, Lincoln & London: University of Nebraska Press, 1995.

Bates, Samuel P. *The Battle of Chancellorsville*: Meadville, Pennsylvania. Edward T. Bates, 1882, Reprint. Gaithersburg, Maryland: Ron R. Van Sickle Military Books, 1987.

———. *History of the Pennsylvania Volunteers 1861-5*, 5 vols. Harrisburg, Pennsylvania: B. Singerly, State Publisher, 1870. Reprint, Wilmington, NC: Broadfoot Publishing Co., 1994.

Bosbyshell, Oliver C. *Pennsylvania at Antietam*. Harrisburg, Antietam Battlefield Memorial Committee, Harrisburg Publishing Company, State Printer, Harrisburg, PA, 1906.

Doubleday, Abner. *Chancellorsville and Gettysburg*. New York: Charles Scribner's Sons, 1882. Reprint. New York: DaCapo Press. 1994.

Page, Charles D. *History of the Fourteenth Regiment*. Meriden, Connecticut: Horton Publishing Company, 1906. Reprint, Salem, Massachusetts: Higginson Book Company, 1998.

Gibbs, James M. *History of the First Battalion Pennsylvania Six Months Volunteers and 187th Regiment Pennsylvania Volunteer Infantry*, n.p. Reprint Salem, Massachusetts: Higginson Book Company, 1998.

Hemminger, John D. *Cumberland County Pennsylvania in the Civil War: 1861–1865*. Harrisburg: State Library of Pennsylvania, 1926.

Palfrey, Francis W. *The Antietam and Fredericksburg*. New York: Charles Scribner's Sons, 1882. Reprint. Harrisburg: The Archive Society, 1992.

Pennsylvania Antietam Battlefield Commission. *One Hundred and Thirtieth Regiment Pennsylvania Volunteer Infantry: Ceremonies and Addresses at Dedication of the Monument at Bloody Lane, Antietam Battlefield, September 1904*. n.p.1904. USAMHI, Carlisle Barracks, Pennsylvania.

Spangler, Edward W. *My Little War Experience*. York, Pennsylvania: York Daily Publishing Company, 1904.

Walker, Francis A. *History of the Second Army Corps*, New York: Charles Scribner's Sons, 1887. Reprint Gaithersburg, Maryland: Olde Soldier Books, Inc., 1997.

Washburn, George H. *A Complete Military History and Record of the 108th Regiment N.Y. Vols*. Rochester, New York: E. R. Andrews, 1894. Reprint, Salem, Massachusetts: Higginson Book Company, 1998.

Manuscripts:

Brehm, Samuel H. diary, Cumberland County Historical Society, Carlisle, Pennsylvania.

Bratton, George, K., diary, York County Historical Society, York, Pennsylvania.

Hemminger, John D., diary, Michael Winery Collection.

Landis, John B., memoirs, Antietam National Park, Sharpsburg, Maryland.

Laughlin, William, Captain, information paper, Newville Historical Society, Newville, Pennsylvania.

Laughlin, Willian, letters, Newville Historical Society, Newville, Pennsylvania.

Masonheimer, Lewis, diary, in possession of Dorothy Bonafield Synder.

Miller, Harman R., letter, 130th Regiment, Pennsylvania Volunteer file, National Archives and Records Administration, Washington, D. C.

Turner, John R., letters, Cumberland County Historical Society, Carlisle, Pennsylvania.

Weiser, John S., letters, Civil War Miscellaneous Collection, Cumberland County Historical Society, Carlisle, Pennsylvania.

Newspapers:

The Baltimore Sun, Baltimore, Maryland, Newspapers.com.
Brooklyn Eagle, Brooklyn, New York, Newspapers.com.
The Carlisle Evening Herald, Carlisle, Pennsylvania, Newspapers.com
The Chronicle, Shippensburg, Pennsylvania, Newspapers.com.
The Daily Item, Sunbury, Pennsylvania, Newspapers.com.
The Daily Notes, Canonsburg, Pennsylvania, Newspapers.com.
The Earth, Brookville, Kansas, Newpapers.com
The Evening Sentinel, December 28, 1929, The State Library of Pennsylvania, Harrisburg, Pennsylvania.
Evening Times-Republican, Marshalltown, Iowa, Newspapers.com.
The Gazette, York, Pennsylvania, Newspapers.com.

Appendix E: Regimental Roster

The Hanover Spectator, 1862-1863, The State Library of Pennsylvania, Harrisburg, Pennsylvania.
Harrisburg Telegraph, Harrisburg, Pennsylvania, Newspapers.com.
The Herald, 1862-1863, The State Library of Pennsylvania, Harrisburg, Pennsylvania.
The Hutchinson News-Herald, Hutchinson, Kansas, Newspapers.com.
Lancaster Intelligencer, Lancaster, Pennsylvania, Newspapers.com.
Lewistown Gazette, Lewistown, Pennsylvania, Newspapers.com.
Muscantine News-Tribune, Muscantine, Iowa, Newspapers.com.
The News-Chronicle, Shippensburg, Pennsylvania, Newspapers.com.
The Philadelphia Inquirer, Philadelphia, Newspapers.com.
The Reporter, Lansdale, Pennsylvania, Newspapers.com.
Richmond Dispatch, Richmond, Virginia, December 22, 1862, Newspapers.com.
The Scranton Tribune, Scranton, Lackawanna County, Pennsylvania, Newspapers.com.
The Sentinel, Carlisle, Pennsylvania, Newspapers.com.
Shippensburg News, 1862–1863. The State Library of Pennsylvania, Harrisburg, Pennsylvania.
The Star and Enterprise, Newville, Pennsylvania, Newspapers.com.
The Valley Star, Newville, June 18, 1863, The Newville Historical Society, Newville, Pennsylvania.
The Valley Sentinel, Carlisle, Pennsylvania, Newspapers.com.
The York Daily, York, Pennsylvania, Newspapers.com.
York Democratic Press, York, Pennsylvania, Newspapers.com.
The York Dispatch, York, Pennsylvania, Newspapers.com.
The York Gazette, York, Pennsylvania, Newspapers.com.

Federal and State Government Documents:

130th Pennsylvania Regimental Records, Pennsylvania State Archives, Harrisburg, Pennsylvania, RG-19, Box 81.
Roll of the Regiment, 130th Regiment Pennsylvania Volunteer Infantry, Roll #517, Record Group 19, Pennsylvania State Archives, Harrisburg, Pennsylvania. Microfilm.
Courts Martial Records, National Archives, Washington, DC.
Pension Records, National Archives, Washington, DC.
Service Records, National Archives, Washington, DC.
The Civil War CD-ROM: *The War of the Rebellion: A Compilation of the Official Records of the Union and Confederate Armies*. Carmel Indiana: Guild Press of Indiana, Inc. 1996.

The Civil War CD-ROM: Frederick H. Dyer, *A Compendium of the War of the Rebellion.* Carmel Indiana: Guild Press of Indiana, Inc. 1996.

SECONDARY SOURCES
Books:

Boatner, Mark Mayo III, 1921 *The Civil War Dictionary.* New York: David McKay Company, Inc., Revised Edition, 1988.

Brooks, Victor D. *Marye's Heights: Fredericksburg.* Conshohocken, Pennsylvania: Combined Publishing. 2001.

Cooling, Benjamin Franklin III and Walton H. Owen II, *Mr. Lincoln's Forts, A Guide to the Civil War Defenses of Washington,* Shippensburg, PA: White Mane Publishing Company, Inc., 1988.

Ferguson, Ernest B. *Chancellorsville 1863.* New York: Vintage Books. 1993.

Gallagher, Gary W. *The Battle of Chancellorsville.* Washington, Pennsylvania: Eastern Acorn Press. 1995.

Hays, Raphael S. II. *John Hays.* Cumberland County Historical Society, Carlisle, Pennsylvania. 2000.

Linderman, Gerald, F. *Embattled Courage.* New York: The Free Press, 1987.

McPherson, James M. *For Cause & Comrades.* New York: Oxford University Press Inc., 1997.

Miller, William J. *The Training of an Army: Camp Curtin and the North's Civil War.* Shippensburg, PA: White Mane Publishing Company, Inc., 1990.

O'Reilly, Francis A. *The Fredericksburg Campaign: Winter War on the Rappahannock.* Baton Rouge: Louisiana State University Press. 2003.

Priest, John M. *Antietam: The Soldiers Battle.* New York: Oxford University Press. 1989.

Rable, George C. *Fredericksburg! Fredericksburg!* Chapel Hill & London: The University of North Carolina Press. 2002.

Sears, Stephen W. *Chancellorsville.* Boston & New York: Houghton Mifflin Company. 1996.

Sears, Stephen W. *Landscape Turned Red: The Battle of Antietam.* Boston & New York: Houghton Mifflin Company. 1983.

Snell, Mark A. *Union Soldiers and the Northern Home Front.* New York: Fordham University Press, 2002.

Stackpole, Edward J. *Drama on the Rappahannock: The Fredericksburg Campaign.* New York: Bonanza Books. 1957.

———, *The Battle of Fredericksburg.* Harrisburg: Eastern Acorn Press. 1965. Reprint, 1981.

United States Army, *American Military History, Army Historical Series*, Washington, DC, US Government Printing Office, 1989.

Maps:

Dove, John. *Battle of Chancellorsville*. National Park Service. 1998. Historical research by Frank A. O'Reilly and Eric J. Mink, Illustrated by John Dove. 12 Map Set.
———, *Battle of Fredericksburg*. National Park Service. 2001. Historical research by Frank A. O'Reilly and Eric J. Mink, Illustrated by John Dove. 5 Map Set.

Websites:

22nd Cavalry Volunteers, Company B. <www.pa-roots.com/pacw/22cacvob6mos.html> (September 30, 2002).
A Genealogy Biography of Hon. Levi Maish Pennsylvania Volunteer of the Civil War. <http://www.pacivil war.com/bios/maish_levi.html> (October 1, 2004).
PA-Roots, 130th Regiment Pennsylvania Volunteers, https://www.pa-roots.com/pacw/infantry/130th/130thorg.html/.
Find-A-Grave, Henry I. Zinn, https://www.findagrave.com/memorial/20724662/henry-i-zinn./.
Find-A Grave, Mary Ann Clark Zinn, https://www.findagrave.com/memorial/34957563/mary_ann_zinn/.
Find-A-Grave, Elsie M. Zinn, https://www.findagrave.com/memorial/34957568/elsie-m-zinn/.
https://www.ancestry.com
https://www.findagrave.com
https://www.fold3.com
https://www.loc.gov
https://www.newspapers.com

INDEX

Allison, Walter M., Corporal, 190
Anderson, George B., Brigadier General, 61
Anderson, Richard H., Brigadier General, 66
Andrews, John W., Colonel, 116
Antietam Creek, 52–54, 61, 64
Aquia Creek, 102, 104
Aurora Borealis, 123

Barksdale, Willian E., Brigadier General, 109
Barr, John, Hospital Steward, 177–78, 203
Belle Plain, Virginia, 99, 100, 102–4, 106–7
Berry, Hiram G., Major General, 147, 150
Best, Frank, Corporal, 195
Bolivar Heights, 80–82, 85, 87, 95
Bowman, Issac, Private, 201
Brehm, Samuel H., 21, 29–30, 34, 36, 46, 49–50, 72, 74, 79, 87, 89–91, 93, 95, 97–98, 102, 104, 110, 124, 126, 130–31, 133–34, 138, 187
Burnside, Ambrose, Major General, 48, 49, 92, 94, 95, 96, 97, 102, 105, 114–15, 119, 124, 128, 130–32

Camp Curtin, 17–18, 23, 27, 83
Camp Defiance, 43
Camp Simmons, 18, 21–23, 27, 81, 134
Camp Wells, 29
Carr, Joseph B., Brigadier General, 149
Chalifant, George W., Chaplain, 84–85, 87, 121, 136–37, 162, 174–75
Chancellor house, 141–42, 144–45, 147, 152, 154
Clemmens, William, Private, 119
Cobb, Howell, Brigadier General, 69
Cobb, Thomas R., Birgidier General, 118, 120
Corman, Leander C., Private, 190
Couch, Darius N., Major General, 84, 87, 94, 114–15, 117, 124, 147, 155
Culpeper Court House, 89

Curtin, Andrew G., Governor, 8, 9, 23, 25, 81, 86

Ege, Joseph, A., Second Lieutenant, 196
Eighteenth Georgia Infantry Regiment, 120
Eighth Ohio Infantry Regiment, 54, 69
Eisenhart, William H., Sergeant Major, 154, 176
Eleventh Corps, 143–45
Eleventh New Jersey Infantry Regiment, 142, 149

Falmouth, Virginia, 98–99, 101–4, 106, 110, 123–24, 126–28, 130–31, 135, 137, 153, 156
Farner, John M., Private, 199
Fifth Alabama Infantry Regiment, 61–62
Fifth Maryland Infantry Regiment, 54, 61–62
Fiftieth New York Engineers, 109
Finkenbinder, William, Private, 196
First Delaware Infantry Regiment, 54, 61–62, 66
First New York Light Artillery, 142
Flyer, Jacob M., Private, 197
Fort Ethan Allen, 36
Fort Marcy, 33, 35–41, 43, 53, 77, 81, 85, 160
Fourteenth Connecticut Regiment Volunteers, 43–44, 54, 57–58, 62, 79, 95, 117–18, 122, 125, 134, 138, 142, 145
Fourteenth Indiana Infantry Regiment, 54, 69
Fourteenth North Carolina Infantry Regiment, 62
Fourth New York Infantry Regiment, 54
Fourth North Carolina Infantry Regiment, 62
Fourth United States Artillery, 142
Franklin, William B., Major General, 96, 115
French, Michael W., 161
French, William H., Brigadier General, 24, 42, 44, 55–56, 79, 82, 87, 91–92, 115, 117–18, 122, 147, 160

Index 273

Givler, William A., Second Lieutenant, 73, 78
Gordon, John B., Colonel, 62
Gordonsville, Virginia, 97

Halleck, Henry W., Major General, 96
Hancock, Winfield S., Brigadier General, 87, 92, 94, 115, 122, 155
Harper's Ferry, West Virginia, 39, 79–81
Harris, Daniel, Second Lieutenant, 193
Haupt, Frederick L., Assistant Surgeon, 81, 95, 173
Hayes, Willaim, Brigadier General, 129, 135, 147, 150
Hays, John, Adjutant, 13–15, 147–48, 154–55, 160, 171
Hays, John, Sergeant, 193
Hemminger, John D., 12–13, 19–20, 26–28, 30, 32–33, 35, 37, 39–42, 46–47, 49–50, 57–58, 63, 66–71, 73, 160–62, 184
Henderson, J. H., Reverend, 46
Hill, D. H., Brevel Major General, 56, 60–61
Hooker, Joseph, Major General, 96, 132–33, 139–41, 143–44, 149, 154–55
Horn, Henry, 160
Hovetter, Josiah, 160
Hunt, Henry, Brigadier General, 94, 109

Ilgenfritz, Samuel, Sergeant, 58
Irwin, William, Colonel, 69

Jenkins, Joseph, S., Major, 159–60, 169, 179
Johnson, R. C., Colonel, 128

Kennedy, Alexander, Private, 196
Kennedy, Cyrus, Private, 196
Kimball, Nathan, Brigadier General, 44, 54–55, 115, 117–18
Kirk, John, 161
Knisley, Peter T., Private, 135
Kyle, Augustus, G., Musician, 198

Lacy House, 105, 110–11, 135, 138
Landis, John B., 16–18, 20–21, 26, 28, 32, 36–37, 39–40, 46–47, 50, 52, 54–55, 57–61, 70–72, 74, 77, 79, 82, 86, 186–87
Laughlin, William, Captain, 18–19, 31, 38–39, 124, 180
Lease, Ephriam, 160

Lee, John, Major, 54, 120, 134, 136, 168–69
Lee, Robert E., General, 30, 32, 40, 45, 62, 71, 73, 101–2, 124, 140–41, 143–44
Lincoln, Abraham, 7–8, 13, 82–83, 89, 97, 126, 132, 138, 155, 182, 184
Longenecker, John H., Assistant Surgeon, 82, 95, 173–74
Longstreet, James, Lieutenant General, 101, 115
Low, John S., Captain, 170–71, 181
Lowe, Thaddeus, Professor, 105–6
Lowkart, Abraham, Private, 159

Maish, Levi, Colonel, 134–35, 154, 167–68, 183
Marshall, Clay H., Adjutant, 104, 170
Marshall, George C., Captain, 182
Maryland, Boonsboro, 51
Maryland, Clarksville, 46
Maryland, Frederick, 42, 45–47, 49, 160
Maryland, Hyattstown, 46
Maryland, Keedysville, 51–52
Maryland, Urbana, 47
Maxwell, J. R, 160
Marye's Heights, 117–19, 121–22, 129
McCall, M. H., 160
McClellan, George B., Major General, 7, 36, 47–48, 52, 71–72, 89, 92, 95
McCoy, Abraham H., Private, 199
McCune, William A., Private, 159
McKeehan, Thaddeus, Private, 159
McLaws, Lafayette, Brigadier General, 143
McLean, George, Third Corporal, 194
Meade, George G., Major General, 155
Miller, Samuel A., Private, 200
Miller, William H., Private, 202
Mitzell, Andrew, 104
Morgan, Charles A., Private, 159
Morris, Dwight, Colonel, 44, 54–55
Mud March, 129
Mumma Farm, 55, 57, 62, 69, 75
Myers, Eli W., Private, 119

Numbers, Thomas, Private, 192

Oiler, Samuel, Private, 200
One Hunded and Thirty Second Pennsylvania Infantry Regiment, 54, 207

One Hundred and Eighth New York Infantry Regiment, 43, 54, 57, 64, 78–79, 116–18, 142, 150, 159
One Hundred and Twenty-Seventh Pennsylvania Infantry Regiment, 38

Palmer, Oliver H., Colonel, 116, 129, 150
Patchell, Samuel, First Lieutenant, 192
Pender, William D., Major General, 148–50
Pennypacker, Samuel W., Honorable, 161
Pierce, F. E., Major, 159
Pleasanton, Alfred, Major General, 147
Pope, John, Major General, 36, 39
Porter, John Fitz, Major General, 40, 71
Porter, William A., Captain, 34, 121–22, 134, 178
Potomac Creek, 99
Powers, Charles P., Colonel, 150–51
Pry Ford, 53

Quigley, Edwin, D., Private, 201

Raffensberger, D. D., Private, 135
Ramsey, John S., Surgeon, 104, 172
Ransom, Robert, Brigadier General, 120
Rappahannock River, 98, 101–2, 105, 109–10, 112, 114, 116, 123, 127, 130, 135, 140–41, 153, 156
Rectortown, Virginia, 93
Revere, Joseph W., Brigadier General, 149–50, 152
Richardson, Israel B., Major General, 45, 53, 64, 79
Rodes, Robert E., Brigadier General, 61–62, 64, 67–68, 79
Roulette Farm, 55–58, 60–61, 63–64, 67, 69–70, 163

Salem, Virginia, 93
Second North Carolina Infantry Regiment, 62–63
Sedgwick, John, Major General, 45, 54–55
Seipe, David Z., Captain, 58–59, 183
Seventh West Virginia Infantry Regiment, 54
Sharpe, Joshua, Captain, 18–19, 37, 124
Sigel, Franz, Major General, 40, 42
Sixteenth Massachusetts Infantry Regiment, 142

Sixteenth North Carolina Infantry Regiment, 148
Sixth Alabama Infantry Regiment, 61–62, 67
Slaysman, George M., Chaplain, 136, 175
Snickersville, Virginia, 90
South Mountain, Battle of, 49–51
Spangler, Edward W., Private, 13, 15, 20, 29, 32, 42–43, 47, 51, 53, 55, 59, 63, 66–71, 91, 103, 110, 112–14, 118–19, 122, 124, 145–46, 152–54, 162, 185
Stewart, Alexander, Private, 194
Stoey, Washington, L., Private, 160, 191
Stoneman, George, Brigadier General, 139
Stuart, J. E. B., Major General, 91–92, 101, 143, 151
Sumner, Edwin, V., Major General, 25, 42–43, 55, 79, 84, 94, 96, 110, 115, 128

Third Alabama Infantry Regiment, 61
Third Arkansas Infantry Regiment, 69
Thirteenth Mississippi Infantry Regiment, 109
Thirteenth North Carolina Infantry Regiment, 148, 150
Thirty Fourth North Carolina Infantry Regiment, 148
Thomas, Samuel B., Colonel, 86
Toben, Thomas, Private, 159
Torbert, Franklin, G., Lieutenant, 119
Tray, John, Private, 159
Turner, John R., Quartermaster, 5, 107, 125, 131, 172
Twelfth Alabama Infantry Regiment, 61
Twelfth New Jersey Infantry Regiment, 128, 142, 150
Twenty Eighth North Carolina Infantry Regiment, 148
Twenty Fourth Georgia Infantry Regiment, 120
Twenty Second North Carolina Infantry Regiment, 148
Twenty Second Pennsylvania Cavalry Regiment, 188
Twenty Seventh North Carolina Infantry Regiment, 69
Twenty Sixth Alabama Infantry Regiment, 61

United States Ford, 141, 153
Upperville, Virginia, 91–93

Index

Warrenton, Virginia, 93–97, 137
Weber, Max, Brigadier General, 44, 53, 55–57, 62, 67
Weiser, John S., Private, 26, 31, 47, 54, 72, 85–86, 88, 124, 131–32, 188
Whistler, Samuel, Private, 32, 161–63
Winter, Peter, Assistant Surgeon, 174
Wiseman, Adam, 160

Wolf, George W., Private, 195

Zeigler, John H., Private, 191
Zinn, Henry I., Colonel, 14, 22–24, 30–31, 34–35, 39–40, 45, 53–54, 72, 75, 79–80, 82–86, 88, 91–92, 95, 98, 103–4, 106, 118, 120–21, 134, 161–62, 166–68, 207

ABOUT THE AUTHOR

TERRENCE W. BELTZ, born in Canton, Ohio, a resident of Earlysville, Virginia, completed his Bachelor of Science in Business Administration at Bowling Green State University in 1972 and his Master of Arts (History) at the University of Richmond in 2004. He retired from the Virginia Housing Development Authority in Richmond, Virginia, and is a retired U.S. Army Colonel with an ardent interest in 19th Century American history, particularly the Civil War. He is the paternal great-grandson of Private William H. Seifert, who served in Company C of the regiment. He is a member of the Sons of the American Revolution (SAR) and the Sons of Union Veterans of the Civil War (SUVCW). In his spare time, he works on family genealogy and is a volunteer with "Find-A-Grave". He is married to Patricia Beville Beltz, together they have two daughters.

www.ingramcontent.com/pod-product-compliance
Lightning Source LLC
Chambersburg PA
CBHW032037150426
43194CB00006B/311